Accomack County, Virginia Court Order Abstracts

1663–1666
Volume 1

JoAnn Riley McKey

HERITAGE BOOKS
2012

HERITAGE BOOKS

AN IMPRINT OF HERITAGE BOOKS, INC.

Books, CDs, and more—Worldwide

For our listing of thousands of titles see our website
at
www.HeritageBooks.com

Published 2012 by
HERITAGE BOOKS, INC.
Publishing Division
100 Railroad Ave. #104
Westminster, Maryland 21157

Library of Congress Cataloging-in-Publication

McKey, JoAnn Riley
  Accomack County, Virginia court order abstracts

  v.1. 1663-1666. – v.2. 1666-1670. – v.3. 1671-1673. – v.4. 1673-1676. – v.5. 1676-1678. –
  v.6. 1678-1682. – v.7. 1682-1690. – v.8. 1690-1697. – v.9. 1697-1703. – v.10. 1703-1710.
  – v. 11. 1710-1714. – v.12/13. 1714-1719. – v. 14. 1719-1724. – v. 15. 1724-1731. – v.16.
  1731-1736. –v.17. 1737-1744. –v18. 1744-1753. –v19. 1753-1763.
  Includes bibliographical references and index.
1. Accomack County (Va.) – Genealogy. 2. Court records – Virginia – Accomack County. I. Title.
F232.A2 2011 929.375516 20

International Standard Book Numbers
Paperbound: 978-0-7884-0448-1
Clothbound: 978-0-7884-9102-3

This book is for my father

Hugh Marshall Riley

whose Accomack County ancestors
lurk among these pages.

INTRODUCTION

Accomack County Court

An original Virginia county, "Accawmak" had been formed in 1634 but was renamed Northampton County in 1642/43. In 1663, Northampton County was divided, with the northern part receiving the original name of Accomack.[1] The court sessions, which started in April of that year were held almost every month and were well attended; at the court held 16 April 1664, Col. Edm. Scarburgh declared that "most of the county" was present.

The good attendance at court is hardly surprising. The sessions provided news, entertainment and social interaction for the isolated inhabitants. These court actions are still interesting; one gets glimpses of real people as they break the Sabbath, commit fornication, speak out in their depositions or quote their neighbors. In wills and deeds the genealogist can learn about his ancestors' relatives and possessions; in court orders he can learn about his ancestors.

Tobacco and Livestock

The world of seventeenth century Virginians revolved around tobacco, corn, horses, cattle and pigs.

The whole economy was based on tobacco, which was also used as a medium of exchange. Fines were paid with tobacco, as were debts and wages. A day's labor was worth 25 lbs of tobacco; the neglect of 32 days of work cost William Onoughton 800 lbs tobacco. Although needing a workman to hew timber, David Williamson refused to pay the 30 lbs/day that Cornelius Watkinson requested. Cured tobacco was packed into casks or hogsheads, which when full weighed about 370 lbs. It was expected that a large payment of tobacco would include the casks in which it was packed. In 1663, ten pounds of tobacco was worth one shilling. (p. 8)

Cattle and hogs, turned loose to forage in the woods, bore their owner's marks on their ears. Even so, they presented a temptation; a large number of court orders dealt with stolen, killed or unlawfully transported animals. Three colonial cows involved in ownership disputes even had their names recorded at court: Py, Butterflower and Sweetlips.

At least one horse abused the freedom that he was allowed; Mr. Dolby's horse had long shown a preference for Thomas Smith's corn field, even breaking down the fence to enter it. Smith had threatened to kill the horse, but when it was found "very much shot and dead" near the broken fence, there was not enough evidence for the jury to convict Smith.

Names

Spelling was very flexible in the 1660's; a person's name was often written several different ways in the same court entry. With a name like Devorax or Ratcliff, the possibilities were almost endless. Because names in this volume are written as they appeared in the original document, it is important that the researcher check the index for every conceivable spelling, getting creative with vowels and even the initial letters.

Christian names were commonly abbreviated. Many of the short forms are still in use; more archaic is "Jno." for John, and "Xper." for Christopher.

Many residents were illiterate, so made marks for their signatures. These marks, as far as possible, appear in parenthesis between the given and surnames. These mark-signatures can be valuable in distinguishing between individuals with the same name; there were at least two, and perhaps three, men named John Watts mentioned in Accomack County records: John Watts, the tailor/planter, who signed with a pair of scissors; John Watts, the cooper; and John Watts, servant and butcher for Dr. Hack, who could write his name.

Titles

Although there was no order of nobility in Virginia in the 17th century, it was a class-conscious society, and the titles used with the names of the colonists held a great deal of significance.
- The term "Honorable" was applied to a man holding a high office such as governor, secretary, auditor or treasurer; his wife was called "Madam."
- The term "Esquire" seems to have been used for a member of the Upper House of the General Assembly, whose position was comparable to a member of the English House of Lords.
- A military title was considered so honorable that it was usually not necessary to use an additional term.
- Precisely defined, and never used lightly, the terms "Gentleman" and "Mr." were generally interchangeable in court documents and were applied to those entitled to use a coat-of-arms. Men of this class were influential in the social life of the community.
- A "Yeoman" occupied a social position between that of the gentleman and common laborer; while he might be called "Mister" on some

occasions, the use of that term in legal documents was reserved for a person of higher social status than that of yeoman.
- In the earlier years the term "Planter" was applied equally to landholders large and small, but gradually it acquired greater status.[2]

Tithables

We have no census for Accomack County during the 1660's; however, we do have tax lists. These lists of tithables, having been compiled by region, tend to have neighbors listed together. For that reason the tax lists in this volume are published as originally written, so unlike the lists of transported persons, they have not been alphabetized.

During the 17th century it was customary to estimate the population as triple the number of tithables.[3]

Head-rights

In 1618, to encourage settlement in the colonies, the head-right system was inaugurated. A person was awarded the right to 50 acres of land for each person whose passage he paid; the certificate he received gave him the right to stake out land wherever he could find it. Loopholes were exploited; a colonist returning from a vacation in England could claim a head-right, as could the sailors in the tobacco ships. "A head-right might require no more than taking an oath in a county court before a friendly judge....No one checked for duplicate entries. Fraud became an integral part of land acquisition."[4] Duplicate names occasionally appeared in the Accomack County entries. Even when the names were not duplicated, some curious coincidences occurred; Mr. Edmond Bowman, himself a justice, transported a group of 24 individuals, three of whom were named Moore Dennis, Morris Dennis and Dennis Morris.

Punishment

The court's panel of judges, or sometimes a jury, would dispense justice and punishment.

In July 1663, Anto. Hodgkins was ordered to employ workers to build a pillory, stocks and whipping post; George Crump agreed to build the ducking stool. The next month Alice Boucher along with Robert Brace, and his servant Elizabeth Leverit, were sentenced to be ducked for scolding and fighting on the Sabbath day. Brace paid 100 lbs tobacco and escaped the punishment, but Alice Boucher was not so fortunate; that November she complained that the ducking had caused her to suffer a miscarriage. A year later Brace had another brush with the ducking stool; for contempt of a court warrant, he was ordered to repair it and stand one hour on the pillory with his fault in capital letters upon his hat.

Fines of between 12 and 50 lbs tobacco were the typical punishments for minor crimes such as non-attendance at church, not clearing the highways, swearing in the face of the court, and drunkenness.

Libel was taken seriously, so people indulging in gossip would sometimes state their stories indirectly. Wm. Alworth, in spreading the rumor of adultery between Mrs. Foxcroft and Mr. Geo. Watson, said that a "bare" was foul of a woman, and it took nine men to rescue her. He later stated it more plainly and was sued by Foxcroft.

James Atkinson, implying that Robert Hewitt killed animals not his own, reported that Hewitt would kill two cows and carry four hides to the tanner. Atkinson also hinted that Hewitt tried to pass off an unlawfully killed pig as a dead raccoon when he reported that Hewitt killed a raccoon as big as two men could carry.

Animals in dispute were central to many court actions, some involving prominent men like Dr. George Hack. Killing a stray cow was considered equal with hog stealing and was punishable by a fine of 2000 lbs tobacco. Even though the ears of hogs and cattle were marked, a hog thief could always claim that the dogs had torn the ears off. Culprits were sometimes seen running away with the head of a pig or were accused of otherwise hiding the evidence.

Dogs, often mentioned in conjunction with hunting, also found their way into court records. When George Brickhouse carelessly fired a gun and killed the dogs belonging to Richard Hinman, the court ordered that he replace them and post a bond for good behavior.

Heavy fines were levied on persons transporting cattle illegally. Dr. Hack and John Meccary, were fined 1000 lbs tobacco for each cow. John Carew paid the same amount for not tending corn.

Twenty-five lashes "well applied to the naked shoulders" was a common punishment for fornication, but such whippings were avoidable when the culprit could pay a fine of 500 lbs tobacco.

Occasionally the most severe punishment would be meted out to servants, who in addition to an extension in their time of servitude, could be "whipped and worked." In November of 1665, Thomas Roberts courageously spoke out against the treatment of William Jones, a servant whipped by four men who took turns beating him till they could no longer stand.

In December 1664, the court was criticized for not building a prison. The following April, Capt. Parker, the new high sheriff, demanded that one be built. The court complied, but one might question the sturdiness of that jail; in November Wm. Onoughton broke out of it and stole Capt. Parker's cutlass.

Fornication

Fornication was a common crime, especially among the servant class; indentured servants were not allowed to marry before their terms expired.[5] This offence was not limited to servants, however; charges of fornication were often leveled against a man and his wife. The county magistrates apparently took careful note of wedding and birth dates, as the case of Gausalin and Bridget Van Nitsin makes clear. They were accused of fornication but were acquitted when the midwife confirmed that Bridget had delivered a "seven month child." All other married couples so accused paid the customary fine of 500 lbs tobacco each; clearly a wedding ceremony did not erase the guilt of fornication that had occurred before the nuptials.

The court was careful to save the parish the expense of raising illegitimate children; often the father would have to post a bond to "save the parish harmless." Although Japhet Cooke declared himself innocent of fornication with Norah and avoided the fine, he was still ordered to support the child and pay court costs.

When fornication crossed racial lines, the penalties were doubled and more. When John Johnson, a married Negro, fathered a child with Hanah Leach, he was imprisoned and worked. His wife Susanna succeeded in obtaining his release, but only on the condition that he support the child, pay all damages, provide a nurse for the child, and post bond for his good behavior. Hanah Leach avoided corporal punishment when she arranged for Col. Scarburgh to pay her fine of 1000 lbs tobacco.

Whether planter, worker, servant or slave, the fornicators of the 1660's were in good company; by 1672, their King, Charles II, had fathered twelve known illegitimate children by seven different women.[6]

Servants

There were various levels of servitude. Some workers were "hired servants," who were paid a wage and were free to work for masters as they chose. (p. 166) Many servants were indentured; before leaving for Virginia they had signed an agreement to serve for a specified period of time in exchange for their transportation. Jane Pitts had a three year indenture, while John Major apparently had been indentured for fourteen years; Wm. Smith purchased him for thirteen years from his first master, Mr. George Hack. Others who arrived without an indenture were expected to serve five years, the "custom of the country." (p. 91, 133)

Some servants were criminals sent to the colonies, and still others had been captured and transported against their will. Young servants, who were brought to the court to have their ages officially judged, would have to serve their masters until adulthood. Some servants were very young; Ruth, the wife of Richard Bundick, wrote a heart-rending letter assigning her illegitimate son to Mrs. Jordan. Ruth regretted that she could not be at court, but "my husband will be there who can dispose of my child." Jane Merideth, a hired servant, died leaving a five-year-old daughter, who Edw. Hamon agreed to take--if he could keep her till she was twenty-one. Others like William Chase, became masters of infant servants. Once the indentured servants had served their time, their masters were to send them on their way with "corn and clothes." (p. 92)

Harshly treated servants had little recourse. Organized search parties hunted for runaways; Indians who captured errant servants were paid for their trouble. (p. 85, 115) John Manington, a servant of Thomas Leatherberry, was abused by both his master and fellow servants; in his case the treatment proved fatal. Other servants, like Edw. Whittell, sick and devoid of hope, chose suicide: he hanged himself in a tobacco house.

Servants could complain to the court, but they were at a definite disadvantage. The master usually received little more than a reprimand while the servant was generally sent back to the abusive master. If the servant misbehaved, he could be whipped, have years added to his time of service or even, like Patrick Huies, be fitted with an iron collar.

Occasionally a servant would turn upon a master. Hanah Snowswell, after delaying a trip to get a pail of water, was struck by her mistress. Hanah turned on her, putting one arm around her neck and the other around her middle. For this offence and telling false tales about her mistress, Hanah received 25 lashes "well applied to her naked shoulders" and one more year of servitude. When Major Tilney criticized his work, Daniell Clansie, a hired servant, grabbed Tilney, struck him and attempted to hit Tilney and another man with a hoe. Clansie got 20 lashes.

Some servants, however, displayed a great deal of loyalty to their masters. John Die had his face bloodied by John Watts' servant, who suspected Die of stealing his master's animals. Watts defended his servant, saying if he'd been in his servant's place, he would have done better. Nineteen year old Phillip Quinton happened upon the servants of Dr. Hack as they were singeing a sow that belonged to Quinton's master. Though outnumbered, he confronted them, demanding to know why they had killed his master's sow. He won the ensuing argument and carried the carcass home on the mare he had with him.

Illness and Insanity

Death and sickness were common, but specific mention of a medical condition was rare. Porky Jane, servant to Col. Scarburgh, died in childbirth; another of his servants, Hugh Bowin, got syphilis from a prostitute. Witnesses observed that John Manington, Leatherberry's dead servant, had been scalded and had the marks of scurvy upon his body.

Two cases of mental illness are recorded: William Onoughton trembled as he loaded his gun and ranted about the enemies before and behind him. He shot at Mrs. Hodgkins' house and crept through a corn field with a large knife to attack John Williams. Dogs prevented that assault, and Onoughton was taken into custody. In another case, Wm. Jones was declared to be unsound of mind and incapable of making decisions.

Indians

Residents of Accomack County in the 1660's took care not to offend the Indians. John Devorax lost his job as an interpreter when he stole a gun from an Indian. John Walthom was dismissed from his position as constable for his actions among the Indians. When Indians apprehended runaway servants they were rewarded with hoes or lengths of shell beads. Several land owners, though already holding patents, exchanged fur mantles to Indian "Kings" for rights to their land. The Indians of Pokomoke complained to the court that John Williams intruded on their land; it was shown that the Indians had sold the land to Williams, but he was ordered to pay them, keep off the land for a year and not to incite them.

All was not peace, however. In November of 1663, the King of Pokomoke came to the commissioners, and producing a medal and document given him by the Governor, complained that his own great men were trying to poison him and incite a rebellion. A party of horse and foot soldiers were sent to his aid, mainly to let him know that he was under the protection of Virginia and not Maryland.

Two months later John Die complained to the court that he had been abused by the King of Matomkin and his great men. Die had been with the Indians about two weeks when they wrested an axe from him and forced him to the ground where he was held by his hair for about an hour while Indians put dirt in his mouth and ears. When the Indians had finished tearing down his "house," the King commanded that he be released.

Defense

Defense was naturally a priority with the county leaders; arms were purchased by the county for resale to the citizens. (p. 99) Only the colonel of the regiment could excuse fines that were imposed on persons failing to provide powder and shot. (p. 106) The fines thus collected from delinquents at musters provided a new drum for the regiment in 1665. (p. 137)

Virginians were suspicious of both the Indians and their neighbors to the north. Debtors and Quakers could elude the grasp of Virginia law by crossing the border into Maryland; the uncertainty of that border proved to be yet another problem. Mr. Edmund Scarburgh recorded the incident at Anamessecks and Manoakin; in October 1663, he and about forty horsemen entered and claimed territory previously considered Maryland's. Some of the residents indicated their willingness to become Virginians and welcomed improved protection from the Indians--others, especially Quakers, were strongly opposed. The intolerance shown by Scarburgh, a county leader, makes the Quaker opposition quite understandable.

Negroes

In September 1666, Mr. Jno. Robins received a certificate for transporting thirty-six people; two of them were Irishmen and fifteen were Negroes. While some Negroes, both men and women, are mentioned as servants, others were free--Antony Johnson and John Johnson both owned land, and Richard Johnson built houses.

Entertainment

In August 1665, Cornelius Watkinson, Phillip Howard and William Darby performed a play called *The Bear and the Cub*. Three months later they were arrested at the complaint of Edward Martin and were ordered to appear in costume at the next court to re-enact the play. After seeing the evidence and listening to the charges, the justices found the three actors not guilty of fault. Edward Martin, the accuser, had to pay the court costs.

Christmas of 1662 was notable for the community hog hunt that took place in Nandue Neck. It was agreed among the neighbors that all hogs good for meat should be killed, regardless of owner. Things were sorted out later with the help of the court.

Richard Buckland, in January of 1664/65, declared that he had set up a house for the "entertainment of inhabitants or strangers." He apparently extended credit to his customers; the sheriff was empowered to collect debts due to Buckland.

Many incidental references indicate that smoking and drinking were common indulgences. Pipes were used for smoking and even bribing--Richard Buckland gave six pipes to a "boy" for pointing out the best of his master's cows. William Price and Thomas "Snudge" carried a coal to light their tobacco; trouble came when they threw it into straw at Col.

Scarburgh's barn door and then stood by while the barn full of corn burned to the ground. Wort, beer in the making, was spilled by the abused servant John Manington when he stumbled over an andiron. Several cases of drunkenness attest to the general availability of strong drink.

Highways

In spite of the extensive use of water for transportation, roads were viewed as essential. In January 1664/65, Mr. Anto. Hodgkins was appointed supervisor over three county road surveyors. Persons owning land on the main road were responsible for clearing a path forty feet wide, or else 10 feet wide with brush cleared 100 feet on each side. One year later it became obvious that the road building standards were too high, and the requirements were eased.

Education

It is interesting that the only real reference to education concerns the schooling of a girl. A cow and calf was the price for teaching Richard Kellum's daughter to write, figure and knit. These arrangements may have been commonplace; it was only because of a dispute concerning the cow that this transaction was recorded.

Calendar and Paging

Until 1752, Britain used the Roman or Julian calendar. Like their legal counterparts in England, the court at Accomack considered the new year to begin on Lady Day, the 25th of March--so December 1664 was followed by January 1664. To avoid confusion in this volume, dates falling between 1 January and 24 March will include both years. A date originally written as 16 January 1664 will appear as 16 January 1664/65.

Court Orders

These Accomack County Court Order abstracts were taken from microfilms of the original handwritten documents. Following each abstract are the original page numbers; an "a" indicates a left-hand page and a "b" indicates a folio or right-hand page. Occasionally words were obliterated by ink blots or were otherwise unreadable. A partially legible word or one with a questionable spelling is followed by a question mark in this volume.

These abstracts are intended as a guide to the original documents. Microfilms of the originals are available through inter-library loan from the Archives Branch, Library of Virginia, 11th St. at Capitol Square, Richmond, VA 23219, or at local Family History Centers.

1. *Ancestry's Red Book: American state, county and town sources*. (Ancestry Incorporated, 1989), p. 690.

2. Philip Alexander Bruce, *Social Life of Virginia in the Seventeenth Century*. (Bowie, Maryland: Heritage Books, 1995 reprint), pp. 105, 112-123.

3. Bruce, p. 14.

4. Ted Morgan, *Wilderness at Dawn: the Settling of the North American Continent*. (New York: Simon & Schuster, 1993), p. 125, 126.

5. Morgan, p. 149.

6. Antonia Fraser, *Royal Charles: Charles II and the Restoration*. (New York: Dell Publishing Co., 1980), p. 411, 412.

Accomack County Court--April 21, 1663

Present: Mr. Anto. Hodgkins   Capt. Geo. Parker
          Mr. Devorx Browne   Mr. Jno. Wise (p. 1)

The oath for administration of justice as commissioners of Accomack County was taken by Mr. Brown and Mr. Wise. Mr. Hugh Yeo, though summoned three times, refused to take the oath. (p. 1)

Surveyors for the highways were appointed as ordered by Northampton County Court 23 March 1662/63:
- Charles Ratcliffe from Dolby's Branch to William Taylor's Bridge from bay to sea
- William Taylor from William Taylor's Branch to Pungoteage Branch at Mr. Hodgkins' from bay to sea
- Edward Revell from Pungoteage Branch at Mr. Hodgkins' house and upwards from bay to sea. (p. 1)

Constables appointed:
- Phillip Fisher from Mr. Dolby's to the Otterdams
- John Waltham from Otterdams to Cradock Creek
- John Druman from the head of Cradock to the head of Pungotege
- Thomas Leatherberry from Mr. Hodgkins' Branch to the head of Pungotege upwards. (p. 1)

Ralph Dow was to construct over the waters of Otterdam a bridge wide enough for a cart and horse to pass and was to be finished by the end October. Payment: 2500 pounds of tobacco. (p. 1, 2a)

Sheriff Henry Jones and Mr. West were to give an account of the estate of Mr. Gerard Bucknor at the next court. (p. 2a)

John Sturgis was granted a certificate for 200 acres for transporting:
John Sanderfer   Joan Mills
Joan Murry   Thomas Evans (p. 2a)

Bill of sale recorded: Alexander Wilson sold a brown mare to Olester Southland and Ralph Doe on 7 November 1662. Witnesses: John King, Henry (B) Browne, Alexander (B) Wilson.

Henry Brown and his wife Ellen, the administratrix of the late Alexander Southland, signed the rights of the above bill of sale to Ralph Doe,

1 April 1663. Signed: Henry (HB) Browne, Ellen (B) Browne. (p. 2a)

Mrs. Anne Toft was granted a certificate for 1200 acres for transporting:

Mary Bridgnorth	James Knowles	John Smith
Thomas Chandler	Michael Loues	Peter Strong
Tobias Dunster	Morgan Mahn?	Abram Vincent
Mary Esthop	Thomas Messenger	James Westgate
John Hartford	William Outred?	Michael White
Atlanta Hues	Richard Porter	Jeffry Wilkins
Even Jones	Margret Roxby	Owen Williams
John Jones	Thomas Rouse	Mary Willis
		(p. 2b)

Persons receiving accommodations during the court sessions were ordered to pay the sheriff when he collected taxes. (p. 2b)

Richard Burdick received a certificate for 600 acres for transporting:

John Aspinall	Thomas Mallowes	Easter Phillips
Henry Horsingham	James Mathews	Jonas Robinson
John James	Martha Milford	James Trustell
John Mallowes	Edwin Montford	William Wright
		(p. 2b)

Ordered that a grand jury attend the next court to inquire into the breach of penal laws and give an account of the persons offending. (p. 2b)

John Savedge was granted a certificate for 250 acres for transporting:

William Haelington	Michaell Lichfield	Abraham Watson
John Howell	James Merecraft	(p. 2b)

John Gerding was granted a certificate for 250 acres for transporting:

Edgar Hine	Edward Smith	Jeffry Wallsingham
Robt. Miller	John Taylor	(p. 2b)

Robert Hicknett was granted a certificate for 250 acres for transporting:

Morris Mathews	James Southfield	Mary Williams
Joan Mills	Theodorik White	(p. 2b)

Ordered that the sheriff summon to the next court: 12 vestrymen, the surveyors of the highways, and the constables. (p. 3a)

William Gowers was granted a certificate for 600 acres for transporting:

Martha Atkins	John Evans	Owen Hopkins

John Markton	Even Powell	John Walford
Margret Mathews	James Powell	James White
Jeffery More	Thomas Smith	Aline Wilson
		(p. 3a)

Ordered that Phillip Fisher, Richard Bayly, Bulbegger Alworth and other Sabbath breakers charged by Major Tilney appear at the next court to answer charges. (p. 3a)

Ordered that the next court be held May 22 at Mr Anto. Hodgkin's house and that the sheriff notify the clerk. (p. 3a)

Accomack County Court--22 May 1663
Mr. Anto. Hodgkins

Present: Major Jno. Tilney   Mr. John Wise

               Mr. Devorax Browne   Mr. Jno. West (p. 3a)

Ordered that the inhabitants of the county bring a list of tithables:
- Major Jno. Tilney's list: from Mr. John Dolby's house to the Otterdam including Bay Side and Sea Side
- Mr. John West's list: from the Otterdam to Mr. Bowman's at the head of Craddock, including Bay Side and Sea Side
- Capt. George Parker's list: from Mr. Bowman's to Mr. Hodgkins including Bay Side and Sea Side
- Mr. Anto. Hodgkins' list: the uppermost part of the county including Bay Side and Sea Side. (p. 3a)

Ordered that Col. Edmund Scarburgh be possessed of the estate of Robt. Wright until administration was legally granted. (p. 3b)

Capt. Geo. Parker entered the court. (p. 3b)

Mr. Randall Revell petitioned for administration of John Nichols' estate and showed depositions indicating that John Nichols desired his estate to go to Randall and Anne Revell, Mr. Revell's children. The court suspended the probate of the oral will and gave Mr. Revell 30 days to bring three of the witnesses to swear before Mr. Anto. Hodgkins, Capt. George Parker, and Mr. John Wise, and in the meantime be possessed of the estate. (p. 3b)

Capt. Parker left while his servants' ages were judged by the court: Thomas Britain, 13 years old; Robert Weste, 11 years old. (p. 3b)

John Williams' servant, Thomas Brook, was judged by the court to be 12 years old. (p. 3b)

Charles Ratcliffe declared against former surveyor Richard Kellum, whose section of the road was not sufficiently cleared. Kellum was fined 500 lbs. of tobacco. (p. 3b)

Ordered that Thomas Tunell give security to Samuel Carter, to whom Tunell owed 2000 lbs. of tobacco for the purchase of a servant. Tunell paid court costs. (p. 3b)

Maj. Tilney exited the court. (p. 3b)

Ordered that the Hungar's Parish levy (which was ordered by the Northampton Co. Court in November 1662) be received by this court. (p. 3b)

Ordered that Philip Fisher remain in the sheriff's custody until he entered a bond for good behavior and paid court costs. (p. 4a)

A complaint, attested to by Maj. Jno. Tilney, was made by the vestry of Hunger's Parish against the following for breaking the Sabbath:

Mary Carrell	Phillip Fisher's wife
William Alworth	Anne Madox
Rich. Bayly	Edmond Kelly
Morgan Dowell	Roger Michel
John Mekittrik	Denis Selevant
Samuell Showell	Philip Fisher's servant William

Each was fined 50 lbs of tobacco and paid court costs. (p. 4a)

John Rany, surveyor, presented Mr. Brookes, Mr. Jacob, and Anthony Johnson, who did not sufficiently clear their roads. Ordered that each pay 50 lbs. of tobacco and court costs. (p. 4a)

Col. Edm. Scarburgh and Mr. Hugh Yeo entered themselves fiefs in trust for the estate of John Nichols in behalf of Randall and Anne Revell, children of Mr. Randall Revell. (p. 4a)

Thomas Leatherberry, Phillip Fisher, John Drumon and John Walthom took their oaths as constables to officiate as ordered on 21 April 1663. (p. 4a)

William Chase acknowledged judgment of 1350 lbs. of tobacco due to Col. John Stringer along with court costs. (p. 4a)

An appeal was granted to Nehemiah Coventon in the difference between him and Mr. John West. (p. 4a)

Mr. Browne exited, and Major Tilney entered the court. (p. 4a)

Folcot Obin acknowledged judgment for 417 lbs. of tobacco due to Mr. Deverx Browne along with court costs. (p. 4a)

In the case of Mr. Devorax Browne, plaintiff, and Capt. Edw. Baker, defendant: Upon Baker's motion, appeal was granted for the next general court at James City with Baker giving security. (p. 4a)

Mr. Browne re-entered the court. (p. 4b)

Ordered that Edward Moore pay George Hamling six barrels of corn and court costs. (p. 4b)

Capt. Parker exited court for the following action:
In the case of Mr. George Hack, plaintiff, and Capt. Geo. Parker, defendant, it was ordered that Parker deliver to Hack a cow and calf. After the calf was weaned, it was to be returned to Parker who was to pay court charges. (p. 4b)

Because Richard Stevens was sued by Nathaniel Bradford without cause, the suit was dismissed with Bradford paying court costs. (p. 4b)

Major Tilney exited court for the following action:
Upon the petition of Major John Tilney, it was ordered that Samuel Showell give security for the payment of 614 lbs of tobacco that he owed Tilney. Showell was to pay court costs. (Extension was issued 12 May 1664 and was satisfied by the payment of Capt. Bowman 12 Sept. 1664. Signed by Mr. Jno. West, high sheriff.) (p. 4b)

Accomack County Court--23 May 1663
Mr. Anto. Hodgkins

Present: Major Jno. Tilney   Mr. Devorax Browne
              Mr. Jno. West   Mr. John Wise (p. 4b)

Capt. Geo. Parker failed to attend the court and was fined 300 lbs of tobacco. (p. 4b)

Ordered that the parish vestry appoint certain days between this day and Whitsuntide[1] to go in procession. (p. 4b)

The case of Capt. Geo. Parker vs. Capt. Edward Baker was referred to the next court.
Ordered that the sheriff take Mr. Edward Baker into custody for his misdemeanor until further order. (p. 4b)

Ordered that John Die deliver to William Silverthorne two barrows and two pigs if they belonged to a sow that Elizabeth Die sold to Silverthorne's wife. John Die was to pay court costs and Silverthorne was to pay 60 lbs of tobacco to Die for corn fed the animals. (p. 5a)

John Watts consented to pay 50 lbs of tobacco and court costs for his servant's breaking the Sabbath. (p. 5a)

Mr. Edward Baker, under a good behavior bond for irreverent behavior to the court, was released from his commitment; he promised better behavior and paid court costs. (p. 5a)

Capt. Parker entered the court. (p. 5a)

John Watts was ordered to pay court charges for harassing John Die and pretending that Die had beaten Watts' servant. The contrary appeared to be true by the following depositions:
Deposition of Thomas Leatherberry, 22 May 1663: About May 2, when John Watts' servant was at Leatherberry's house looking for cattle, Leatherberry asked the servant if he knew that John Die hunted the Leatherberry cattle, to which the servant replied yes, and that his master and mistress knew it. Leatherberry replied that John Die denied it. The servant said that he, his master and dame would execute justice and went his way. Leatherberry presently heard a noise and the words "rogue" and "thief," but did not know who spoke them. Soon John Die came to Leatherberry's house all bloody, claiming that John Watts' servant had beaten him. Signed, Thomas (T) Leatherberry.
Deposition of Daniel Till aged about 28 years, 23 May 1663: As Till was coming from Leatherberry's house, John Die requested him to help him

---

[1]*The week beginning with Whitsunday, the fiftieth day after Easter.*

home with his cattle. Till went back to light his pipe and then went to
help, but not meeting John Die, went to Die's house. When Die came
home he was all bloody about the face. John Watts happened to be there,
so Die told Watts that Watts' servant had beaten him. Watts replied, "If
[I] had been in [my] man's stead, [I] would have done better." Signed,
Daniel (3) Till.

Deposition of Robert Houston, 22 May 1663: John Watts sent for Houston
to view his servant. One of the servant's hands and his left shin were
swollen, and his belly was very hard. Coming home, Houston met John
Die and told him that he had done well to cripple John Watts' servant.
Die said that he did the servant no harm, but that the servant threw Die
down and stood astride him facing away. Die kicked Watts' servant off
him and got up. Seeing the servant unable to resist, John Die said,
"Being thou art another man's servant, go like a rogue as thou art." (p.
5a, b)

Robert Brace was found guilty of mismarking a heifer belonging to Robert
Bayly. Ordered that Brace pay 1000 lbs tobacco to Bayly and a fine of
1000 lbs tobacco. Brace was to remain in the sheriff's custody until
posting bond for good behavior and paying court costs.

Deposition of John Drumond aged 26 years, 22 May 1663: About April
1st, Drumond went with John Barnet to Brace's to take notice that Brace
had marked Robert Bayley's calf. They found a calf formerly marked by
Bayley tied and with ears freshly bleeding. Brace acknowledged that he
marked it. Signed, John Drumond.

Deposition of William Aborne aged 26: Said the same as John Drumond.

Deposition of John Barnet aged about 30 years, 22 May 1663: Going to
Brace's house, Barnet asked if Brace had marked any animals lately.
Brace answered, "What need [you] care?" Barnet saw Bayly's heifer with
ears bloody from Brace's mark. Asked why he did it, Brace said he
might as well claim all he could. Signed, John (B) Barnet.

Deposition of Tobias Sellvey, 22 May 1663: Robert Bayley's wife
requested him to view a calf marked by Robert Brace. "We found Robert
Bayley's mark old made and Mr. Brace's mark new made bleeding."
This calf had been in Sellvey's field all year, and he knew it to be
Bayley's by mark and color. Signed, Tobias Sellvey.

Deposition of John Smally, 23 May 1663: Last winter four yearlings came
home "to my master Robt. Brace, and I told him of them, for I took
them to be my master's by the color, but their marks I know not."
Signed, John Smally. (p. 5b-6a)

Henry Jones assumed power of attorney for the executors of Mr. Gerard
Bucknor. Jones was to give account of Bucknor's estate the next Monday

at the house of Capt. Parker.

The estate of Mr. Gerard Bucknor owed Capt. William James seven pounds twelve shillings sterling. Henry Jones, attorney, was ordered to pay, if not money, then tobacco at ten shillings per hundred. He was also to pay court charges. (p. 6a)

Because William Jones was of unsound mind and not capable of making bargains, Ralph Dow did not have to meet the obligation of paying William Smith 1000 lbs tobacco for him. Ralph Dow was to keep Jones and give the court a yearly account of his labor and living costs. (p. 6b)

Richard Kellum admitted killing Richard Buckland's cow and was ordered to pay a fine of 1000 lbs tobacco and to pay Buckland 1000 lbs tobacco and a new cow. Kellum was to remain in the sheriff's custody till posting a bond for good behavior and paying court costs.

The jury considered the difference between Buckland and Kellum and found the cow called Butterflower to be Buckland's.

The jury, sent out again, considered Kellum's confession and found it to be a matter of fact.

Deposition of John Jenkins, 22 May 1663: Two years ago last March Jenkins accompanied Buckland to Kellum's, and Kellum asked what Buckland would charge to teach his daughter to write, figure, and knit. Buckland asked for a cow and calf, to which Kellum agreed. About a month later the cow, Butterflower, and a calf was brought to Buckland by John Burt, Kellum's servant. Buckland marked the calf with his own mark. Signed, John (II) Jenkins.

Deposition of John Burt servant, 22 May 1663: John Jenkins was not at "my master's house when I carried the cow away to Richard Buckland's for to give the child milk." Signed, John Burt.

Deposition of Richard Welch, 22 May 1663: "To the best of my knowledge, John Jenkins was not at my master's house" the day the cow was driven to Buckland's. Signed, Richard (x) Welch.

Deposition of Daniell Dorman aged about 22 years, 22 May 1663: Because he was at William Bosman's to "fetch guns home" that day, he knows nothing of the matter. Signed, Daniel (CC) Dorman

Deposition of Dorothy Churchill aged about 20 years, 23 May 1663: Dorothy was in the cowpen when Buckland came in and she knew of no sale or bargain or of any delivery of a cow by her master to anyone. John Jenkins was not there at any time. Signed, Dorothy (~) Churchill.

Deposition of John Burt aged about 24 years, 22 May 1663: "I never knew Richard Kellum to deliver a cow and calf to Richard Buckland or ever sell him one." Signed, John Burt.

Deposition of Richard Welch aged about 19 years, 22 May 1663: Said the same as John Burt. Signed, Richd. (e) Welch. (p. 6b-7a)

Capt. George Parker (who exited court) complained that Mr. George Hack
   had killed hogs belonging to Parker. The jury found Dr. Hack guilty and
   ordered him to pay Parker 2000 lbs tobacco and remain in the sheriff's
   custody till he posted bond for good behavior and paid court costs.
Evidence for Capt. Parker:
Deposition of John Marshall aged 20 years, sworn before Edm. Scarburgh
   14 June 1662: Marshall was hunting in the woods with Dr. George
   Hack, George Truett and Thomas Newton. The dogs took hold of a
   white boar which Dr. Hack claimed to be his, and he caused Marshall
   to kill it. The same day Dr. Hack claimed a white sow, asking his
   servant Edward if he did not know his sow that had been gone so long.
   Edward agreed, and Dr. Hack asked George Truet to kill it. As the
   servant was beginning to carry it home, Marshall looked at the ears and
   told Dr. Hack that the sow belonged to Capt. George Parker. "It is so,"
   said Dr. Hack, and was going to leave it, but Marshall and Truett carried
   it to safety for Capt. Parker. As they were hunting they found a boar
   bound, and Dr. Hack said it was his, but Marshall told him it was not
   his mark. Then Dr. Hack said it was his boy Brian's. Signed, John
   (circle with +) Marshall.
Deposition of Thomas Newton aged about 36 years, 22 May 1663: Newton
   said the same, only he did not see the mark of the boar that was tied.
   Signed, Thomas (e) Newton.
Deposition of Cristopher Calvert, 22 May 1663: Around last July Dr.
   Hack's servant, John the butcher, came to Calvert's house complaining
   of bad usage and said that Dr. Hack sent him into the woods to kill any
   hog he could find. Signed, Cristopher (+) Calvert.
Deposition of Phillip Quinton aged about 19 years, 22 May 1663: About a
   year ago his master sent him for a mare at Mr. Littleton's, and in
   returning he met Dr. Hack's Negro woman coming from William
   Boucher's with fire. When Quinton demanded to know where she was
   going with it, she answered to singe a hog. He went with her into the
   swamp where "I found Dr. Hack's butcher by a sow of my master's
   which they had killed, and I demanded wherefore they had killed my
   master's sow, and so big with pig, upon which they gave me ill
   language, calling me lying rogue, and said it was their master's mark."
   An argument ensued, with Hack's servants saying it might be James or
   Richard Woodworth's mark. On parting Quinton said he would have the
   sow or the ears to carry home, which being refused, he said he would
   send his master. One of the servants called him back and put the sow on
   the mare Quinton was taking home. The servants told him that Black
   Jack, Mr. Littleton's Negro, was out with the dogs looking for more.

Signed, Phillip (W with an arch) Quinton.

Deposition of John Parker aged about 28 years, 22 May 1663: About two years ago Parker was with John Nichols at Mr. George Parker's house when they heard a great cry of hogs. Looking out, they found Dr. Hack's dogs upon Parker's hogs, wounding them. John Parker immediately took one of the dogs and killed him. Signed, John Parker.

Evidence for Mr. Hack:

Deposition of John Watts aged about 22 years, sworn 13 April 1663 before J. Custis: Watts stated that he knew Mr. George Hack had a white boar that used to use Hack's old field, but being harassed by hogs and dogs, left the field. About a year ago Watts went hunting for Hack's hogs and saw the boar with two barrows. Watts told Mrs. Hack of it in the presence of George Truett. Watts testified that George Hack always gave him strict order not to kill any hog but his own. Signed, John Watts.

Deposition of William Chase aged 25 years, 22 May 1663: Chase knew that Mr. George Hack had a large white boar which a year ago last summer used Hack's old field. It was always fighting with Hack's blue boar "and made such a tumult in the tobacco house as if the devil was in it." Being torn at the ears by hogs and dogs, the boar left the plantation and Chase saw it no more. Signed, Wm. (O) Chase.

Deposition of John Rickets, 22 May 1663: Last Christmas Rickets' master sent him into the woods to look for a boar killed the day before by John Michill. Richets did not find it, so his master sent for John Michill and George Truet with their dogs. Michell found the boar and said it was not Capt. Parker's and advised Rickets' master to cut off the left ear to satisfy Parker that it wasn't his. Signed, John Rickets.

Deposition of Edward Dale aged about 20 years, 22 May 1663: The day before George Truet and Dale (who was George Hack's servant) hunted hogs, Capt. Parker's servant said that he had been hunting hogs with dogs. When Dale went to George Truet's he found a hog tied, but he did not know by whom. Signed, Edw. (2) Dale.

Deposition of William Boucher aged about 56 years, 22 May 1663: Last Christmas evening when the neighbors had been hunting, John Machell told Boucher that he'd had no luck for George Truet, but Machell had killed two barrows and a boar for Mr. Hack and a sow for Capt. Parker. Machell further stated that he knew Hack had a white boar that had been torn at the ears by dogs and that there was nothing left of the right ear, only a piece. Signed, William (line with arch) Boucher. (p. 7b-9a)

Petition by Mr. John West for satisfaction from Mr. Bucknor's estate: West was to get 8 lbs tobacco per 100 received and 2 lbs more per 100 for the lack of a man to go with him as promised. If Bucknor's attorney, Mr. Jones, found a man, the two pounds would not be allowed. (p. 9a)

Ordered that John Die be fined 12 lbs tobacco and court costs for swearing in the face of the court. (p. 9a)

Deposition of Thomas Benthall aged about 50 years, 23 May 1663: A year ago last February John Die's wife sold a sow to William Silverthorne's wife for a pair of French shoes, three ells of linen and three yards of canvas. Silverthorne's wife failed to take the sow, so Die's wife asked Benthall to remind her. Silverthorne's wife neglected till after the sow had five pigs. It was concluded that Die's wife should have two of the pigs for looking after the sow and that Silverthorne's wife should have two with the sow. They were to kill the fifth pig and eat it together. Signed, Thomas Bentall. (p. 9a)

Henry Smith discharged Mrs. Dorithy Jorden from all debts "from the beginning of the world to this day," 13 March 1662/3. Signed by Henry Smith. Witnesses: John Shepherd and John Yeo. Recorded 23 May 1663, by Robt. Hutchinson. (p. 9a)

Henry Jones, agent for executors of Mr. Gerrard Bucknor, discharged John Fawsett from all debts except a bill of 1217 lbs tobacco dated 12 May 1663. Signed, Henry Jones. Witnesses: John Walthoum and Richard (RK) Kellum. Recorded 23 May 1663 by Robt Hutchinson. (p. 9b)

Edmund Scarburgh sold to Mrs. Anne Toft a bay mare colt with a white star on the forehead 27 October 1662. Signed, Edm. Scarburgh. Witnesses: James Cade, Jon. Alexander. Recorded 23 May 1663. (p. 9b)

Richard Bundick, planter, and his wife Dorothy sold to Richard Jacob, planter, recently of Northampton Co., 500 acres on the southern branches of Pungotege Creek between the deep branch and the main branch. The neck of land was originally purchased from Nicholas Waddelow, planter. Richard Jacob died before the completion of the agreement, but the Bundicks had already received payment for all but 100 acres. Jacob had bequeathed the land in his will, and the Bundicks confirmed the sale. Signed 23 May 1663, Richard (backwards B,R) Bundick and Dorithy (backwards B) Bundick. Witnesses: Will. Jones, Tho. Fowkes. Recorded 25 May 1663 by Robt. Hutchinson. (p. 9b, 10a)

Richard Bundick and wife Dorithy sold to the heirs of Richard Jacob, deceased, 350 acres originally granted to them by Gov. Francis Moryson 20 October 1661, and bounded by the land of Nicholas Waddelow. The sale included "house and housing, orchard and all the edifices." Signed 23 May 1663, Richard (backwards B,R) Bundick and Dorithy (backwards B) Bundick. Witnesses: Will. Jones, Tho. Fowkes. Recorded 25 May 1663, by Robt. Hutchinson. (p. 10b)

On 4 October 1662, appearing before John Daniell, Notary of London, were Ralph Allen and Thomas Bucknor gentlemen of London and the executors of Gerrard Bucknor, deceased merchant of London. Letters of administration bore date 13 September 1663, for probate of wills. They granted the power of attorney to Robert Pitts, mariner of London, and Devoroux Brown and Henry Jones merchants of Virginia. Signed, Ra. Allen, Thos. Bucknor, J. Dickinson, Nic. Hayward, Joes. Daniel.

John Fredericke, Knight Lord Mayor, attested that John Daniell was a notary, sworn and admitted, and that these documents were credible, dated 7 October 1662. (p. 11b)

Accounts received of Mr. James Wingfield, 1662: 30018 pounds tobacco.

Debts for 1662/63 included payments to: Nathaniel Coledick, Commander for tobacco shipped on the *Vincent* of London; Mr. John West for receiving tobacco; William Jones for Mr. Wingfield's accommodation; Mr Devorax Browne for physic and Mr. Wingfield's accommodation; Mr. George Hack for physic for Mr. Wingfield; the sheriff and clerk concerning Mr. Wingfield, and necessary expenses. Signed, Hen. Jones.

The 1662 listing of cargo for the account of Mr. Gerrard Bucknor included some of the following: a quarter cask of Rhenish wine and four loaves of sugar sent to Col. Scarburgh as a gift; prunes used at sea for sickness; sugar used at sea for the servants; nutmeg, pepper, cloves, cinnamon and currants; cotton cloth and canvas; hats and shoes.

The 1662/63 expenses included payments to: Nathaniel Coledick, commander bound for Accomack in Virginia; John West for receiving tobacco; Mr. John Fawcett for selling goods and for the use of his horse; Col. Scarburgh for physic. Also mentioned is a bond of Mr. James Cades' for 41 pounds 19 shillings 6 pence sterling. (p. 11b-12a)

Accomack County Court--25 May 1663

Present:
                    Mr. Anto. Hodgkins
        Capt. Geo. Parker   Mr. John West
        Mr. Devorx. Browne   Mr. John Wise (p. 13a)

Mr. Henry Jones swore 25 May 1663, that the account presented was the whole account of the estate of Mr. Gerrard Bucknor in the counties of Accomack and Northampton. Signed, Henry Jones. (p. 13a)

Deposition of Owen Mackra aged about 23 years, 16 May 1663: About last January as they were crossing over a branch at Pungotege, Mackra asked

John Nichols, "What if you should fall into this branch and then should
die, what would you give me?" Nichols said he had already disposed of
his estate to his brother Randall and his sister Anne, and added that he
had no reason to give his brother Edward anything. Signed, Owen ([][])
Mackra. Witnesses: Edward Dickenson, William Thorne, Thomas Davis.
Sworn 13 June 1663, before Anto. Hodgkins, Geo. Parker, Jno. Wise.
(p. 13a)

Deposition of Elizabeth Munt aged about 38 years, 16 May 1663: About 23
   March, John Nichols came to her house to see his brother and sister.
   "He took his brother Randall on the one knee and his sister Anne on the
   other and said, 'Alas, poor rogues, they have no luck with their sheep,
   but if I live I will recruit their store, and if I die I will give them all that
   I have betwixt them, for I love them as dear as if they were my own
   natural brother and sister.'" Then he and the children wept while Nichols
   embraced them both. Elizabeth Munt then told him his fondness would
   spoil the children, and he replied, "I should be very sorry to do them
   wrong, but all the good I can. Nor anyone else shall do them wrong
   whilst that I live." Signed, Elizabeth Munt. Witnesses: Edw. Dickenson,
   Wm. Thorne, Tho. Davis. Sworn 13 June 1663 before Anto. Hodgkins,
   Geo. Parker, Jno. Wise. (p. 14a)

Accomack County Court--16 July 1663

Present: Anto. Hodgkins   Mr. Devorax Browne
                  Mr. John Wise   Major Jno. Tilney
                       Capt. Geo. Parker   (p. 14a)

Kathrin Scarborow in 1659, had placed in the custody of Nehemiah
   Covington two heifers that she had given to her son Henry Scarburgh.
   Mr. John West petitioned in behalf of Henry for the possession of the
   heiffers. Ordered that Covington deliver the heifers with their increase
   and at the next court give an account of the rest of the estate in his
   possession and of his expenses in caring for it so satisfaction could be
   made. (p. 14a)

The suit brought against Denis Selevant by Nicholas Rogers was dropped
   because Rogers failed to enter complaint. Rogers paid court costs. (p.
   14a)

The suit brought against George Hamling by Edward Moore was dropped;
   Moore failed to enter complaint. Moore paid court costs. (p. 14a)

Mr. West Entered court. (p. 14a)

The suit brought against Joseph Pitman by James Atkinson was dropped because Atkinson failed to enter complaint. Atkinson paid court costs. (p. 14a,b)

The suit brought against Jonah Jackson by John Rogers was dropped because Rogers failed to enter complaint. Rogers was to pay court costs. (p. 14b)

Edward Smith had in his possession Morris Mathews' heifer, which Smith claimed was sold by Mathews. Being unable to prove this, Smith was ordered to deliver the heifer and her increase and pay court costs.

Deposition of Phillip Fisher, 16 July 1663: Fisher knew of no cow on his plantation belonging to Richard Archer, but knew of Morris Matthews' cow, which Fisher had held while Matthews marked it as a calf. Signed, Phillip Fisher.

Deposition of Samuell Showell, 16 July 1663: Claimed that Morris Mathews sold a calf to Richard Archer who asked Showell to bear witness. Signed, Samuell Showell.

Deposition of John Mekittrick, 16 July 1663: Said he was ordered by Richard Archer to receive a calf from Morris Matthews. It was among wild cattle. Signed, John (0=) Mekettrick. (p. 14b)

The case of John Jenkins, plaintiff, and John Rogers, defendant, was referred to the next court so the parties could bring in evidence. (p. 14b)

Ordered that James Atkinson be fined 50 lbs tobacco for breaking the Sabbath. (p. 15a)

The case of William Blake, plaintiff, and Jno. Prittyman, defendant, was referred to the next court for collection of evidence. (p. 15a)

Mr. George Hack's servant Peter York was judged to be 13 years old.

Mr. George Hack requested the court to judge the age of his servant John Craine, but as Craine had an indenture, the court ordered he serve only the length of time in the signed indenture. (p. 15a)

The suit against John Johnson was dropped because Nich. Rogers failed to enter a bill of complaint. Rogers paid court costs. (p. 15a)

For her lying and scandalous speech about the disagreement between Robert Huitt and James Atkinson, Issabella Ware was ordered into the sheriff's custody to receive fifteen lashes upon her naked shoulders and to pay court costs. (p. 15a)

Ordered that Richard Bundick pay his debt of 400 lbs tobacco to Robt. Bayly and pay court costs. (p. 15a)

Major Tilney exited the court for the following action: (p. 15a)
Mr. Jno. Dolby had Thomas Smith arrested for a horse found dead by Smith's field. The jury found that Dolby had no cause for action. The suit was dropped with Dolby paying court charges.
The names of the jury:

Alex Addison	Ralph Dow	John Renny
Nath. Bradford	Tho. Foolkes	John Smith
Cristopher Calvert	Geo. Johnson	Arthur Upshott
Timothy Coe	James Paine	Mr. Geo. Watson

Verdict: The jury found it not a matter of fact by these evidences:

Deposition of Major John Tilney, 6 July 1663: About the beginning of May, he met Mr. John Dolby, whose horse was killed. Tilney went with him to Thomas Smith's old field where he saw "the horse, very much shot and dead." About a hundred yards away Tilney saw a newly broken fence with horsetracks in the field. Signed, Jno. Tilney.

William Major, on 6 July 1663, said the same as Major John Tilney. Signed, William Major.

Deposition of George Brickhouse, 16 July 1663: Last spring he and Thomas Smith saw Dolby's horse come into Smith's field. Smith said he would fix the fence and warn Dolby to control his horse, and if the horse came back after the warning, let "him stand to the adventure." After the horse was dead, Dolby's servants claimed that Brickhouse heard Smith say he would kill Mr. Dolby's horse. George Brickhouse asked Smith and his wife whether they had said this. They replied that they did not say they would kill him, but that they would pepper his hindparts. Signed, George Brickhouse.

Deposition of Margret Morgan aged about 25 years, 16 July 1663: On Sunday afternoon the 3rd of May, the day that her master's horse was killed, she went to the horse, and on the way met George Brickhouse and his wife, who both turned back and went with her to where Dolby's horse lay dead. Brickhouse set his foot upon the horse, said it was a great pity and added, "I see Thomas Smith is as good as his word, for he threatened a great while ago that he would shoot this horse." Signed, Margret (MM) Morgan.

Deposition of Thomas Johnson aged about 20 years, 16 July 1663: Said that last April he had gone many times to the house of George Brickhouse to fetch his master's horse. Brickhouse asked Johnson to tell his master

Dolby to keep his horse at home, for a neighbor threatened to kill it. Signed, Thomas (O) Johnson.

Deposition of Derrick Costianne aged about 15 or 16 years, 16 July 1663: On Easter Day, April 19, he was at the house of George Brickhouse looking for his master's horse for him to go to church. Thomas Smith and his wife were also there. Brickhouse said that the horse had been in his field and was now by his fence. Thomas Smith remarked that if the horse came into his field, he would shoot him. "'Nay,' quoth his wife, 'we will pound him.'" Smith answered that the horse would not come off so well and repeated that he would shoot him. Signed, Derrick (O) Costeanne. (p. 15a-16a)

Ordered that Richard Kellum be released from his bond for good behavior with him paying court costs. (p. 16a)

Ordered that Phillip Fisher be released from his bond for good behavior with him paying court costs. (p. 16a)

The suit against Henry Jones was dropped because Mr. West failed to enter a bill of complaint. West paid court costs. (p. 16a)

Henry Jones presented an account of Mr. Gerrard Bucknor's estate. Col. Edmond Scarburgh objected to it as false. Ordered that Jones attend an inquiry the first day after the next court. (p. 16b)

A jury found Jno. Goring and Robert Hignet guilty of marking pigs not their own. Ordered that Goring and Hignet pay a fine of 2000 lbs tobacco and post a bond for good behavior and pay court costs. Edmond Kelly claimed the pigs but had no proof. Col. Scarburgh, His Majesty's treasurer's deputy, laid claim to the pigs for the use of the King. Kelly was referred to the next court to prove them his or be censured by the court. The names of the jury:

Alex. Addison	Ralph Dow	John Renny
Nath. Bradford	Tho. Foolkes	John Smith
Cristopher Calvert	Geo. Johnson	Arthur Upshott
Timothy Coe	James Paine	Mr. Geo. Watson

Deposition of Phillip Fisher, 16 July 1663: Edmund Kelly came and asked Fisher to view three of his pigs that went out with his sows unmarked and returned marked. Morgan Dowell, who was present, said it was Robert Hignet's mark. Fisher said to pen the pigs and go to Hignet's to see his mark. He did; Robert Hignet and John Goring went with him. Signed, Phillip Fisher.

Deposition of Robert Dow, 16 July 1663: Said that Robert Hignet acknowl-

edged that he marked one of the pigs claimed by Edmond Kelly, and that
Jno. Gording marked two of them. When asked, he said, "I own the
mark but disown the pigs." Signed, Ralph (R) Dow.

Deposition of Denis Selevant, 16 April 1663: Said that Robert Hignet admitted marking pigs claimed by Edmond Kelly, and said he was sorry,
for he took them for wild pigs. Selevant said that John Goring asked to
buy the pigs from Kelly. Signed, Denis (N with circle on top) Selevant.

Deposition of Cristian Stampherron, 16 July 1663: Said that Edmond Kelly
found two of his pigs marked with John Goring's mark and one with
Robert Hignet's. Hignet admitted the one mark and said he was sorry if
they were Kelly's pigs. John Goring had said they belonged to wild
sows. Signed, Cristian (t) Stampheron.

Deposition of Roger Michell, 16 July 1663: Michell was requested by Kelly
to view three pigs with his sows that returned with the marks of Robt.
Hignett and Jno. Goring. Signed, Roger (RM) Michell.

Deposition of Thomas Carrell, 16 July 1663: Carrell was requested by
Kelly to view the pigs with Robt. Hignet's mark. The marked pigs
followed Edm. Kelly's sow. Signed, Thomas (|--|) Carrell. (p. 16b-17a)

Judgment against Henry Jones at the suit of Col. Edm. Scarburgh,
collector: Jones transported six hogsheads of tobacco across the bay
without certificate. Ordered that he pay six hogsheads of tobacco and
court costs. (p. 17b)

With his consent, it was ordered that George Crump provide a ducking
stool before the next court, thereby acquitting his servant Issabella Wall
from a court-ordered whipping. Crump to pay court costs. (p. 17b)

The suit against William Silverthorne was dropped because Tho. Bentall
failed to enter his petition. Bentall paid court costs. (p. 17b)

George Brickhouse fired a gun unlawfully and killed Richard Hinman's
dogs. Ordered that Brickhouse post a bond for good behavior, replace
the dogs and pay court costs. (p. 17b)

Mr. West left the court for the following action:
The order of nonsuit against Mr. West obtained by Henry Jones appeared,
after examination and the testimony of Mr. Edm. Bowman, to be falsely
obtained. The order was reversed with Henry Jones fined 100 lbs tobacco
and court costs for his abuse of the court. (p. 17b)

Ordered that the sheriff send for Elizabeth Leveret to appear in court. (p.
17b)

William Smith petitioned to be discharged as guardian of Richard Hinman. As Timothy Coe was willing to be guardian, it was ordered that Coe should receive Hinman's estate and that he give a yearly account of it. (p. 17b)

Deposition of Edmond Bowman, 17 July 1663: Bowman was requested by Mr. Henry Jones to arbitrate between Jones and Mr. John West. Bowman went to the house of West, who said he wanted something from Col. Scarburgh that might enlighten the agreement, and that Scarburgh would bring it to court. Bowman went to court and told Jones that he would end the business if they were ready. (p. 18a)

Ordered that the case of John Jenkins and John Rogers be suspended till the next court so evidence could be produced. (p. 18a)

Ordered that the sheriff give Elizabeth Leveret thirty lashes on her naked shoulders for rebellion to her master and insolence to her fellow servant. (p. 18a)

Richard Bundick, who had been ordered to pay 400 lbs of tobacco to Robert Bayly, made a motion to have the order reversed and have a trial at the next court. It was granted. (p. 18a)

Upon the request of Jno. Prityman, it was ordered that the case between him and Wm. Blake be suspended till the next court. (p. 18a)

John Jenkins petitioned to bring to court the heifer in controversy between him and John Rogers. Considering the trouble that might arise, the court appointed Richard Buckland, Wm. Andrews and Edward Hazard to view the heifer and give a report at the next court. (p. 18a)

Ordered that Robert Brace's bond for good behavior be returned, with him paying court costs. (p. 18a)

Oath of administration of justice as commissioner of Accomack County was taken by Hugh Yeo, who then entered the court. (p. 18b)

Complaint was made by Robert Brace against his servant Thomas Cottingham for his stubbornness and swearing. Upon Cottingham's confession and promise of better behavior, punishment was remitted. Ordered that the next time he was heard swearing, he was to have twenty-one lashes on his naked shoulders and punishment for his former offense. (p. 18b)

Ordered that Mr. Watson replace Richard Hill as foreman of the grand jury, and because Hill acted insolently to the court, he was ordered committed into the sheriff's custody till posting bond for good behavior, paying a fine of 300 lbs tobacco, and court costs.

Ordered that Richard Hill pay the fees for his arrest at the suit of Capt. Parker. (p. 18b)

Anto. Hodgkins was given the power to employ workmen to build a pillory, stocks and whipping post. (p. 18b)

Mr. Hugh Yeo exited the court for the following action:

Col. Edm. Scarburgh and Mr. Hugh Yeo, bound over John Nichol's estate for the security of Edward Revell against any trouble coming from James Bonwell, who had purchased land from John Nichols. (p. 18b)

Murrin Cornelius had repeated several "speeches" disparaging the wife of Robert Huit. Cornelius confessed and said she had heard them from Mary White, but could not prove it. Cornelius was ordered to make her contrition by acknowledgement in court and in both Occahannock Church and Nanduce? Church. She was to pay court costs. (p. 18b, 19a)

William Smith, guardian of Richard Hinman, was taken to court by Mr. Leving Denwood concerning land belonging to Hinman and claimed by Denwood. The court examined the title and found that Denwood formerly sold the land to Coale. Ordered that the suit be dropped and Denwood pay court costs. (p. 19a)

Deposition of Daniell Mackare, 16 July 1663: According to Murrin Cornelius, Mary White said that Goody Huitt, when she was in England, had stolen a gown and hood.

Deposition of Joseph Pitman, 16 July 1663: Murrin Cornelius told Pitman that Mary White reported that Dame Huitt, when she was in England, stole a gown, a hood and a smoothing iron. While at Daniell Makare's, she also reported that Robert Huit (Pitman's master) and Pitman had stolen thirteen or fourteen hogs. Two days later Cornelius came to Huitt's house where Dame Huitt spoke to her about her words. Cornelius replied that she said them out of spite. Signed, Joseph (2) Pitman.

Deposition of Susan Hall, aged about 19 years, 16 July 1663: Murrin Cornelius told Hall that Mary White said Dame Huitt (Hall's mistress) had stolen a gown, a scarf, a hood and a smoothing iron in England. Afterwards Murrin admitted she had told about the hogs and the thefts out of spite. (p. 19a)

The case between Robert Huitt, plaintiff, and James Atkinson, defendant, concerning hogs and cattle was referred to a jury, which found Huitt guilty of killing hogs and cattle other than his own. Ordered that Robert Huitt pay 1000 lbs tobacco to James Atkinson and a fine of 1000 lbs tobacco. Huitt was to be held in the sheriff's custody till posting bond for good behavior and paying court costs.

The names of the jury:

Alex. Addison	Ralph Dow	Jno. Renny
Nath. Bradford	Thomas Foolkes	John Smith
Cristopher Calvert	Geo. Johnson	Arthur Upshott
Timothy Coe	James Price	George Watson

Deposition of Hugh Cornelius and Marrion his wife, 16 July 1663: About a year ago Mary White related that Richard Hill's barrow got into Undimon's field, where Huitt killed it and with his men carried it home. When the hog was dressed, they saw Richard Hill's daughter coming to the house, so they cut off the hog's head and ran into a little room with it. As Capt. Baker and Hill were at Huitt's house the next Sabbath, they were invited to stay to dinner. Hill asked if that was part of the same poor sow that Huitt had sent Hill's wife a piece of. Mary White also related that Huitt had killed only one poor sow that year. She added that Robert Huitt's wife sent for her and asked what her nephew had said about her. Mary White told her what had been related. Huitt's wife said that if Mary had told her in private, she would have liked Mary well, but now Richard Hill and everyone would hear it. Signed, Hugh (x) Cornelius, Marrion (backward 3) Cornelius.

Deposition of John Lecatt aged about 21 years, 16 July 1663: Last Christmas "my Dame Milby sent me" to Robert Huett's house, and while there Lecatt saw hanging at the door a singed hog with both ears cut off. Signed, Jean Le Cat.

Deposition of Charles Ratcliff, 16 July 1663: A month ago Robert Huit's servant brought a cow hide with the ears and cheek torn away. He said that Mr. Tropmill bought it from his master. Signed, Charles Rackleff.

Deposition of Hugh Turpin, 16 July 1663: About a year and a half ago Turpin was at Robert Huett's house, and Mary White said to the maid servant, "What shall we do, for we shall want meat." The maid replied that they would have enough, for last year her master went out and brought home two hogs in the evening and had them in the curing tub before morning. Signed, Hugh Turpin.

Deposition of Isaac Dix, 16 July 1663: Isaac Dix said the same as Hugh Turpin. Signed, Isaac Dix. (p. 19a-20a)

The following persons were ordered to appear at the next court for fornication and "other crimes":

For fornication[2]:

Roger Dickenson and Mary Trotman
Daniell Curtis and Mary Green
Mr. Cade and Mary Chambers
Jno. Tick and Alice Roberts
Tho. Davis and Jane his wife
Van Netsin and Bridget his wife
Jno. Watts and Mary his wife
Wm. Onoughton and Eliza. Shepway
Jno. Rogers and Mary his wife
Edw. Revel and Frances his wife
Jno. Willis and Jane Scoffull
Ab Church and Mary Scading
Mihill Gray with Mrs. Anne Toft's servant
Wm. Browne and Japhet Cook with Norah

Thomas Wally and wife for fighting with Jno. Paramore on the Sabbath.
Edward Smith for breach of the Sabbath.
Mr. George Hack for a stray beast. (p. 20a)

Deposition of William Silverthorne, 17 July 1663: In June he was at William Taylor's cowpen where he saw a young cow with Mr. Revell's mark. He had the ears in his hand and took notice of it. Signed, Wm. (M) Silverthorne (p. 20a)

Col. Edm. Scarburgh petitioned on behalf of Mr. Charles Scarburgh for determining the outset of the main branch of Pungoteage Creek. Ordered that a jury including one or more surveyors seek the place in question and return a verdict at the next court. (p. 20b)

Mr. West exited the court for the following:

For transporting 16 people into the colony, Robert Brace had been granted 800 acres by Sir Wm. Berkeley. The land was bounded by Chinconessecks and Deep Creeks and by the Bay. Signed 12 April 1661, William Berkelry (sic) and Tho. Ludwell, secretary. Robert Brace signed this land over to John West. Signed 23 June 1663, Robert (RB) Brace. Recorded by Robt. Hutchinson. (p. 20b)

John West bargained a black mare colt to Robert Brace. The bill of sale dated 24 June 1663, was signed by John West and recorded 29 July 1663, by Robt. Hutchinson. (p. 20b-21a)

---

[2]*Five of these couples were married; the arrival of a child too soon after marriage subjected the parents to charges of fornication.*

John West gave his nephew Henry Scarberough a 14 month-old dark red mare with a black mane and tail. The colt came from a mare called Tatte in Occahannock Neck. If Henry died before reaching age 21, the colt was to be returned to West or his heirs. The colt was to be managed by Mrs. Anne Charlton, grandmother of Henry, during her lifetime, and afterwards by whoever West thought fit. Signed by John West, 17 July 1663. Recorded 29 July 1663 by Robt. Hutchinson.

John West gave to his son Scarbrough West a 15 month old iron gray mare with a small star on the forehead. If the son died before reaching age 16, the colt was to be returned to West or his heirs. Signed by John West, 10 July 1663. (p. 21a)

For transporting eight people, John Nicholas had been granted 400 acres bounded by the south branch of Anoncock Creek, Ekees Branch and the land of Wm. Melling. Signed 3 November 1660, William Berkeley and Tho. Ludwell, secretary. John Nicholas of Pungoteage Creek, for 4000 lbs tobacco, sold this land to James Bonwell. Signed 18 September 1661, John Nichols, witnesses: Henr. Voss and Tho. Rydnig. Acknowledged in court 17 July 1663, by Col. Edmond Scarburgh and Mr. Hugh Yeo, fiefs in trust for the estate of John Nichols for Randolph and Anne Revell. Recorded 29 July 1665, by Robt. Hutchinson. (p. 21b)

Nowchetrawen, king of Checconestick, sold to Devorax Browne, patent holder, the land on the north side of Deep Creek. Signed 4 July 1663, by Nowchetrawen (circle with teardrop), witnesses: Iscc.? Alexander, George Truett and Geo. Watson. Acknowledged in court 17 July 1663, by Nowchetrawen and his great man Awossereurus (circle with line) before Robt. Hutchinson. (p. 22a)

Teage Omiscall provided funds for William Onoughton's payment for 1000 lbs tobacco and the splitting of 404 logs. So Onoughton bound over to Omiscall his present crops of corn and tobacco, except what he owed John Jenkins, a cow and calf, a ewe lamb and a sow. Signed 27 June 1663, Wm. (X) Onoughton. Witnesses: John Parker, Wm. (W) Silverthorne. (p. 22a)

Accomack County Court--17 August 1663

Present:
Mr. Anto. Hodgkins
Capt. Geo. Parker   Mr. Hugh Yeo
Mr. Jno. West   Mr. John Wise (p. 22a)

Certificate was granted to Mr. Devorax Browne for 1500 acres for transporting:

Stephen	Wm. Foard	Wm. Newworth
Anthony (a boy)	Wm. Ford	Henry Permaine
John Beale	Absolom Gandy	Peter Presly
Eliday Blunt	Wm. Goodchild	John Road
Arthur Brandlow	Thomas Greene	Griffin Savage
Samuell Capmaker	Jno. Hammond	William Smith
Ruth Coledge	Jasper James	Cristoph. Tompson
Arthur Edwards	William Jones	Sarah Turnor
Jonathan Eton	Timothy Lowe	Ellias Virgania
Kathrin Fisher	John Loyd	Roger Ware
		(p. 22b)

Mr. Browne entered and Mr. West left during the following: (p. 22b)

Certificate was granted to Mr. John West for 1500 acres for transporting:

Richard Fele	John Juell	Jno. Stevens
Wm. Abtill	Alex. Kinshman	John Stixon
Barbara Batty	Hanna Knowell	Cristopher
Thomas Bell	Bons Markes	Strobridge
Mathew Bennit	Teage Morcarta	Nicholas White
Giles Boones	Cristopher Moses	Tho. Williams
Owen Colona	Thomas Palmer	Wm. Williams
Edw. Coock	William Palmy	Wm. Williams
Nich. Coward	Edw. Prestidge	Jno. Wilton
Patrick Haies	John Rooe	(p. 22b)
Eliza. James	John Say	

Certificate was granted to John Renny for 400 acres for transporting:

Abraham Dotson	William Freeman	Thomas Middleton
Henry Ellins	Margrett Hall	John Mitick
Martha Eyres	Ellinor Jackson	(p. 22b)

Certificate was granted to William Chase for 300 acres for transporting:

Francis Branson	John Dickeson	Ellin Porket
John Colby	Sarah Gill	Mary Trotman
		(p. 23a)

Major Jno. Tilney entered the court. (p. 23a)

The suit brought against George Hamling by Edward Moore was dropped for lack of cause with Moore paying court costs. (p. 23a)

The suit brought against Jonah Jackson by John Rogers was dropped for lack of cause with Rogers paying court costs.

Deposition of John Walthoum aged about 26 years, 17 August 1663: Walthoum was at John Rogers' house when Jonah Jackson bargained with Rogers for some work; Jackson was to give Rogers a cow that would not kick till she lifted up her foot. Signed, John Walthoum. (p. 23a)

Ordered that the case between John Rogers and John Jenkins be suspended till the afternoon. (p. 23a)

Richard Hill was released from his bond for good behavior. He paid court costs. (p. 23a)

Mary Trotman confessed fornication with Roger Dickenson and requested a delay till the next court when Dickenson could appear, her father being security for her till then. (p. 23a)

Daniell Curtis confessed fornication with Mary Greene; he was fined 500 lbs tobacco and ordered to support the child and post a bond for good behavior. (p. 23a)

Mary Green confessed fornication with Daniell Curtis; she was granted a year to pay the fine of 500 lbs tobacco and court costs. (p. 23b)

Mary Chambers swore that James Cade was the father of her child, which was born at George Truett's house. When Cade returned to the county he would have to answer the charge.

George Truitt, Mary Chamber's master, agreed to pay 500 lbs tobacco for Mary's fornication, but asked to do so at the end of January. Mary Chambers was acquitted from corporal punishment with Truitt paying court costs. (p. 23b)

Thomas Davis and his wife confessed the sin of fornication. Ordered that he pay 1000 lbs tobacco, post bond for good behavior, and pay court costs. (p. 23b)

Japhet Cooke denied that he committed fornication with Norah. With Col. Scarburgh witnessing to his innocence, he was acquitted from the fine, but it was ordered that he pay court costs and put in security so the parish would not be liable. (p. 23b)

John Tick confessed fornication with Alice Roberts; it was ordered that he pay 500 lbs tobacco, post bond, and pay court costs. (p. 23b)

William Browne denied that he committed fornication with Norah, but she
swore that he was father of her child, so it was ordered that Browne be
fined 500 lbs tobacco, post bond for the child's support, be committed
to the sheriff's custody till he post bond for good behavior, and pay
court costs.

Norath (sic) confessed the sin of fornication but asked to be released from
corporal punishment by paying a fine. As William White promised to
pay 400 lbs tobacco for Norah, she was acquitted from the punishment,
but was to pay 100 lbs tobacco herself, with court costs. (p. 24a)

John Kirke confessed fornication with Jane Savage. Kirke's mistress,
Dorothy Jordan, agreed to pay 500 lbs tobacco, be security for his good
behavior and support the child along with court costs, so Kirke was
acquitted from corporal punishment. (p. 24a)

Jane Savage confessed fornication with John Kirke, but since Mrs. Jordan
promised to pay 500 lbs tobacco, she was acquitted from corporal
punishment. (p. 24a)

Hugh ---? agreed to support the child laid to the charge of Japhet Cooke
until she came of age so the parish would not be liable. Signed, Hugh
(X) --- 17 August 1663. (p. 24a)

Gausalin Van Nitsin and Bridgett his wife were accused of fornication; he
affirmed that they had been married seven months before the child was
born. The sentencing was suspended till the next court when Van Nitsin
was to appear along with the women attending the birth to testify that it
was a seven month child. (p. 24b)

In the case of James Atkinson, plaintiff, and Joseph Pitman, defendant, the
jury found that Atkinson had no cause for action. The suit was dismissed
with Atkinson paying court costs.

The names of the jury:

Alex. Addison	Ralph Dow	Charles Rackleff
Nath. Bradford	Thomas Foolkes	John Renny
Cristopher Calvert	Geo. Johnson	John Smith
Timothy Coe	James Price	George Watson

Deposition of William Browne, 17 August 1663: About three months ago
in Craddock Swamp, he saw Joseph Pitman with an unknown black
object under his arm, but when Browne came near, Pitman let it fall.
Daniell Mackare's dog was there with a pig in her mouth, and Browne
caused her to let it go. After he beat off the dog she went into the swamp
after other pigs. Signed, Wm. (|) Browne.

Deposition of John Charles, 17 August 1663: About three months ago

Charles was in Craddock Swamp with William Brown. There Charles saw Daniell Mackare's dog with a pig in her mouth, which he made her release. Then the dog ran into the swamp. Before this he saw Joseph Pitman throwing rocks at the dog. Signed, John (X) Charles.

Deposition of James Taylor, 17 August 1663: About three months ago William Browne and John Charles were at Taylor's house where James Atkinson was present. Brown asked Atkinson why he didn't look after his pigs, for the dogs were harassing them in Craddock Swamp. Joseph Pitman was there with an unknown black thing under his arm. Signed, James ([][]) Taylor.

Deposition of Daniel Mackeris, aged about 25 years, 17 August 1663: About the first week of May, Mackeris borrowed Robert Huitt's servant, Joseph Pitman, to go to Mr. Fookes for a cow with two dogs. While hunting in the swamp they fell foul of some pigs. As Mackeris asked Pitman to take the dogs off, William Browne and John Charles came by. Signed, Daniel (O) Mackeris. (p. 24b-25a)

George Brickhouse asked to be released from his bond for good behavior; ordered that his bond be delivered to him, with him paying court costs. (p. 25a)

John Watts confessed committing fornication with his wife. Ordered that he post bond for good behavior, pay 1000 lbs tobacco for him and his wife, and pay court costs. (p. 25a)

William Onoughton denied committing fornication with Elizabeth Shepway, but she made oath that he was the father of her child. Ordered that Onoughton pay 500 lbs tobacco, put in security for the support of the child, post bond for good behavior and pay court costs. (p. 25a)

Elizabeth Shepway confessed fornication with William Onoughton. As she could not pay the fine, ordered that she have twenty-five lashes on her naked shoulders and pay court costs. (p. 25b)

John Rogers confessed committing fornication with Mary his wife. Ordered that he post bond for good behavior, pay 1000 lbs tobacco for him and his wife, and pay court costs. (p. 25b)

Edward Revell confessed committing fornication with Frances his wife. Ordered that he post bond for good behavior, pay 1000 lbs tobacco for him and his wife, and pay court costs. (p. 25b)

John Willis committed fornication with Jane Scaffall. Since Mr. Bowman had agreed to pay 500 lbs tobacco, it was ordered that Willis be acquitted from corporal punishment. Bowman was to put up security for the child's support, pay court charges and transport Willis out of the county.

Jane Scaffull committed fornication with John Willis, and as Mr. Bowman had agreed to pay 500 lbs tobacco and court charges, she was acquitted from corporal punishment. (p. 25b)

AbChurch committed fornication with Mary Scading, who confessed. As Col. Scarburgh promised payment of the fine, AbChurch was acquitted from corporal punishment, but had to put up security for good behavior and pay court charges. (p. 25b)

Mary Scading confessed fornication with AbChurch. As she could not pay the fine, it was ordered that she have twenty-five lashes on her naked shoulders and pay court costs. (p. 26a)

John Paramore confessed to breaking the Sabbath. Ordered he pay 50 lbs tobacco with court costs. (p. 26a)

Thomas Wally and his wife confessed to breaking the Sabbath. Ordered that they pay 100 lbs tobacco with court costs. (p. 26a)

Edward Smith confessed to breaking the Sabbath. Ordered that he pay 50 lbs tobacco with court costs. (p. 26a)

Ordered that Elizabeth Leverit be committed to the sheriff's custody and be ducked for fighting and scolding, and also to pay court costs. (p. 26a)

Ordered that Alice Boucher be committed to the sheriff's custody and be ducked for fighting and scolding, and also to pay court costs. (p. 26a)

Robert Brace's servant, Elizabeth Leverit, was incorrigible and impudent, and upon Brace's complaint at the last court was punished for insolent behavior to her master. Since that time Leverit, Alice Boucher and Robert Brace have "lawlessly scolded, fought, and misdemeaned themselves on the Sabbath day." Ordered that Leverit and Boucher be ducked, and because Brace had "degenerated so much from a man," and could not govern his house, he would be censured and ducked along with them and pay court charges. (p. 26a)

Ordered that John Rogers, for insolent behavior to the court and irreverent words, stand with his hands in the pillory for one hour and pay court costs. (p. 26a)

Certificate was granted to Thomas Leatherberry for 500 acres for transporting:

John Collins	Ellinor Hooke	Robt. Satchell
Alice Goasior	Henry Michell	Richard Stevens
Mordica Hamond	Sarah Naylor	(p. 26b)
Gartrid Hand	Thomas Pettet	

Mrs. Anne Voss, administratrix of her husband's estate, agreed to pay Mrs. Dorothy Jordan 4014 lbs tobacco. (p. 26b)

Mary Paramore, formerly Mary Studson, and her son John Studson requested in open court that Col. Edm. Scarburgh evaluate their 250 acres of land in Arrococo Neck and to do as he sees fit concerning their land lying between Mr. Hugh Yeo and Mr. Tho. Fookes. (p. 26b)

Mr. Browne left the court for the following action:
Stephen Warren ran away from his master, Mr. Devorx Browne; ordered that he receive twenty-five lashes on his naked shoulders. (p. 26b)

Mr. West left the court for the following action:
Patrick Huies ran away from his master, Mr. John West; ordered that he have twenty-five lashes on his naked shoulders. Because of his incorrigible behavior to his master, it was also ordered that he wear an iron collar around his neck till he behave better toward his master. (p. 26b)

Thomas Bunny petitioned to be removed from Mr. George Hack and to live with Mr. James Fookes to learn the trade of carpentry. Ordered, with the consent of Fookes and Bunny, that Bunny be a "true and faithful" servant for four years to Fookes, who was to employ him only in the trade of carpentry. (p. 26b)

Mr. Browne left the court for the following action:
Complaint was made by Mr. Browne against his servant Ruth Colledge, that she was pregnant and refused to name the father. She behaved "obstinately and audaciously" to the court. Ordered that she be sent to the house of correction for a month and pay court costs. (p. 26b-27a)

Certificate was granted to Robert Hill for 400 acres for transporting:

John James	Mary Thompson	James Willbrooke
Thomas James	Edward Wallis	Mathew Williams
Henry Mathews	Jeffry Whitly	(p. 27a)

Robert Brace, ordered by the court to be ducked, supplicated the court to

be remitted from the punishment. Ordered in place of ducking that he be
fined 100 lbs tobacco and pay court costs. (p. 27a)

Mr. Wise left the court for the following action:
Certificate was granted to Mr. John Wise for 250 acres for transporting:

John Fenn	William Layton	Wm. Watson
Richard Ingrum	Ellinor Leftwich	(p. 27a)

Accomack County Court--18 August 1663

Present: Mr. Anto. Hodgkins
      Major Jno. Tilney   Mr. Devorx Browne
      Capt. Geo. Parker   Mr. Hugh Yeo
      Mr. Jno West   Mr. John Wise (p.27a)

A jury convicted John Rogers of mismarking a heifer belonging to John
Jenkins, and the "court taking into their serious consideration the bad
consequence of such evil practices and to deter others from the like"
ordered John Rogers be committed to the sheriff's custody and to stand
one hour with his head in the pillory with his fault posted over his head,
"For mismarking a heifer which was none of his own." Rogers was to
return the heifer to Jenkins and pay court costs.

The names of the jury:

Alex. Addison	Ralph Dow	Charles Rackleff
Nath. Bradford	Thomas Foolkes	John Renny
Cristopher Calvert	Geo. Johnson	John Smith
Timothy Coe	James Price	George Watson

Deposition of Richard Buckland, 17 August 1663: John Rogers came to
Buckland's house and asked if John Jenkins' heifer was there. Buckland
said it was. Rogers claimed to have purchased the heifer and wished to
take possession of her. Buckland asked Rogers to stay, for the heifer
would come home with Buckland's cattle. Rogers did this and took
delivery of the heifer. Signed, Rich. Buckland.

Richard Buckland's wife was able to testify the same. Signed, Charity (C)
Buckland.

Deposition of Alphonsoe Balles, 17 July 1663: Balles viewed a "beast"
claimed by John Jenkins and judged her to be about three years old next
March. She had Jenkins' mark, was coal black except for white markings
from her udder to her forelegs and on the tip of her tail. She was
branded with I on the hip. Signed, Alphonsoe Balles.

Deposition of Richard Hill, 17 August 1663: Hill and Thomas Osbourne
went to William Taylor's house where Osbourne said, "Old man, here

is the beast that you do look for, and I hope you will not be worse than your word with me." Taylor replied, "Did not John Jenkins give the order the last court for to deliver me the beast that was at your pen?" Then Osbourne got a rope and helped brand the beast. Signed, Richard (RH) Hill.

Deposition of William Onoughton, 16 July 1663: Said that the cow John Jenkins sold to John Rogers was coal black except a little white at the end of the tail. Signed, William (X) Onoughton.

Deposition of William Anderson, aged about 18 years, 16 July 1663: Said the heifer that John Rogers accepted was coal black with only a little white on the udder and the tail. Signed, Will. Anderson.

Deposition of William Anderson, 17 August 1663: Said that the heifer John Rogers bought from John Jenkins was about three years old or more last March or April. Signed, Will. Anderson.

Deposition of John Cropper, aged about 18 years, 17 August 1663: Said that he never heard Thomas Osbourne say that he was ordered by John Jenkins to deliver any beast to John Rogers. When John Rogers had branded the heifer, she broke her rope and ran into the woods, and he said that he didn't care where she went now that he had branded her. Then Cropper heard Osbourne say to Rogers, "Old man, ye had best have a care that ye go not abroad and say that I, Thomas Osbourne, deliver to you another man's beast, for I will not do any such thing." Signed, John Cropper.

Deposition of John Kirk, 17 August 1663: Kirk lived at Mrs. Jordan's house, where he saw a three year old heifer branded on the left hip with John Jenkins' mark. The heifer was black with white under the belly from the udder to the brisket and on the end of the tail. Signed by John (|-|-|) Kirke.

Deposition of Thomas Bentall, 17 August 1663: About last June 22, John Rogers was at Bentall's house and was asked why he was out so late. Rogers said he was going to his "Countryman John Jenkins" for a bill of sale for a beast he was buying. Bentall asked if the beast was weaned, and Rogers answered, no, but there were two belonging to John Jenkins at Mrs. Jordan's, and as soon as he had his bill of sale he would go and take the one he liked best. Signed, Thomas Benthall.

Deposition of Edward Hazard, 17 August 1663: When Hazard lived with Mihill Ricketts last year, there was a heifer that John Rogers claimed to have purchased from John Jenkins. The heifer was black with a little white under her belly on her udder and at the end of her tail. Signed, Edward Hazard.

Deposition of Mihill Ricketts, 17 August 1663: Said that when John Rogers was at Ricketts' house, "I asked John Rogers why he told the court that the heifer at my Uncle Taylor's was the beast he accepted of John

Jenkins at first." Rogers said that he knew it was not the heifer that he first accepted from John Jenkins. Signed by Mihill (MR) Ricketts. (p. 27a-28b)

John Johnson's suit against John Rogers was dropped because the value sought was under 200 lbs tobacco. Ordered that John Johnson pay court charges. (p. 28b)

Major Jno. Tilney exited the court for the following action:
A jury found John Prittyman not guilty of stealing a sow in the case of William Blake, plaintiff, and John Prittyman, defendant. A sow originally owned by Prittyman was given to Richard Archer, who gave it to William Blake. Prittyman, who declared that it belonged to Archer, killed it because it trespassed. Prittyman promised to give Archer another sow, but since Archer had given it to Blake, Prittyman was ordered to deliver one to Blake and pay court costs.
The names of the jury:

George Watson	John Renny	Geo. Johnson
Ralph Dow	Cristopher Calvert	Timothy Coe
James Price	Alex. Addison	Nath. Bradford
Thomas Foolkes	Charles Ratkleff	John Smith

Deposition of Richard Smith, aged about 40 years, 17 August 1663: Smith, who lived at John Prittyman's house, said that Prittyman and his wife went into the woods to look for hogs and killed a sow that belonged to Richard Archer. Prittyman came home and asked Smith to help fetch it. Prittyman asked Smith to notice that the sow belonged to Archer, and said that if Archer came again, Smith would give him another sow to replace it. Signed, Rich. (O) Smith.

Deposition of Mary Bell, aged about 40 years, 17th of August 1663: Said that she came to Prittyman's house and saw a singed hog hanging up. Bell spoke to Prittyman's wife, who said that it was a sow that her husband had given to Richard Archer as a pig. They were forced to kill it, she said, because it was so wild that "they could have no benefit of their own hogs." She further said that if Richard Archer ever came again, her husband would give him another sow. When Bell asked how the sow became so wild, Prittyman's wife replied that it was the one that Richard Archer had chosen. Signed, Mary (--O) Bell.

Deposition of Major Jno. Tilney, 16 July 1663: John Prittyman came to Tilney's house, and Tilney asked why Prittyman didn't resolve his difference with William Blake. Prittyman answered that he would willingly do so. Tilney replied that according to Blake, Prittyman had offered only a sow shoat. Prittyman replied that it was false, for he had confessed that he killed the sow and offered a sow to Blake. Prittyman said, "Let him do his worst, [I] care not." Tilney said it would go bad, as Prittyman had been formerly accused of the same thing. Prittyman replied that he would make Blake prove that Archer had given him the sow. Signed, Jno. Tilney.

Deposition of John Mackettrick, 16 July 1663: Said that he was with William Blake and Richard Archer when Archer gave a sow to Blake. It was the sow John Prittyman admitted to killing. Signed, John (Q) Micketrick.

Richard Ward, 16 July 1663, swore that he was there when Richard Archer gave William Blake a sow. Signed, Richard (W) Ward.

Deposition of William Smith, 16 July 1663: About two months ago at Smith's house he spoke with John Prittyman about William Blake. Prittyman said that Blake intended to sue him for killing a sow. Smith asked if Prittyman had killed Blake's sow, and Prittyman replied that he did not kill Blake's hog, but that he killed a hog he had given to Richard Archer, which William Blake now claimed had been given to him by Archer. Signed, William Smith. (p. 28b-29b)

Edmond Kelly claimed pigs marked by John Goring and Robert Hignet. Because he could not prove his assertion, it was ordered that the pigs "remain to His Majesty's use" and that Kelly pay court charges. (p. 30a)

Mr. Yeo left the court for the following action:

According to the testimony of Mr. Hugh Yeo, Richard Bundick owed Robert Bayly 400 lbs tobacco. Ordered that Bundick make payment and pay court charges.

Attestation of Mr. Hugh Yeo, 16 August 1663: When Mr. Yeo made up the accounts between Robert Bayly and Richard Bundick on 26 April 1660, the bill due to Mr. John Willcocks was about 10,000 lbs tobacco. The balance was to be equally paid between them. Signed, Hugh Yeo.

Robert Bayly requested that Tobius Sellvey demand from Richard Bundick a debt of 400 lbs tobacco. Sellvey advised Bundick to pay because Bayly was threatening arrest. Bundick said that this year (1661) he could not pay, but the next year, 1662, he would be sure to pay Bayly. Signed, Tob. Sellvey.

Deposition of William Wheler, 15 August 1663: Said he was with Robert Bayly at Mr. Willcocks' when Bayly took in the joint bill between Richard Bundick and Robert Bayly. Bayly gave his bill for the remainder. Willcocks gave some tobacco to Bayly's daughter to buy a breeder, and Bayly said, "You cannot give it to one, except you give to both." Wilcocks said, "I will give Richard's wife nothing, for his wife hath abused me." (p. 30a)

Ordered that the suit brought against Mary White by Hugh Cornelius be dropped for lack of cause, with Cornelius paying court costs. (p. 30a)

Ordered that Mary White, who "scandalized and abused" Goody Huit, her aunt, be committed into the sheriff's custody until she asked her aunt's forgiveness three times: once in open court, once before the congregation of each church in the county on succeeding Sabbath days. Mary White was to pay court costs.

Deposition of Dority Watts aged about 28 years, 18 August 1663: Said that last November when she came to William White's house late at night, both William and his wife asked her to stay all night. She accepted, and after a short time she heard White's wife say that her aunt stole a hood and a scarf in England, and if she had not left when she did, she would have been stopped. Mrs. White also said that her aunt stole a doctor's case of instruments. Signed, Dority (D) Watts.

Deposition of Marrion Cornelius, aged about 25 years, 18 August 1663: Mary White told her that Mary's Aunt Goody Huitt, while in England, stole a gown, a hood, and a scarf, and if she had not hastened out of England, she would have been stopped. Also she stole the doctor's instruments aboard the ship she came in and put them in Mary White's box in case the ship's master found it out. Signed, Marrion (O over arc) Cornelius. (p. 30a-30b)

Robert Hignet asked to be released from his bond for good behavior. After proclamation was made three times in court with no objection, his bond was returned with him paying court charges. (p. 30b)

John Gourdon asked to be released from his bond for good behavior. After proclamation was made three times in court with no objection, his bond was returned with him paying court charges. (p. 30b)

Robert Huit asked to be released from his bond for good behavior. After proclamation was made three times in court with no objection, his bond was returned, with him paying court charges. (p. 30b)

Capt. Parker left court for the following action:
Ordered that Capt. George Parker be fined 12 lbs tobacco for swearing in the face of the court. Parker paid court charges. (p. 30b, 31a)

Mr. West exited the court. (p. 31a)

The difference between Mrs. Anne Charlton and Nehemiah Covington was, upon Covington's request, referred to the next court. (p. 31a)

Mr. George Hack's servant Mary Trotman, who was presented to the court for bastard bearing, was sold by Mr. Hack to William Chase, who had kept the child and mother for about seven months. For this the court thought it fitting that William Chase be allowed 500 lbs tobacco by Mr. Hack. Since Chase promised to keep the child without further charge to anyone else, it was ordered that he may be its master till it came of age. (p. 31a)

Nehemiah Covington brought an account of the cattle belonging to Henry Scarburgh, the son of Mr. Charles Scarborough in England, and requested that he might be paid for his care. Ordered that Covington be paid 300 lbs tobacco by Mr. West, the person intrusted for Henry Scarborough. An account of the increase of two heifers since 3 years ago last spring: 4 cows, 3 yearlings, 3 calves, 1 steer over two years old. One bull calf was killed by his grandmother, and one other calf died. The account was sworn and delivered by Nehemiah Covington 18 August 1663. (p. 31a)

Mr. West entered the court. (p. 31a)

Col. Edm. Scarburgh declared he could prove false the account presented by Henry James. Ordered that Henry James bring to the next court his books, especially the ones kept by Mr. Fawset for sale of goods on behalf of James. (p. 31a)

Sued in the name of the King by Col. Edm. Scarburgh, Mr. George Hack, was, by a jury, found guilty of killing a stray cow. Being equivalent with hog stealing, it was ordered that Mr. Hack pay 2000 lbs tobacco for the use of His Majesty and post bond with security for good behavior and pay court costs.
The names of the jury:

Alex. Addison	Ralph Dow	Charles Ratkleff
Nath. Bradford	Thomas Foolkes	John Renny
Cristopher Calvert	Geo. Johnson	John Smith
Timothy Coe	James Price	George Watson

Deposition of John Rogers, 18 August 1663: Said that the beast that Dr. George Hack fetched from his pen and killed was marked: one ear had a hole and the other had a swallow fork in it. Signed, John Rogers.

Deposition of Robert Bayly, 17 July 1663: While at Dr. Hack's house he heard Mr. George Hack and Abraham Morgan's wife discuss changing four cattle. A pied one bore Tobius Sellvey's mark, the two red ones were at Tobius Sellvey's plantation. Mr. Hack said, find them and I will give you as many. Signed, Robert (B) Bayly.

Deposition of Tobius Sellvey, 16 July 1663: Two heifers were at his plan-tation off and on for part of a year. One was a two year old red heifer cropped on one ear with two holes in the other, and one was a three year old red heifer with Abraham Morgan's mark. The two heifers were taken at the instructions of Dr. Hack. Signed, Tobius Sellvey.

Deposition of William Chase aged about 28 years, 18 August 1663: Three years ago last April, Chase went to Tobius Sellvey's to fetch a cow. Dr. Hack sent his servant Bridget Williams with him to fetch two red heifers that Hack bought from Abraham Morgan, one three years old with a calf, and the other two years old. These cattle remained on Hack's plantation till about the end of August and then returned to Tobius Sellvey's. The next spring Chase was at John Rogers' and there saw the two year old heifer and told Rogers that it belonged to Hack. Rogers said she had lost a calf and that he had worked hard to save the heifer. The next fall Mr. Hack sent his servants to fetch her from John Rogers. Chase killed her in Mr. Hack's cowpen. Signed, William (O) Chase. (p. 31b-32a)

A mistake was made in the process of the last court in the case between Robert Huit and James Atkinson. It was formerly ordered that James Atkinson should have 1000 lbs tobacco for informing against Robert Huit, but it appears that Robert Huit informed against himself, so the fine would accrue to His Majesty. Ordered that the former order be repealed and that Robert Huit pay 2000 lbs tobacco for the use of His Majesty along with court charges. (p. 32a)

Timothy Coe requested that part of the estate of Richard Hinman be sold at auction to pay for some of Hinman's land which was recently escheated. Ordered that a part of his estate that could best be spared be sold, but no more than necessary for the payment. Major Jno. Tilney was requested to be present at the auction. (p. 32a)

Richard Hill declared his sorrow for his late offence and requested that his 300 lb tobacco fine be remitted. Ordered that this be done, with him paying court costs. (p. 32a)

Thomas Bunny, who yesterday was ordered to live with Mr. James Fookes for four years, came today requesting his liberty, so if his friends in England sent for him he could go home to them. In view of the danger of such liberty, the court ordered that Bunny return to Dr. Hack, to whom he was committed by Capt. Edward Baker, and to remain there till Christmas. (p. 32a)

Mr. Jno. Tilney left the court. (p. 32a)

Certificate was granted to Col. Edmond Scarburgh for 2850 acres for transporting:

Jno. Angell	Jno. Evans	Wm. Pearle
Wm. Ashley	Hen. Farrington	Hen. Porter
Wm. Banister	Edw. Fleetwood	Tho. Pory
Elza. Bidolph	Robt. Fleetwood	Jonathan Samwaies
Jno. Birum	Anne Fonne	Saml. Short
Jno. Casher	Jno. Hancock	Ja. Silverlocks
Robt. Casher	John Hody	John Smith
Jno. Castick	Ja. Jolley	Peter Solme
Ralph Castleton	Thomas King	Jno. Sparkes
Phillip Coles	Robt. Masters	Agnes Taylor
Tho. Coles	Jone Mazed	John Tizard
Tho. Corus	Rich. Me--s?	Robt. Twiggs
Jno. Courtney	Jenken Morgan	William Wall
Fran Crawly	Edw. Morris	Jno. Wells
Thomas Crisp	Roger Nowell	Cristian Winters
Jno. Dickenson	Jone Ossett	Nich. Woodward
Jno. Difnesh	Ellnor Packett	Damon? Worthy
Robt. Drury	Anne Paine	(p. 32b)
Robt. Drury	Ezard Paine	
John Dry	Robt. Parker	

Capt. George Parker exited the court. (p. 32b)

Robt. Hutchinson sued the estate of John Milby for 1054 lbs tobacco. The estate of John Milby was attached for that sum, and if it were to be found in Accomack County, it would be paid along with court costs. (p. 32b)

Major Tilney and Capt. Parker entered the court. (p. 32b)

Protest was made 17 August 1663: An agreement was made in 1662 between Randall Revell, Thomas Benthall and Edm. Scarburgh on behalf of John West. As several articles had not been performed, the protest was as follows:
Against Thomas Benthall, tanner
    - for abusing and not using servants committed to his trust. Among other things he lamed a good Negro and allowed a lazy boy, Tom Bell, to deride him to his face. This boy placed with another tanner was a good servant.

- for not tanning in two and a half years as much as he agreed to tan in one year, as witnessed by the curriers[3], shoemakers and the account of leather.
- for spoiling hides and not tanning them.
- for eight shoemakers' time and cost in not having leather to work for four months in 1662.
- for ten shoemakers' time and cost in not having leather to work five weeks in five months in 1663, as witnessed by the shoemakers.
- for spoiling 500 hides and more, which got wormy because they were not tanned in time in 1662 and 1663, as witnessed by the curriers and shoemakers.
- for 800 and more days work needed to prevent the loss of everything, as witnessed by the servants employed and paid per the account.
- for embezzling and disposing of leather contrary to the covenant, as witnessed by Silverthorne and the servants.
- for sending green hides by horses and boats on the pretext of impregnating them with fat to make good leather, and when the hides were brought, dried them, as witnessed by Edward Revell and the servants.
- for neglecting to get enough bark in 1662, and consequently starving the leather being impregnated with fat, and leaving hides unwrought. Witnesses: Mr. Yeo, from whom bark was borrowed, the currier and servants.
- The protest against Thomas Benthall and Randall Revell concluded with all other costs, charges and damage according to the conditions given 15 March 1662. Signed by Edm. Scarburgh for John West; read & published in open court 18 August 1663. (p. 32b-33a)

Deposition of John Marvell, 18 August 1663: Said that about five or six weeks ago he was at John Waltham's house where he saw Capt. Batts and others with him, but did not see any weapons or hostile behavior. Signed, John Marvell.
Deposition of David Gibbins, aged about 20 years, 18 August 1663: At his master Jno. Waltham's house, Gibbins saw Capt. Batts and his men, who were not armed and did not stand guard. Signed, David (2) Gibbins. (p. 33a)

Evidence for Robt. Huit versus Jno. Atkinson:
Deposition of Eliza. Bowman, aged about 50 years, 17 July 1663: Said that about the last of December, Robert Huit had a three or four year old hog that went with her hogs. Huit's hog was unruly and had no ears, for

---

[3]*A currier dresses leather after it is tanned.*

Bowman's dogs had pulled them off. Eliza. Bowman sent word to Huit about that time asking him to take care of the hog. Huit sent a servant and a freeman who took the hog with a rope, killed him in Bowman's pen, and carried him home. Signed, Eliza. (M) Bowman. (p. 33a)

Deposition of Roger Barter, 16 July 1663: Said that the hide that was carried to Charles Ratclif's belonged to a cow that died in calving. After it was taken off the cow, his master Robert Huitt hung it in an old house where the dogs pulled it down and tore it. Barter's master killed only two cattle this year, one hide went to Col. Edm. Scarburgh, and the other to Capt. Parker. A sheep hide was sent to Scarburgh. Barter also said that a boar staying at Richard Bayle's had no ears because the dogs tore them. Bayly sent notice to Huitt, who sent Barter and a fellow servant to fetch home the hog. Signed, Roger (W) Barter.

Deposition of Wm. Dine, 16 July 1663: Said the same as Roger Barter, except for bringing the hog home from Rich. Baly's. But he saw that the hog brought from Bayly's was without ears. Signed by William (\) Dine.

Deposition of Richard Bayly, 16 July 1663: Said that Robert Huitt had at Bayly's house a boar whose ears had been torn off by dogs. Bayly asked Hewitt to take him, so when the boar was caught, Bayly sent word to Hewitt, who sent two servants to kill him and carry him home. Signed, Richard Bally (sic).

Deposition of John Carry, aged about 22 years, 16 July 1663: Said that Robert Hewitt showed him a red barrow's ears nailed up in his house. Carry asked why he did that, and Hewitt replied that he and James Atkinson had had some words about hogs. The ears bore Huitt's mark, only one hole was torn out. Carry saw the hog before it was dressed. Testified to Robt. Hutchinson, signed by John Carry.

Deposition of Joseph Pitman, 16 July 1663: James Atkinson said that Pitman's master, Robert Huett, had killed Richard Hill's hog, cut off the head and ran away with it; that Huett would kill two cows and carry four hides to Col. Scarburgh, and that Huett killed a raccoon as big as two men could carry.[4] Pitman affirmed under oath that his master killed only two cows, one hide going to Col. Scarburgh and the other to Capt. Parker. Concerning the hog described by John Carry, Pitman said he and one of his fellow servants fetched a boar from Richard Bayly's. It had been there three years and the dogs had pulled its ears off. Signed, Joseph (V) Pitman.

---

[4]*Atkinson is suggesting that Huit killed pigs and called them raccoons.*

Deposition of James Taylor, 16 July 1663: Said that James Atkinson told Taylor and several others that Robert Huitt had killed Richard Hill's hog and run away with the head, that he had killed two cows and carried four hides to Col. Scarburgh, and that Huitt killed raccoons as big as two men could lift. Signed, James ([][]) Taylor.

Deposition of Joseph Pitman, 16 July 1663: Pitman heard Atkinson's words as reported above by James Taylor. Signed, Joseph (V) Pitman.

Deposition of Norah Mackare, 16 July 1663: Norah lived in Huitt's house for nine months, and in that time never saw a misdemeanor committed by Huitt or his wife or family. Signed, Norah (inverted V) Mackare.

Deposition of William White, 16 July 1663: White said he had lived in this country several years and had never heard ill reports of Robert Huitt and his wife till this rumor was spread. Testified to Robt. Hutchinson. Signed, William (M) White. (p. 34a)

On 29 May 1661, Wm. Berkeley had granted Nathaniell Bradford 400 acres between Ockahannock Creek and Nuswattocks Creek on the Bay Side next to the land of Henry Edwards. The original patent, granted for transporting eight people, was dated 10 October 1658. On 18 August 1663, Nathaniell Bradford and his wife Alice sold the land to Henry Eldridge. Signed, Nathaniell Bratford (sic) and Alice (O) Bradford. Recorded 20 August 1663, by Robt. Hutchinson. (p. 34b)

A list of Tithables in Accomack County 1663:

Mr. Anto. Hodgkins	4	John Lewis	5
John Rany	6	Walter Taylor	5
George Truitt	5	Hone Collony	2
Jno. Williams	4	Wm. Alworth	1
Jno. Jenkins	3	Abraham Taylor	4
Tho. Leatherberry	1	John Eyre	3
Edward Revell	3	Robt. Hewitt	6
Wm. Silverthorne	2	Wm. White	1
Anto. Longe	1	Daniell Macra	1
Robert Hill	4	Jno. Milby	3
Teage Andrews	5	Jno. Major	3
John Watts	2	Jno. Durman	3
Thomas Benthall	5	Robt. Brace	3
Wm. Chase	6	Mr. Jno. West	7
Wm. & Francis Benstone	3	Mr. Devorx Browne	12
John Parker	6	Mrs. Charlton	1
Richard Hill	6	Tobius Sellvey	1
John Die	1	Robt. Bayly	2

Richard Johnson	1	Jno. Fawsett	2
Anto. Johnson	1	Jno. Waltham	6
Mihill Ricards	4	Alphonso Balls	3
Mr. Jno. Wise	7	Jno. Cobb	1
Jno. Alford	3	James Camell	1
Mr. Southee Littleton	5	Nath. Bradford	4
Geo. Crump	2	Samuell Taylor	2
Tho. Tunnell	2	Robt. Richinson	3
Jno. Macele	2	Mr. Edm. Bowman	9
Tho. Newton	2	Wm. Major	3
Jno. Holding	2	Obedience Johnson	3
Mr. Geo. Hack	9	Hen. Edwards	4
Rich. Buckland	1	Jno. Weler	3
Cristopher Calvert	3	Andrew Finke	4
Capt. Geo. Parker	8	Mrs. Jordon	8
Jno. Brookes	1	Tho. Bloyes	2
Hendrick Johnson	4	Jonas Jackson	2
Ol? Richard at		Richard Stevens	4
Wm. Whelor's	1	Tho. Davis	1
Mr. Tho. Fookes	10	Jno. Paramore	3
Mr. Hugh Yeo	7	Folcot Obin	2
Daniell Ograham	1	Tho. Solne	1
John Croft	1	Ralph Dow	2
Simon Miller	1	Jno. King	1
Rich. Hill	1	Robt. Hicknet	2
Bartholomew Man	1	Phillip Fisher	4
Jeames Atkinson	1	Mr. Haggaman	1
John Smith	4	Jno. Johnson	2
Arthur Upshott	3	Tho. Carrell	2
Henry Smith	6	Edm. Kelly	4
Alex Adison	3	Major Jno. Tilney	8
Edw. More	2	Timothy Coe	4
Charles Ratclife	5	Wm. Smith	2
Geo. Johnson	4	Hen. Stott	2
Wm. Rodolphus	2	Richard Smith	2
James Price	4	Mr. Leving Denwood	5
Wm. Taylor	4	Tho. Browne	3
Hen. Bishop	5	Wm. Roberts	5
Edw. Smith	2	Henry Browne	2
Derman Shellowan	2	Wm. Blake	2
Jno. Lewis	5	Benjamen Larance	1
Jno. Turnor	2	Robt. Watson	2
Rich. Kellum	7	Henry White	1

Tho. Wally	2	Jno. Stutson	4
Jno. Prittyman	2	Jeffry Minshall	3
Tho. Smith	1	Tho. Bell	1
Geo. Brickhouse	2	sum total: 409 (p. 35a)	

The jury appointed to find the main branch of Pungoteage, for the most part residents along the coast of Chesapeake Bay in Virginia, determined that the main branch of Pungoteage ran between Mr. Anto. Hodgkins and Mr. Edw. Revell's plantations by an observation taken at Randolph's Bridge. The course of the branch was "north by east half a point easterly" according to the bay. Signed 30 July 1663, by Thomas Perkes.

The names of the jury:

Cristop. Calvert	Tho. Leatherberry	Jno. Raney
Jno. Drumon	Southe Littleton	Mehill Ricards
Mr. James Foux?	Jno. Parker	Wm. Taylor
Mr. Thomas Foux?	Mr. Tho. Perkes	Geo. Truet (p. 35a)

Accomack County Court--10 November 1663

The justices of the peace for Accomack County: Col. Edm. Scarburgh, Capt. George Parker, Mr. John Tilney, and Mr. John West were "of the quorum."[5] Other justices were Mr. Edm. Bowman, Mr. Devorax Browne, Mr. Hugh Yeo, and Mr. John Wise. Commissioned at James City, 25 September 1663. Signed, William Berkeley. (p. 35b)

Present:
Capt. Geo. Parker	Mr. Devox Browne
Major Jno. Tilney	Mr. Hugh Yeo
Mr. John West	Mr. John Wise (p. 35b)

The oath for administration of justice as commissioner was taken by Mr. Edmond Bowman, who then entered the court. (p. 35b)

Certificate was granted to John Graves for 100 acres for transporting: John Graves and Dorothy Graves. (p. 35b)

Richard Stevens was indebted to Mr. Isaac Foxcroft for rent and other dues on 300 acres for three years; ordered that Richard Stevens pay 300 lbs tobacco and court costs. (p. 35b)

---

[5] *A select group of justices, some of whom were required to be present at court sessions.*

The suit brought against William Benstone by Phillip Smith was dismissed because Smith failed to enter his complaint. Smith paid court costs. (p. 35b)

Edward Revel petitioned for the return of his bond for good behavior; ordered that it be done, with him paying court charges. (p. 35b)

Thomas Davis petitioned for the return of his bond for good behavior; ordered that it be done, with him paying court charges. (p. 36a)

Edw. Smith petitioned for the return of his bond for good behavior; ordered that it be done, with him paying court charges. (p. 36a)

John Watts petitioned for the return of his bond for good behavior; ordered that it be done, with him paying court charges. (p. 36a)

William Onoughton petitioned for the return of his bond for good behavior; ordered that it be done with him paying court charges. (p. 36a)

John Kirk petitioned for the return of his bond for good behavior; ordered that it be done with him paying court charges. (p. 36a)

Ordered that Gausalin van Nitsin be acquitted of the judgment of fornication made at the last court, as it appeared by the testimony of the midwife Elizabeth Williams, that his wife's child was born before its time.
Deposition of Elizabeth Williams, aged about 40 years, 16 November 1663: Said that Gausalin Van Nitsen's wife Bridget had a child before its time. Signed, Elizabeth (EW) Williams. (p. 36a)

Mr. Devorax Browne's servant, Griffith Savage, complained that he was commanded contrary to conditions of agreement, but he could not prove the assertions; ordered that the case be referred to the next court so necessary evidence could be presented. In the interim he was to lawfully serve his master. (p. 36a)

William Browne confessed to stealing from Abraham Taylor; ordered that Browne be committed to the custody of the sheriff and "have twenty-five lashes well applied upon his naked shoulders." (p. 36b)

Ordered that Mr. Anto. Hodgkins, attorney of Mr. Simon Carpenter, who in turn was attorney of Walter Dixon and Thomas Powell, give bond for their suit of William Chase.
Upon the petition of Mr. Anto. Hodgkins, it appeared that William Chase

was indebted to Walter Dixson for 1000 feet of sound pine boards one inch thick, which were to be delivered to Dickeson's plantation on Patapsco River. Ordered that Walter Chase deliver the lumber and pay court charges. Dickeson was to pay Chase according to their agreement upon the delivery.

Upon the petition of Mr. Anto. Hodgkins, it appeared that William Chase was indebted to Thomas Powell for 1000 feet of one inch pine boards and two steers which should have been delivered at Patapsco River. Ordered that William Chase deliver the lumber and steers and pay court costs. Upon delivery Powell was to pay Chase according to their agreement. (p. 36b)

John Stockly paid a heifer to Richard Buckland for the use of John Coulston's children, but because Buckland had not used the heifer for the good of the orphans as was intended, it was ordered Buckland pay a good three year old heifer with calf next spring. Capt. Parker and Mr. Wise were requested to witness the delivery of the heifer for the good of the children, with Buckland paying court costs. (p. 36b)

Tho. Maddox chose for his guardian, Mr. Edmond Bowman, who the court ordered to give a yearly account of the orphan's estate. (p. 37a)

In the case of Richard Kellum, plaintiff, and Richard Hill, defendant, it was ordered with the consent of both parties that the cow and calf that Kellum delivered to Hill in exchange for carding and spinning wool be returned to the cattle of Kellum, with Hill paying court costs. (p. 37a)

Mr. Bowman left the court for the following action:
Certificate is granted to Mr. Edmond Bowman for 1200 Acres for transporting:

Moses Barrell	John Illes	Dennis Morris
Robt. Bridges	Elisa. Jackson	Danll. Nech
Deborah Catchme	Ellinor Johnson	Denam. Scotch
Eliza Cooke	Dorothy Lamb	Joshua Smith
Moore Dennis	Ellinor Lucas	Jane Suffill
Morris Dennis	Rich. Marrinor	Abraham Taylor
Jone Griffing	Walter Marton	Ja. Whettum
Anne House	Anne Morgin	Thomas Woodfill
		(p. 37a)

Mr. West left the court for the following action:
Mr. John West and Mrs. Matilda West attested, and Nehemiah Covington confessed that he owed Mrs. Anne Charlton four years rent on land at

Kikotanck in Northampton Co. At 400 lbs tobacco per year, the debt totaled 1600 lbs tobacco. Ordered that Covington pay the rent and court costs. (p. 37a)

Thomas Powell and Walter Dickeson of Baltimore County, Maryland, assigned power of attorney to Simon Carpenter of the same place, so he could purchase from William Chase of Accomack Co., Virginia, 2000 feet of pine boards and two steers. Signed 16th day of the "12 month" 1663 (sic), by Thomas Powell and Walter Dickenson. Witnesses: Sam. Goldsmith and Fra. Wright.

Simon Carpender, on behalf of Thomas Powell and Walter Dickeson, assigned power of attorney to Anto. Hodgkins to conclude the matter with William Chase. Signed 15 March 1662/3 (sic) by Simon Carpender. Witnesses: Michaell (MR) Richards, Anthony (TS) Johnson. (p. 37b)

Evidence for Mrs. Charlton versus Covington:

Deposition of Mr. Jno. West, aged about 20 years: Said that Nehemiah Covington came to West's mother and agreed about the time he stayed and planted at Kikotanck and to pay 400 lbs tobacco per year. If he should "have any more besides them" he would "pay 100 lbs tobacco for every one entertained." Signed, John West.

Deposition of Mr. Jno West: Said that about a year and a half ago his mother, Mrs. Anne Charlton, requested him to demand the rent due from Nehemiah Covington, who said he was willing to pay, but hoped "she would forbear him another year." He used the same words several times, and "in consideration of his pretended want," West persuaded his mother accordingly. Signed, John West.

Deposition of Mrs. Matilda West, 16 November 1663: Said that about a year ago she was with her mother-in-law, Mrs. Anne Charlton, at Nehemiah Covington's house and heard her demand the rent due her. He answered that he had a tobacco house burned and could pay nothing. Mrs. Carlton offered to let him pay two hogsheads of tobacco and then let him pay the rest when he was able. He did not promise to pay her any that year except for one hogshead if he could. He said he would pay it all the next year. Signed, Matilda West. (p. 37b-38a)

Accomack County Court--November 11, 1663

Mr. West entered court. (p. 38a)

The suit brought against Thomas Leatherberry by Mary Paramore was dismissed because Paramore failed to enter her complaint. Paramore was to pay court costs. (p. 38b)

Capt. Parker left the court for the following action:

Alice Boutcher confessed to speaking "scandalous words against the court" and pleaded the court's favor, promising to behave better in the future. The court took the promises into consideration and acquitted her. She paid court costs.

Deposition of Joane Brookes aged about 50 years, 10 November 1663: She was at William Wotton's house last Monday along with Alice, the wife of William Boutcher. Alice said that she was pregnant with a child as big as her fist when Capt. Parker caused her to be ducked. She miscarried and said she would be revenged on him within a year. Joane told her she should do it soon and not keep it in her breast so long. Alice said, "He kept malice in his breast three years, for which I was ducked." Alice wanted to have it tried in another place. Signed, Jone (O) Brookes. (p. 38a)

The suit brought against Jno. Carew by Mihill Ricketts was dismissed because Ricketts failed to enter his complaint. Richetts was to pay court costs. (p. 38b)

William Chase had been taken to court several times by Mr. George Hack and desired compensation for it. Ordered that Hack make satisfaction to Chase and pay court charges. (p. 38a)

Ordered that John Walthom be dismissed from the office of constable and enter bond for good behavior. Richard Kellum was appointed constable instead. (p. 38a)

By the governor's command, John Walthom, Peter Walker and Richard Stevens were questioned about their actions among the Indians in the south. They acknowledged their actions and submitted to the court's censure. There would be no further proceedings till the governor's pleasure was known. (p. 38b)

John Walthom was charged for entertaining Nathaniell Batts and his company at his house. Walthom submitted to the mercy of the court which deferred further proceedings till the governor's pleasure was known. (p. 38b)

The suit of John Jenkins against John Rogers was dismissed because Jenkins did not prove his bill of complaint. Jenkins was to pay court charges.

The suit of John Rogers against John Jenkins was dismissed because Rogers had no apparent cause for action. Rogers was to pay court costs. (p. 38b)

Edm. Scarburgh received from "Leist Coll. Wm. Waters" 800 lbs tobacco in full satisfaction for all debts due to Scarburgh and others he had to receive for, including Mr. Valentine Hill of New England. The payment was from Col. Obedience Robins formerly of Accomack, who had now paid in full on 10 October 1663. Signed, Edm. Scarburgh. Recorded 12 November 1663, Robt. Hutchinson. (p. 38b)

Tabeteaby sold John Jenkins 400 acres between Thomas Leatherberry and Cristopher Calvert. Signed 10 November 1663, Tabetaby (W with loops) and Mr. Johns (zigzag). Recorded 12 November 1663, by Robt. Hutchinson. (p. 38b)

Gov. Francis Moryson granted William Waters 1200 acres between Anancock Creek and Chessanessecks Creek for transporting 24 people. Signed 20 February 1661/62 by Francis Moryson and Tho. Ludwell. On 10 July 1663, Waters and his wife Dorothy sold half the land to Mr. Jno. Wise. Signed, William Waters and Dorothy (D) Waters. Witnesses: Thomas Ball and Nich. Webbe. Recorded 12 November 1663 by Robt. Hutchinson. (p. 39a)

Ekeekes, King of Onancock and Chicconesseck, sold John Wise rights to 600 acres on the south side of Checconesseck that had been taken up by Major Wm. Waters and was bordered by John Michael. Signed 3 July 1663, Ekeekes (v with swirl). Witnesses: George Truet and Alice (R) Truet. Recorded 12 November 1663 by Robt. Hutchinson. (p. 39b)

William Chase assigned to George Parker two servants named Frances Branson and Ellinor Pocket, to serve out their full time. The conditions were as follows: If William Chase delivered to Geo. Parker 3200 feet of sawed pine planks on his new plantation in Onancock Creek by the end of next March, for which he had already been paid, then the assignment of the servants would be void. If the planks were not delivered, then the servants would be turned over to Parker in perfect health with payment for their service since 28 October 1663. Signed, William (O) Chase. Witnesses: John (I) Grames and Morris (M) Matthew. Acknowledged in open court 10 November 1663. (p. 39b)

Mr. Jno. West paid a mare colt and two cows and calves to Robert Brace for land described in the patent dated 12 April 1661. Signed 11 November 1663, Robert (RB) Brace. Recorded 12 November 1663, by Robt. Hutchinson. (p. 40a)

On 21 January 1649/50 Thomas Clifton sold to John Johnson, Jr., the 100 acres on a branch of Nuswattocks Creek, that included the "housing that do properly belong unto Richard Kellum." Signed, Thomas (TO) Clifton. Witnesses: John Tilney and Hans Nicolaij. On 10 November 1663, John Johnson, joiner, and his wife Elizabeth sold the land to Phillip Fisher, planter. Signed, John (II) Johnson and Elizabeth (O) Johnson. Witnesses: Jno. Laurence and Jno. King. Recorded 12 November 1663, by Robt. Hutchinson. (p. 40a)

For two matchcoats [fur mantles] and a shirt, John Watts purchased from Tapatiapon (great Emperor of the Eastern Shore), Kokewise, and Watchesogon all Indian claims to the land on the south side of Anancock known as Quietjanjerk. William Benstone formerly sold this land to Watts. Signed 9 November 1663, Tapatiapon (WN), Kokewiss (Z), and Watchesagon (S). Wittnesses: Robt. Hutchinson, William (WS) Silverthorne. (p.40b)

For three matchcoats [fur mantles], Thomas Leatherberry purchased from Tapatiapon (great Emperor of the Eastern Shore), Kokewiss, and Watchesogon all Indian claims to the land on the south side of Anancock Creek that was formerly granted to Jno. Elzey, who sold it to Leatherberry. Signed 9 November 1663, Tapatiapon (WN), Kokewiss (zig-zag), Watchesogon (uneven oval). Witnesses: Robt. Hutchinson, William (WS) Silverthorne.

Tapatiapon (great Emperor of the Eastern Shore), Kokewiss and Watchesagon, for three matchcoats [fur mantles], sold to Thomas Leatherberry all Indian claims to the land called Ambrotanahotinck on the south side of Anancock. Signed 1 August 1663, Tapatiapon (W), Kokewiss (zigzag), and Watchesagon (zigzag). Witnesses: Robt. Hutchinson, William (WS) Silverthorne. (p. 41a)

John Elzey patented 1200 acres on 3 October 1660; he and his wife Sara agreed to sell it to Mr. Henry Voss for 2500 lbs tobacco on 18 September 1661, but before the payment was made, Voss died. His widow, Anne, found the estate insolvent and could not pay. Elzey then sold the property to Thomas Leatherberry. Signed 2 October 1663, John Elzey and Sara. Witnesses: Edm. Scarburgh and James Fookes. Recorded 12 November 1663, by Robt. Hutchinson. (p. 41b)

John West leased Rand Neck for 19 years and Timber Neck for 50 years to Ogen Collman. The two necks contained 500 acres and were bounded by Richard Bayly, Sara's Neck and Richard Kellum. Signed by John West and acknowledged in open court 11 November 1663, before Robt.

Hutchinson. (p. 41b)

Tabeteaby sold William Anderson 600 acres on the bay bordering Dr. George Hack's land. Signed 10 November 1663, Tabeteaby (W). Witnesses: Rich. Buckland and John (II) Jenkins. Recorded 12 November 1663, by Robt. Hutchinson. (p. 42a)

George Johnson, planter, gave an iron-gray mare with a mare colt to Elisabeth, Mary and Ellinor Meridee, the three daughters of Phillip Meridee, deceased. Johnson's wife Ellinor Johnson, or someone she trusted, could dispose of the gift for the use of the three maids. Any other gift alleged to be given by George Johnson was declared void. Signed, George Johnson. Witnesses: Chris Tompson and Joanes Price. Acknowledged in open court 11 November 1663. Recorded by Robt. Hutchinson. (p. 42a)

Tapeapum (sic), Emperor of the Eastern Shore, sold to Richard Kellum all Indian claims to 800 acres at the head of Matchopungo. Signed 10 November 1663, Topeteapum (W). Witnesses: Tobius Sellvey and George Truett. (p. 42a)

Mr. Edmund Scarburgh presented an account of the incidents at Anamessecks and Manoakin on the Eastern Shore of Virginia:
He was accompanied by Col. Stringer and about forty horsemen who were taken along to repel the "contempt which I was informed some Quakers and a fool in office had threatened." They arrived in Anamessecks Sunday night October 11; on Monday morning at the house of Stephen Horsey, an officer of Lord Baltimore, the commands of the assembly were published by Scarburgh. Because the officer could not read, Scarburgh repeatedly read them to him. Horsey did not comment, but brought out a patent instead of his commission, claiming it was his authority and saying he would not be false to his trust to the Lord Leist of Maryland.
He was informed that Lord Baltimore had no land south of Watkins Point, and all that he needed to do was subscribe his obedience to His Majesty, who would protect him as a subject. If he refused, Scarburgh would arrest him for contempt and rebellion. Horsey appeared startled at this and claimed that if he and others pledged obedience, the governor of Maryland would come as soon as Scarburgh was gone and hang them at the doors.
He was told that he held an unworthy opinion of the Lord Leist, and that such tyranny was unthinkable. Horsey answered that since such things had been done in Maryland, he dared not subscribe. After

consultation among the military and civil officers, it was decided to arrest him and set a broad arrow[6] on his door.

Next they went to the house of Ambrose Dixon, a Quaker. There they found a boat and men from Groome's ship, two "running Quakers," and two Quakers who lived there, George Johnson and Thomas Price.

The Quakers "scoffed and despised" the reverent reading of the act; George Johnson "filled with the spirit of nonsense," spoke and forgot what he had said. Determined not to waste time like Johnson, Scarburgh briefly demanded their obedience. When they all refused, the broad arrow was set at the door, and they were all arrested to appear before the governor's council to answer for contempt and rebellion.

They next marched to Henry Boston's house, where the act was read. Boston agreed to attend after a day or two, so the group went on to Monoakin. There Scarburgh sent a summons for all the householders and freemen to appear, which they cheerfully did. All subscribed except Mr. John Elzey and Capt. William Thorne, both officers for Lord Baltimore who wanted time to return their commissions.

The people then made entries of their lands and requested the protection of the governor of Virginia as His Majesty's subjects, which was assured them as far as possible. They complained of a recent invasion of Indians and the great danger of being cut off. They sent for aid form the Lord Leist of Maryland, who after two weeks' delay sent a letter advising them to stand on their own. So the residents said they were "owned for profit and deserted in distress." They would recently have been cut off if the Indians had not been terrified by the report of Scarburgh coming with troops and the timely arrival of a sloop full of armed men seeking runaways.

Because of the Indians, the nearness of Quakers and their remoteness, the residents requested officers to be appointed for them. Scarburgh assured them this would be done as soon as he could give the governor an account of the affair.

Some residents discussed Maryland's claim to Manoakin and all places to Anancock. They were told that the proclamation was erroneous; the bounds of Lord Baltimore's patent were declared by the act of assembly, and he could be referred to it. The people were not to trouble themselves with things beyond the control of private men. The satisfied residents requested and were promised protection for themselves and against any pretenders from Lord Baltimore.

At that point Hollingsworth Marcham, of a northern vessel, requested

---

[6]*An arrow-shaped mark placed on British ordnance and government property as well as on the uniforms of worn by convicts.*

liberty of trade. Scarburgh suspected that the Quakers, in hopes he would demand customs and other charges, were plotting to disrupt the compliance of the people of Manoakin. Therefore, he presumed to give their "infant plantation" free trade, thus discrediting the Quakers, who had predicted otherwise. Scarburgh hoped it would not be "ill taken" if customs were ordered later.

Then Stephen Horsey and Henry Boston appeared as promised. Horsey said he would subscribe the following day when he had set aside his commission, as Mr. Elzey and Capt. Thorn had done, but Horsey did not return. Scarburgh was informed that he took Boston with him and advised others to rebellion.

Stephen Horsey, an "ignorant and insolent" officer, was a cooper by profession and formerly lived in Accomack County where he was known as a "factious and tumultuous person, a man repugnant" to all government and sects. Constant only in opposing the church and government, his children were at "great ages yet unchristened." He left the lower parts to live at Anamessecks to head rebellion there. He stands arrested, but is defiant and should be dealt with by stricter order.

George Johnson, a changeable heretic, had often wandered in the county, where he was notorious for "shifting schismatical pranks." He eventually settled at Anemesstecks where he made a plantation this year. A known drunkard, he is reported by neighbors to be the father of his negro wench's bastard. Fearing justice, he professed quaking and instructed others, having yet to learn good manners himself. He calls obedient subjects villains and rogues. He is arrested to appear before the governor, but his defiance demands that a stricter course be taken.

Thomas Price, a creeping Quaker, is by trade a leather dresser, "whose conscience would not serve to dwell amongst the wicked" and therefore moved to Anamesticks. "He hears much and saith nothing else but that he would not obey government, for which he stands arrested."

Ambrose Dixon, a caulker by trade, for a long time lived in the lower parts and was often "in question for his quaking profession." He moved to Anamestecks to do what "he could not be here permitted." He is a "prater of nonsense and much led by the spirit of ignorance." He is followed by many Quakers who meet at his house. He conveys or engages persons out of the county, for which he stands arrested. The broad arrow was set on his door, but he "bids defiance until severer course reform him."

Henry Boston, "an unmannerly fellow," stands condemned for fighting and condemning the laws of the country. A rebel to government and disobedient to authority, he recently received punishment. Not subscribing, he hid himself to escape arrest.

This is all "except for two or three loose fellows that follow the

Quakers for scraps, whom a good whip is fittest to reform."

Some days after the people of the Manoakin area requested safety in regards to strange stories spread by Quakers, the court of Accomack on 10 November 1663 ordered the following:

Present: Capt. Geo. Parker   Mr. Devorx Browne
                Major Jno. Tilney   Mr. Hugh Yeo
                Mr. Jno. West   Mr. Jno. Wise
                        Mr. Edmond Bowman

The residents at Manoakin and other remote parts of the county have confirmed their obedience by subscribing to the acts of assembly. This the Quakers and other factious persons have not done, and persisting in their rebellion have spread rumors to disturb the peace, pretending they come from the Lord Leist of Maryland. To prevent the designs of the Quakers, who are declared subversive to the government, and to serve the loyal subjects who requested protection, the following is ordered: Until the government can be fully informed of the affair, Capt. Wm. Thorne, an officer under Col. Scarburgh, Mr. Randall Revell, Mr. Wm. Bosman or Mr. Jno. Rhodes will have authority to call together and command His Majesty's subjects at Manoakin and as far as the Poko-mock River to come together and arm themselves for protection from invaders and those that would disturb their peace or property. The court is assured that these rumors arise more from the Quakers' desires than from the Lord Leist of Maryland:
- That the Lord Leist of Maryland will hang those who subscribed their obedience to the government of Virginia
- That the Governor of Virginia "for meddling hath a piece of green wax[7] sent for him"
- That Jolly intends to settle at Pokomoke River on people's land and hold it by force
- That Col. Scarburgh for executing the command of Virginia's assembly deserves to be hanged, and "more stuff like this"

Scarburgh concluded his account by saying that further action rested with "your honors." He wrote to the Lord Leist of Maryland, sending a copy of the act and offering to meet with Mr. Catlet and Mr. Laurance if his Honor desired. Having received only a "capitulatory letter," he presumes that the Lord Leist to have had representation at Jamestown. He now expected orders or to have the affair left with the court of Accomack. If necessary, the Quakers, "whose interest will never permit their consciences to comply with that government which is inconsistent

---

[7]*A seal of green wax was used on documents issued out of the Exchequer to sheriffs.*

with their affairs," will be brought before "your Honor." Signed, Edm. Scarburgh. (p. 42b-44b)

Accomack County Court--10 November 1663

Present: Capt. Geo. Parker   Mr. Devorx Browne
          Major Jno. Tilney   Mr. Hugh Yeo
          Mr. John West   Mr. Jno. Wise
               Mr. Edm. Bowman (p. 44b)

The King of Pokomoke came to the commissioners and requested aid according to an agreement with the governor of Virginia. He produced the document and a medal given him by the governor. The King of Pokomoke complained that his great men were trying to poison him and cause rebellion among his subjects. He requested a party of horse and foot soldiers. It was ordered that Major Jno. Tilney, Capt. Geo. Parker and Capt. Edm. Bowman take such a company to Pokomoke as soon as possible to aid the king by either punishing or suppressing rebellion, thereby "letting him know under whose protection he is" so he will "conform only to the country of Virginia and not...Maryland." If they found "one Jolly of Maryland" settling at Pokomoke by force of arms, they were to arrest him to answer for his illegal intrusion. (p. 44b)

Henry Ethridge sold to John Trotman the land he had previously purchased from Nath. Bradford. Signed 11 November 1663, Henry (O) Ethridge. Witnesses: Jno. Parker and Will. Anderson. Recorded 12 November by Robt. Hutchinson. (p. 44b)

Matahoquis, the Indian king, sold all Indian claims to the land patented by Thomas Robinson and agreed to bring his great men to the court to confirm it. Signed 23 October 1663, Matahoquis (cursive J). Witnesses: Jno. Williams, Robt. (H) Hill and Robt. (R) Houston. Acknowledged in court 10 November 1663, Recorded 12 November 1663, by Robt. Hutchinson. (p. 45a)

Francis Moryson, Governor, granted John Jenkins 250 acres on the south side of Pungoteage River, bounded by Pokomoke Creek, the land of Thomas Teackle, the land of Anthony Johnson, Negro, and the land of John Johnson, Negro. The land had originally been patented on 17 March 1655, to Jno. Williams. Signed 20 October 1661, by Francis Moryson and Tho. Ludwell. On 5 December 1662, John Jenkins and his wife Margritt sold the land to John Brookes. Signed, John (II) Jenkins and Margrit (mark) Jenkins. Witnesses: Thomas Montfort and John Williams. Recorded 8 December 1662, by Robt. Hutchinson. (p. 45a)

Accomack County Court--16 December 1663

Present: Capt. Geo. Parker   Mr. Hugh Yeo
                Major Jno. Tilney   Mr. Jno. Wise
                     Mr. John West (p. 45b)

The suit brought against Edward Hazard by James Taylor was dropped because Taylor failed to enter a complaint. Taylor was to pay court costs. (p. 45b)

Mr. Browne entered the court. (p. 45b)

Wm. Rodolphus accused Samuell Banton of drinking and spoiling a "case of drames." Banton confessed and was ordered committed to the sheriff's custody and have twenty-five lashes applied to his naked shoulders.

Peter Clavell confessed to being a confederate of Samuell Banton in drinking and spoiling a case of drink belonging to Wm. Rodolphus. Ordered that Clavell be committed to the sheriff's custody and have fifteen lashes "well laid" upon his naked shoulders.

Jenkin Morris confessed to being with Samuell Banton and Peter Clavell and drinking part of the drink belonging to Wm. Rodolphus, but as it appeared he was not as guilty as Banton and Clavell, it was ordered that Jenkin Morris execute the punishment inflicted on Banton and Clavell and be acquitted of further action against himself for this offence. (p. 45b)

The case of Roger Wollford, plaintiff, and Jno. Turnor, defendant, was referred to the next court at the request of Turnor. (p. 45b)

Mr. Yeo exited the court. (p. 45b)

The case of Thomas Teackle, plaintiff, and Jno. Fawsett, defendant, was referred to the next court at the request of Fawsett. (p. 45b)

It appeared to the court that Richard Cox owed Mr. Anto. Hodgkins 240 lbs tobacco for taxes in 1660. Cox claimed that Hodgkins had given him the tobacco, but could not prove it, so he requested and was given ten days respite and paid court costs. (p. 45b)

John Walthoum petitioned to be released from his bond for good behavior. Proclamation was made three times, and no objections being made, his bond was delivered with him paying court costs. (p. 46a)

Mr. Browne exited the court for the following action:
According to contract, John Williams owed Devorax Browne 642 lbs tobacco for the use of Mrs. Anne Cross?. Ordered that Williams pay Browne and court charges. (p. 46a)

Teague Anderson paid to Col. Jno. Stringer for public dues a hogshead of tobacco which some time later proved faulty. As Mr. John Wise testified that the damage was caused by storage, Anderson was excused from the debt. (p. 46a)

Deposition of Mrs. Anne Tofft, aged 20 years, 16 December 1663: About last April Mr. Jno. Custis, Jno. Mellish--master of the ship *Royal Oake*, and Jno. Shepheard came to Col. Edm. Scarburgh at Pungoteage requesting to have their ship released from seizure. Anne understood from their conversation that the ship was seized upon its first arrival, for it had come directly from Holland to Virginia with various goods and had neither a passport from any British port, nor proof that the *Royal Oake* was a free ship of England. Then Mr. Custis went out of the house and talked privately with Col. Scarburgh, then with the master and the merchant by turns, and then sometimes they spoke to Scarburgh together, but what they said, Anne did not know. When they came in again, Mr. John Custis solemnly swore that the *Royal Oake* was the same ship that was in Virginia last year and belonged to the same owners. Then Col. Scarburgh drew a bond, and Anne witnessed that it was signed and sealed by Mr. Mellish, Mr. Shepheard and Mr. Custis and delivered to Col. Scarburgh for His Majesty's use. After that the men talked about hogsheads of tobacco that were shipped on the *Royal Oake* without certificate and were seized according to the Act of Assembly. These Scarburgh said he would not take, but because they needed tobacco, he would put more in if they would carry the amount of tobacco seized for a friend of his and deliver them in Holland without charge. They all left the house and Anne saw them walking together and apart with Col. Scarburgh. When they came in again, she heard them all agree to deliver forty hogsheads clear of charges to Holland. One of them urged Col. Scarburgh to pay two shillings per hogshead of the seized tobacco for Virginia customs, which he agreed to do. The master said he would send his sloops for the tobacco. They stayed an hour or more afterwards merrily eating and drinking and acting very satisfied, saying they were glad they had ended their business this way. A few days later Claus, the

master's mate of the *Royal Oake* came to Pungotege with two sloops and
told Scarburgh he had come for forty hogsheads of tobacco and whatever
more Scarburgh wanted to send. So they carried away tobacco, but how
much Anne did not know. Signed, Ann Toft. (p. 46a,b)

Accomack County Court--17 December 1663

Present: Capt. Geo. Parker   Mr. Devorx. Browne
              Major Jno. Tilney   Mr. Hugh Yeo
              Mr. Jno. West   Mr. Jno. Wise (p. 46b)

Richard Kellum sued Richard Buckland over a cow formerly in controversy. The court considered Kellum's petition, his evidence, and Buckland's
answer, and ordered that there was no cause to overturn the verdict given
by a jury last May. Kellum's suit was dismissed with him paying court
charges.
Evidence for Rich. Kellum:
Deposition of Oneal Dermon aged about 25 years, 11 November 1663: Said
that he was at last May's court after judgment was passed against
Richard Kellum for killing a cow, and heard Kellum's wife and Rich.
Buckland discussing the cow. Buckland declared, and bound it with an
oath, that he gave Kellum permission to kill the cow in question. Signed,
Oneale (C) Derman.
Deposition of Edward Martine, 11 November 1663: On 19 June 1663,
Martin was with Richard Kellum's wife Sarah at Richard Buckland's
house, where he heard Sarah demand a bill from Buckland for seven and
a half bushels of wheat. Buckland called her impudent and told her that
John Jenkins could swear that he had the wheat for the cow in question.
Buckland said that Kellum sent his girl to say that Kellum would kill the
cow, and Buckland said her father could kill the cow if he provided
another for it. Buckland said to Sarah, "Country woman, if you will be
peaceable, I will tell you the bargain." The bargain was made at night in
the inner room in the chimney corner with nobody around except for
Buckland's namesake, who had advised Buckland to get a good milk cow
and allotted Buckland a black pied cow. The next morning Buckland
went to his namesake, the cowkeeper, and asked which was the best
cow, for "your master saith I must have a cow called by the name of
Py." The boy said that wasn't a good cow, so Buckland asked if the boy
could point out the best one, and the boy replied, "What will you give
me?" Buckland agreed to give him six pipes. Signed, Edward (M)
Martine.
Deposition of John Die aged about 36 years, 11 November 1663: Said that

Richard Buckland sent for Sara Turnor as soon as judgment was passed and asked, "Sara, did you tell me that your father would kill the cow named Butterflower?" She answered yes and also admitted that her father would give Buckland another one. Then Buckland bound it with an oath and swore it was the truth and said it was not yet paid. Sara said he might have had it if he had come for it. John (I) Die.

Deposition of Richard Stevens, 16 December 1663: Said that on 19 June 1663, he was with Richard Kellum's wife Sarah at Richard Buckland's house, where he heard Sarah demand a bill from Buckland for some wheat. He replied, "Are you so impudent to demand a bill of me for wheat? Look upon the records and on John Jenkins' oath, and there you shall see what I had the wheat for." Concerning the cow, Buckland said that he borrowed Capt. Parker's horse to fetch the cow home. Goody Kellum asked if it was a black pied cow, and Buckland said he thought it was, and said that he bargained with her husband over night. The next morning he went to the cowpen and asked Richard Welch which was the best cow. Signed, Richard Stevens.

Deposition of Sarah Turnor, aged about 14 years, 11 November 1663: Said she was sent to Richard Buckland's to tell him that her father intended to kill the cow called Butterflower because she was barren, and that her father would give him a pregnant cow or a cow with a calf in exchange. Buckland said a pregnant cow would do him no good, because it would run away, but he would be content with a cow and calf. Signed, Sarah Turnner.

Evidence for Buckland:

Deposition of Christopher Calvert, aged about 48 years, 16 December 1663: About the beginning of last May he heard Richard Buckland demand to know from Richard Kellum how Buckland's cow was doing. Kellum replied, "It is well." The next morning at Kellum's house, Buckland asked Kellum if he had considered what they had discussed last night. Kellum replied, "I will deliver you a heifer with calf or a calf by her side, provided you will have nothing to do with the heifer that I have of yours at my pen." Signed, Christopher (+) Calvert. (p. 46b-47b)

Ordered that the following persons be summoned to the next court by the sheriff:
- Wm. Taylor and Charles Ratclife, surveyors of the highway, for neglecting the repair of the bridge between their bounds, commonly called William Taylor's Bridge
- John Barnet for not tending two acres of corn
- Wm. Gray and Nich. Laurence to give an account to the court "of their manner of living"
- Father Patrick and Anne, Mr. West's servants, for fornication

- Peter Presly, Wm. Jones, Ruth and Lidia, Mr. Browne's servants, for
fornication
- Grand jurymen for not bringing in their presentments: John Renny,
Robert Huett, Jno. Lewis, Edw. Moore, James Price. (p. 47b)

Edmund Scarburgh, collector for the Eastern Shore of Virginia sent notice
to the courts of Northampton and Accomack Counties. He found
occasion for concern and had executed the acts of assembly by examining
hogsheads of tobacco delivered to any ship or boat. He requested a
speedy way of getting from each planter last year's account of all
tobacco, to whom it was sold, and how it was transported. Of special
concern was the ketch *Virginia Merchant*, Robert Ricsdon master, and
the ship *Royal Oake*, John Mellish master, to make full inquiry where
they received tobacco and where they made landings. Signed, Edm.
Scarburgh, Collector. (p. 47b-48a)
Ordered that all inhabitants give a written account to Mr. John Fawsett,
undersheriff, of their tobacco, to whom disposed, and how transported.
The planters were to make oath that this was their full account of last
year's crop and was the whole truth. (p. 48a)

Henry White made entry of land lying between Thomas Leatherberry and
the land belonging to the orphans of Alexander Mattocks. White needed
the aid of Leatherberry and Arthur Upshott, guardian of the orphans, to
discover his boundaries. Ordered that Leatherberry and Upshott show
White the bounds of their land so White could survey. (p. 48a)

The suit of James Hinderson against John King for debt was dismissed
because of the small amount involved. It was ordered that the matter be
referred to Mr. West and Mr. Browne or either of them. (p. 48a)

John White petitioned for the release of his bond for good behavior.
Proclamation was made three times with no objections against him, so
it was ordered that White's bond be delivered, with him paying court
costs. (p. 48a)

The suit brought against Mary White by Murrin Cornelius was dropped at
the request of Mary White because there was no cause of action. (p.
48a)

The suit brought against Mrs. Anne Charlton by Nehemiah Covington was
dropped because Covington failed to enter a complaint. Covington was
to pay court costs. (p. 48a)

Joseph Pitman was accused of perjury, but the court found it was through ignorance, so ordered that Pitman be acquitted and his master make satisfaction for the charge in the suit. Pitman was to repay his master by service after his time of indenture was expired. (p. 48a)

Mr. Hugh Yeo exited the court for the following action:
At the suit of Mr. Hugh Yeo, Mr. Isaac Foxcroft was to appear at court. Since he failed to appear, it was ordered that if the sheriff did not bring Mr. Foxcroft to the next court, the judgment was to proceed against the sheriff for the amount owed to Mr. Yeo. (p. 48a, b)

Richard Kellum was formerly fined 500 lbs tobacco for not completely clearing the highways when he was surveyor. As it appeared the defect was small, it was ordered that the fine be remitted with Kellum paying court costs. (p. 48a)

James Atkinson had Murrin Cornelius subpoenaed to court, and she requested compensation. Ordered that Atkinson pay Cornelius what is due her for providing evidence in behalf of Cornelius, who was ordered to pay court costs. (p. 48a)

Robert Huitt had Daniell Mackare and his wife Norah subpoenaed to court, and they requested compensation. It was ordered that Huitt pay them what was due for providing evidence in his behalf and pay court costs. (p. 48a)

According to the command of the Honorable Governor Sir William Berkeley for rehearing the case between Capt. George Parker, plaintiff, and George Hack, defendant, the court retried the case concerning hogs which had first been determined in May. Several evidences were presented by both sides and the jury found no error in the former verdict, but found the charge of Capt. Parker against Hack to be augmented. Ordered that Hack not only perform the former order, but also pay the costs of the present court.

The jury:

Alex. Addeson	Mr. Geo. Johnson	Wm. Taylor
Timothy Coe	Mr. Southee	Mr. Arthur
Ralph Dowe	Littleton	Upshott
Mr. Tho. Foolkes	Charles Parker	Mr. Geo. Watson
Mr. Richard Hill	Mehill Ricketts	(p. 48b)

Evidences for Mr. Hack:
Deposition of George Truett, aged about 46 years, 11 November 1663: About last Christmas there was a general hunting for hogs in Nandue

Neck. Truett went with his dogs to the hunt where it was agreed among the neighbors that all hogs good for meat should be killed regardless of owner. They found a white sow and asked Mr. Hack if it was his, and he said it was. After she was killed, John Mackele looked at the mark and said it was Capt. Parker's. Then Hack said if it were Parkers, he must have her, so the sow was taken from the woods and laid on a pile of boards. The captain's servants fetched her away. Signed, George Truett.

Deposition of William Boucher, aged about 56 years, 11 November 1663: Said that the sow killed by Mr. Hack's servant John Watts and Mr. Littleton's Negro was the stray sow that Capt. Parker had ordered be killed or captured for him. This sow and others used Mr. Hack's swamp near the branch by Boucher's house. Signed, Wm. (W) Boutcher.

Deposition of Bridgett Van Nitsin, aged about 19 years, 11 November 1663: Said that Mr. Hack had two boars, one white and one blue, that used Hack's old field and often fought together, and by fighting, the white boar lost most of his right ear, so there was only a stump left. Then he went astray. Last Christmas some of the neighbors informed her that they had killed that boar for Mr. Hack. Signed, Bridgett (R) Van Nitsin.

Deposition of Richard Buckland, aged about 41 years, 16 December 1663: At Capt. Parker's, Buckland heard Capt. Baker say that he came purposely to discuss with Parker a sow that was killed by Dr. Hack's servants. Signed, Richard Buckland.

Deposition of Edward Dale, aged about 20 years, 16 December 1663: Said that he saw his master's hogs which were marked with three slits, one of which was grown back together. Signed, Edward (M) Dale.

Deposition of John White, aged about 23 years, 16 December 1663: He saw one of Mr. Hack's hogs marked as described by Edward Dale. Signed, John (O with a dot) White.

Evidence for Capt. Parker:

Deposition of Husalin Van Nitsin, aged about 29 years, 16 December 1663: A year ago last summer at Dr. Hack's cowpen, Dr. Hack's servant John Watts complained to his mistress "of diet." She called him rogue and thief to which he replied, "I was never a thief till I came into this country and you made me a thief to kill other people's hogs." When Van Nitsin lived with Dr. Hack, Hack's servants often hunted for hogs, and Hack himself sometimes went with them. They often killed hogs and singed them in the woods and brought them home. Van Nitsin saw many of different marks and asked whose they were. Hack sometimes said James Caines or Richard Woodsworth. Van Nitsin refused to go hunting with Hack, saying the neighbors lost their hogs and suspected Hack's people. Signed, Husalim Van Nitsin.

Deposition of Bridget Van Nitsin, aged about twenty years, 16 December 1663: Said that about four years ago Mr. Hack killed four or five hogs for Mr. Augustus Barks, but she did not know the marks of the hogs. Signed, Bridget (R) Van Nitsin.

Deposition of William Chase, aged about 30 years, 16 December 1663: Said that he was at Mr. Hacke's cowpen when John Watts, servant to Mr. Hack, and Mrs. Hack had a falling out. She called him a rogue and thief, and he replied that he was never a rogue or thief till he came to Virginia and was made to kill other folk's hogs. Signed, William (O with a dot) Chase. (p. 48b-49b)

At the complaint of Mr. West and with the depositions of Rebecca Hester and Nora Neregon, it appeared to the court that Hanah Snowswell laid violent hands on her mistress, Mrs. West. It was ordered that Hanah Snowswell serve at least a year after her indenture had expired.

Deposition of Rebecca Hester, 17 December 1663: Said that her mistress sent Hanah Snowswell for a pail of water, but Hanah replied, "I'll do my own business first." Her mistress struck Hanah, who turned on the mistress, putting one arm around her neck and the other around her middle. Hanah said, "Mistress, I will not hurt you." Signed, Rebecca Hester.

Deposition of Nora Neregon, aged about 30 years, 17 December 1663: Said that Hanah Snowswell put one arm around her mistress' neck and the other around her middle. The mistress cried, "Murder!" and Hanah said, "I will not hurt you, Mistress." Signed, Norah (m) Neregon.

Because Hanah Snowswell had told the court false tales about her mistress, Mrs. West, it was ordered that the sheriff take her into custody and give her 25 lashes well applied to her naked shoulders. (p. 50a)

Mr. Browne exited the court for the following action:

Governor Wm. Berkley commanded that the court rehear the difference between Col. Edm. Scarburgh at His Majesty's suit, and Mr. George Hack, defendant, concerning a cow killed by Mr. Hack. Last August the court found Hack guilty, but obedient to His Honor's commands, permitted Hack to make further defense. The evidence was considered by the jury, who found no cause to alter their former verdict. Ordered that Mr. Hack perform the former order and pay court charges.

The names of the jury:

Alex. Adison	George Johnson	Mr. Wm. Taylor
Timothy Coe	Rich. Kellum	Mr. Arthur
Ralph Dowe	Mr. Southee	Upshott
Mr. Tho. Foolkes	Littleton	Mr. George
Mr. Richard Hill	Mihill Ricketts	Watson (p. 50a)

Deposition of Mr. Devorax Browne, aged about 25 years, 11 November 1663: About three years ago Anne Morgin came to Browne's house and asked if he had seen any of her cattle or hogs. Browne said he didn't know them, and she said that Henry Eldrige had marked one beast of hers, "for which she said that she would have his ears." For all she knew Eldrige had marked more cattle of hers besides the hogs. Signed, Devorax Browne.

Deposition of Sarah Holding, aged about 25 years, 11 November 1663: About three and a half years ago Anne Morgin came to her master Robert Parker's plantation and was very angry, saying that her husband Abraham Morgin had given orders to Henry Eldrige to mark a red cow calf; Eldridge had mismarked it. Signed, Sarah (O) Holding.

Deposition of Henry Ethridge, aged about 24 years, 11 November 1663: About five years ago Abram. Morgin's wife had asked Ethridge to mark a red cow calf with her husband's mark. Ethridge marked it as near Morgin's mark as he could, and the next year when Morgin's wife came again and saw it, she said that he had mismarked it. Henry (O) Ethridge.

Deposition of William Nayton, aged about 22 years, 17 July 1663: While at work at John Rogers' he heard William Chase say he would prove that the red heifer in his field was Dr. Hack's who had exchanged her for a beast that went up the bay. Signed, Wm. (+) Nayton.

Deposition of Bridgett Van Nitsin, aged about 19 years, 11 November 1663: Said that two red cows in the possession of her Master Hack had once belonged to Abraham Morgin. One cow her master carried up the bay, and the other red cow was killed for Mr. Hack's use as she was told by Wm. Chase. Signed, Bridget (R) Van Nitsin.

Deposition of Charity Buckland, aged 35 years, 16 December 1663: Said that she and John Rogers were at the house of Antony Johnson, Negro, and she demanded to know if the cow he reported belonging to her children was there or not. He said it was not, for it was Mr. Hack's. Buckland asked if it was Mr. Hack's mark, and he said it was Abram. Morgin's mark. Signed, Charity (Ch) Buckland.

Deposition of Gausalim Van Nitsin, aged about 30 years, 11 November 1663: Said he went to John Rogers' plantation with two of Dr. Hack's servants to fetch a red cow for Dr. Hack. John Rogers' wife showed them the cow which they brought home. Gausalim did not know its mark. Signed, Gausalim Van Nitsin.

Deposition of John Parker, aged about 28 years, 11 November 1663: About three years ago Abraham Morgin went out of the county and left four or five cattle in Parker's custody and asked Parker to deliver the cattle to Mr. George Hack for his use. They were delivered accordingly. Signed, John Parker.

Deposition of John Ricketts, aged about 23 years, 11 November 1663: At the June Court, Ricketts heard John Rogers say that he thought there would be a lawsuit between Ricketts' master and Rogers about a cow that Ricketts' master killed. Rogers admitted believing the cow belonged to Ricketts' master. However, Capt. Parker urged Rogers to sue Ricketts' master, saying that Parker would recover the cow for Rogers. Rogers further said that he would not have troubled Ricketts' master, but Capt. Parker "set him on" and would "put a thorn" in the foot of Ricketts' master. Signed, John Ricketts. (p. 50a-51a)

The following persons reported by the church wardens were to be summoned by the sheriff to the next court for not attending church:

Francis Benstone	William George	John Robinson
Wm. Benstone	Jno. Harris	Col. Edm.
Wm. Boutcher	James Henderson	Scarburgh
Mr. Devorax	Henry ye	Daniell ye Turnor
Browne	Dutchman	Gausalin
Jno. Cary	Obedience	Van Nitsin
Japhat Cooke	Johnson	Jno. Waller
William Dine	Thomas	John Watts
John Dye	Leatherberry	Mr. Jno. West
Henry Eldridge	Jno. Major	(p. 51b)

William Taylor obtained an order against John Williams at a Northampton court on 12 November 1660, for 700 lbs tobacco with court charges which remained unpaid. As Williams had been summoned to appear at both the last court and the present court and failed to appear, it was ordered that the suit of William Taylor proceed against John Williams for that sum. (p. 51b)

John Wolford of Monoakin assigned power of attorney to his friends George Watson and Luke Denwood in order to demand and receive of John Turnor all debts owed to Wolford, or in case of nonpayment, to sue. Signed 24 November 1663, by Roger Wolford. Witnessed by Lyving Denwood and John Yeo. Recorded 18 December 1663, by Robt. Hutchinson. (p. 51b-52a)

Francis Moryson, Governor, granted James Kime 500 acres at the head of the south branch of Anoncock bordering Christopher Colvert, Mr. Will. Mellinge and the woods. Robert Bayly had originally patented 200 acres 17 March 1655; the rest was due Kime for transporting six people to the colony. Signed 20 October 1661, Francis Moryson and Tho. Ludwell. On 13 July 1663, Geo. Parker sold the land to John Macell (Scotsman?) as ordered by Kime, who was in Monoakin. Signed, Geo. Parker.

Witnesses: Wm. White and Sarah (m) Johnson DeWitt. Acknowledged 24 November 1663, by James (<) Kime. Witnesses: Geo. Parker, Jno. West, Devorx. Browne and Jno. Wise. Recorded 18 December 1663, by Robt. Hutchinson. (p. 52a)

Letter to Thomas Bunick from London, 22 August 1663: In this letter Edward Baker, "my love to you remembered," orders Bunick to come home with Robert Pitt, being helpful to him and ruled by him both aboard and ashore. Baker had changed his mind for "I am sorry I did not bring you home with me." He pleaded with Bunick to take care of all the things he left at Mr. Hack's including trunks, cases, empty bottles, clothes, wine barrels and three empty hogshead casks, and to give account of them to Mr. John West, who was to dispose of them. With West's permission Bunick could sell them at Mr. Hack's for as much as he could get in tobacco. Bunick was to inform West if Hack had taken up land in Maryland for Baker, who now hoped this was not the case. Signed, "So rest your loving master, Edward Baker." Recorded 18 December 1663, by Robt. Hutchinson. (p. 52b)

Accomack County Court--18 January 1663/64

Present: Major Jno. Tilney   Mr. Hugh Yeo
                  Mr. Jno. West   Mr. Jno. Wise
                      Mr. Devorx. Browne (p. 52b)

Action was entered by Capt. Geo. Parker against John Harris, but he could not be found, so it was ordered that attachment proceed against his estate for 548 lbs tobacco and court charges. If Harris was found, he would be responsible till further trial. (p. 52b)

Capt. Geo. Parker entered court. (p. 52b)

John Turnor owed Roger Woolford 1138 1/2 lbs tobacco, partly by account and partly by contract. Ordered that Turnor make payment and pay court costs. (p. 52b)

Robert Hinderson, mariner, assigned power of attorney to his good friend George Watson to sue David Revell for 1500 lbs tobacco. Signed December 1663 by Robert Hinderson. Recorded 18 January 1663/64, by Robt. Hutchinson. (p. 52b)

It appeared to the court that Edward Revell owed Robert Henderson by contract 1500 lbs tobacco. Ordered that Revell make payment and pay court charges. (p. 53a)

Mr. Yeo exited the court. (p. 53a)

Thomas Bloyes entered action against Richard Stevens, but Stevens was not to be found, so it was ordered that attachment proceed against the estate of Stevens for 1443 lbs tobacco and court charges. If Stevens was found, he would be responsible until further order. (p. 53a)

Major Tilney exited the court for the following action:
It appeared to the court upon the balance of account between John Turnor, plaintiff, and Wm. Rodolphus, defendant, that Rodolphus owed Turnor 338 lbs tobacco. Ordered that Rodolphus pay Turnor and court charges. (p. 53a)

Mr. Browne exited the court for the following action:
Cristopher Calvert acknowledged owing Mr. Devorx. Browne 1752 lbs tobacco. Ordered that Calvert pay Browne and court charges. (p. 53a)

The case between William Chase and Mr. Jno. Michael was referred to the next court at the request of Chase. (p. 53a)

Col. Edm. Scarburgh complained about the poor quality of leather from Nathaniell Bradford, currier, and desiring that it be improved in the future, requested that the leather be inspected. The court appointed Charles Ratcliffe, George Crumpe, Thomas Taylor, Robt. Richardson, and John Parker, tanner, to view the leather and report to the next court whether the fault lay with the tanner, currier or both. (p. 53a)

Mousatran, "King and owner of the land at Chiccanessecks Creek," and Ekeecks, King of Anancock, sold their rights to 1000 acres to John, Sara and Margrett Michaell. Signed 2 November 1663, Mousatran (U), Ekeeks (O), and Wassota (W). Witnesses: Edm. Scarburgh and George Truett. Recorded 15 January 1663/64, by Robt. Hutchinson. (p. 53a)

Mr. Devorax Browne and Mr. Robert Pitts entered action against Mr. Henry Jones, attorney for the executors of Mr. Gerrard Bucknor, but failed to enter their complaint. Ordered that the suit be dismissed with Browne and Pitts paying court costs. (p. 53b)

Mr. Hugh Yeo left the court for the following action:
It appeared to the court by the oath of Mr. Hugh Yeo that Mr. Isaac Foxcroft owed Yeo 1000 lbs tobacco for charges at James City for an

action against him as security for Foxcroft. Ordered that Foxcroft pay Yeo and court charges.

Isaac Foxcroft, merchant of Northampton Co., acknowledged his debt to Hugh Yeo, merchant of the same place, for the amount of 29,940 lbs of "good sound bright and large tobacco." 24 September 1661.

The conditions: this obligation will be void if Isaac Foxcroft or his heirs shall periodically defend Hugh Yeo and his heirs and keep them free from trouble, damage or loss that may accrue to him by becoming bound with Foxcroft in bonds to George Lee, grocer of London, for payment of 7485 lbs tobacco, payable next 20 December at Findall's Point in Yorke River and 7485 lbs tobacco on 20 December 1662. Signed, Isaac Foxcroft. Witnesses: Tho. Breveton and John Appleton. Recorded 18 January 1663/64, by Robt. Hutchinson, clerk. (p. 53b)

Richard Foster of lower Northfolke assigned power of attorney to his "loving friend" Edmond Bowman to collect debts from John Waltham, Jno. Vries?, William Foster and Richard Stevens of Accomack. (p. 53b)

Accomack County Court--19 January 1663/64

Present: Capt. Geo. Parker   Mr. Hugh Yeo
               Mr. Devorx. Browne   Mr. Jno. Wise (p. 54a)

Rich. Foster's attorney Mr. Edm. Bowman, sued Richard Stevens, who could not be found. Ordered that attachment proceed against the estate of Stevens for 754 lbs tobacco. If Stevens was found, he would be responsible till further trial. (p. 54a)

Francis Benstone sued John Harris, who could not be found. Ordered that attachment proceed against the estate of Harris for 260 lbs tobacco. If Harris was found, he would be responsible until further trial. (p. 54a)

Mr. West entered the court. (p. 54a)

In the case between Richard Johnson, Negro plaintiff, and Richard Buckland, defendant, both sides agreed to allow Mihill Ricketts and Jno. Graves to judge the amount due Johnson for building a house for Buckland and give a report to the court. (p. 54a)

Mr. Wise exited the court for the following action:

Isaac Foxcroft acknowledged that Mr. Robt. Parker requested him to ship with Capt. Whitty ten hogsheads of Parker's tobacco. Unable to do so,

Foxcroft shipped four hogsheads, weight unknown, to Holland, and claimed he never took charge of the other six. The court judged the weight to be 370 lbs apiece and ordered that Foxcroft pay Mr. Jno. Wise, attorney for Parker, 1480 lbs tobacco and court costs. If it appeared that Foxcroft made use of more than three hogsheads, he would be accountable for that also. (p. 54a)

Robert Huitt owed James Atkinson for several charges in a suit; it was ordered that Atkinson pay 346 lbs tobacco with court charges. (p. 54a)

John Barnet was accused of not tending corn, but upon examination it appeared that he could not get ground to plant on this year. He was acquitted, but had to pay court charges. (p. 54a)

William Gray, having given an account of his manner of living, was discharged from his notice from the court but paid court charges. (p. 54b)

Nicholas Laurance, having given an account of his manner of living, was discharged from his notice from the court, but paid court charges. (p. 54b)

James Price was excused from his notice from the court because of sickness, but paid court charges. (p. 54b)

Robt. Huitt was discharged from his notice from the court because of lameness, but paid court costs. (p. 54b)

Ordered that the sheriff take Jno. Carew into custody till further notice for insolency to the court and striking Mihill Ricketts, church warden. (p. 54b)

Mr. Browne exited the court for the following action:
- Mr. Browne was cleared of his absence from church because he was out of the county.
- Jno. Major was cleared of his absence from church because he attended Occahannock Church instead of Nanduce Church.
- Gausalin Van Nitsin was cleared of his absence from church because he was lame. (p. 54b)

Mr. West exited the court for the following four actions:
The following persons, having no lawful excuses, were fined 50 lbs tobacco apiece for not attending church:

Wm. Benstone	Wm. Dine	Daniell Mackare
Francis Benstone	Hen. Ethredge	Col. Edm.
Jno. Cary	Wm. Gray	Scarburgh
Japhet Cooke	ObedienceJohnson	Mr. Jno. West
Jno. Die	Tho. Leatherberry	(p. 54b)

The suit brought against Thomas Smith by Robert Foster was dropped because Foster failed to enter a complaint. Foster paid court costs. (p. 54b)

John Die complained to the court that he had been beaten and abused by the King of Matomkin and his great men, which was confirmed by Henry Michell. The court requested Col. Edm. Scarburgh to investigate, do what he thought just and necessary, and give a report at the next court. (p. 54b)

Deposition of Henry Michell, aged about 20 years, 19 January 1663/64: Michell and John Die had spent about two weeks at Matomkin when the King of Matomkin with about 18 or 20 Indians came to John Die and talked together, but Michell could not understand what they were saying. Michell saw the Indians struggle with Die for an axe that he held, and then they threw him down and kept him there "almost an hour by the hair of his head and put dirt in his mouth and ears." Michell said that Die did not strike any of the Indians, but when he was down he struggled and kicked to get clear of them. While he was down, some of the Indians pulled down his house. Then the king said, "He has had enough, let him go." Signed, Henry (H) Michel. Testified to Robt. Hutchinson. (p. 55a)

After the following action, Mr. West entered court:

Ordered that Anne Dix, for fornication with Patrick, the servant of Mr. West, be taken into the sheriff's custody and receive twenty lashes on her naked shoulders. (p. 55a)

The suit brought against William Silverthorne by Mr. Thomas Selby was dropped because Selby failed to enter a complaint. Selby paid court costs. (p. 55a)

Major Jno. Tilney entered the court. (p. 55a)

In rehearing the case between Richard Buckland and Richard Kellum, the court ordered that the charges in the whole suit be shared equally between them, and that the fine remain unchanged. (p. 55a)

Mr. Browne exited court for the following action:

Presented to the court for fornication were Mr. Browne's servants: William Jones, Peter Pressly, Ruth and Lidia. They were spared from punishment because Browne promised to "perform all things required by the Act of Assembly" and pay court costs. (p. 55a)

Dorothy Younge swore before the court that she was with child by James Taylor.

Mr. Anto. Hodgkins' servant Dorothy Young being pregnant with James Taylor's child, Hodgkins petitioned the court, which ordered Taylor's custody till he put in security for all charges and damages that Hodgkins would sustain and "perform according to Act of Assembly." (p. 55a,b)

Capt. Parker and Mr. Wise exited the court for the following two actions:

Robt. Parker owed John Parker 1458 lbs tobacco by arbitration and account, and because Mr. John Wise, the attorney for Robt. Parker, could not prove any payments were made, it is ordered that Mr. Wise pay Mr. Jno Parker and court costs.

Because there was a difference in accounts between Mr. Robt. Parker and his brother John Parker, it was agreed by both parties to end the difference between Mr. Devorx. Browne, Mr. Rich. Bayly and Mr. George Hack and pay them according to the 20,000 lb tobacco bond. Having reviewed the accounts, the court awarded Mr. Jno. Parker's account 1073 lbs tobacco. To be deducted from Jno. Parker's account: 150 lbs tobacco for Abraham Morgin, 133 lbs for Mr. Wm. Whittington, and 200 lbs for shipping. As for the 1000 lbs for the sloop charged by Jno. Parker, the court referred it to the two brothers to settle it themselves. If Jno. Parker could prove that Morgin and Whittington had been paid, then Robt. Parker would owe that much to Jno. Parker. Jno. and Robt. Parker were to give each other a general discharge. The court did not meddle with the account of the grandmother Mrs. Joan Elsey?. Signed by Devorx. Browne, George Hacke, and Rich. (3) Bayly. Recorded 19 January 1663/64, by Robt. Hutchinson. (p. 55b)

John Carry, promising better behavior, was acquitted from his punishment for his insolence to the court and abuse of Mihill Ricketts, church warden. Carry paid court costs. (p. 55b)

Major Tilney exited the court for the following action:

Isaac Foxcroft of Northampton County sold to John Tilney of Accomack County a five year old sorrel mare branded with 2C. Signed 22 July 1663, Isaac Foxcroft. Witnesses: George Smith, John Tilney and Lenord (X) House. Acknowledged in court 19 January 1663/64, and recorded by Robt. Hutchinson. (p. 55b, 56a)

For 1241 lbs tobacco, William Stevens sold Robert Hutchinson 700 acres lying on Matchotanck Creek, also know as Little Anoncock Creek. The property, which included houses, buildings, orchards, gardens and fences, had been inherited by Stevens from his deceased father, William Stevens. Signed 6 November 1663, Will. Stevens. Witnesses: John Fawsett, G. Hack, Geo. Parker, Devorax Browne, Jno. Tilney, Hugh Yeo, Jno. West, Jno. Wise. Recorded 20 January 1663/64, by Robt. Hutchinson. (p. 56b, 57a)

The original patent, granted to William Stevens by Gov. Francis Moryson, was located on the Bay Side on Matchotank Creek near Pungoteage and was renewed 20 October 1662. Signed Francis Moryson and Tho. Ludwell. (p. 57a)

The Great Emperor of the Eastern Shore Tapaliapon, Kokewiss and Watchesagon, in exchange for three matchcoats [fur mantles], released to Robert Hutchinson the land on the south side of Matchotank Creek originally patented to William Stevens, whose son assigned it to Hutchinson. On 9 November 1663, two witnesses made their marks: Thomas (T) Leatherberry and William (WN) Silverthorne. Acknowledged in court 10 November 1663, and signed by Geo. Parker, Jno. Tilney, John West, Edmond Bowman, Devorax Browne, Hugh Yeo, and John Wise. Recorded 20 January 1663/64, by Robt. Hutchinson. (p. 57b)

Accomack County Court--16 February 1663/64

Present: Capt. Geo. Parker

     Mr. Jno. West   Mr. Devorx. Browne
     Mr. Edm. Bowman   Mr. John Wise (p. 58a)

Wm. Roberts' servant boy Henry Knight was judged by the court to be 13 years old. (p. 58a)

Hone? Collony's servant boy Edw. Scinons? was judged by the court to be 13 years old. (p. 58a)

Mr. Bowman exited the court for the following action:
Capt. Edmond Bowman, assignee of Lt. Col. Tho. Lambert, entered action against Capt. Jno. Belgrave, who could not be found. Ordered that an attachment of 2171 lbs tobacco proceed against any estate of Lambert found in the county. (p. 58a)

Thomas Smith acknowledged he owed Robert Foster 455 lbs tobacco. Ordered he pay this to Foster and court costs. (p. 58a)

Mr. Browne exited the court. (p. 58a)

In the difference between Thomas Leatherberry, plaintiff, and Ralph Dow, defendant, concerning a broken contract: ordered that with the consent of both parties, Henry White and Charles Ratcliffe view the damaged sustained by Leatherbery and report to the next court. (p. 58a)

Certificate was granted to John Renny for 100 acres for transporting Edward Whitehill and Elizabeth Penter (p. 58a)

William Benstone, according to a contract dated in Northampton Co. 23 March 1662, owed Henry Smith 844 lbs tobacco with court charges, as well as 170 lbs due per account. Ordered that Benstone pay the full amount and court charges. (p. 58a)

William Benstone was granted a delay till the next court in the difference concerning hogs between him and Mr. Smith. (p. 58a)

Richard Hill entered action against Capt. Anto. Fenn, who could not be found. Ordered that an attachment of 3000 lbs tobacco be granted against any estate of Fenn found in the county. (p. 58b)

Deposition of John Levick, aged about 36 years, 16 February 1663/64: Said that a passenger named Bridget left the ship *Happy Adventure* at the Isle of White. He asked what she wanted done with her things if the ship left her behind. She replied that she left them with Mrs. Hill. The master was ashore and knew nothing of her wishes. Signed, John Levicke.

Deposition of Mary Davis aged about 19 years, 16 February 1663/64: Said that Bridgett Neale, as she went over the side of the ship to go ashore at the Isle of White, gave her keys to Mrs. Mary Hill along with a note saying, that if she never returned, Mrs. Hill was to have all her things, and that she would rather have them thrown into the sea than let the ship's master have them. If she came again she would come to Mrs. Hill. Signed, Mary (M) Davis.

Deposition of Elizabeth Gillman, aged about 19, 16 February 1663/64: Said that when at the Cawes? as Bridget Neale went ashore she gave her keys to Goody Hill along with her receipt for her passage and freight payments. Hill asked Neale if she had friends that her goods should be sent to if the ship sailed without her. Neale replied, "No, I have none but a father-in-law,[8] and he hath too much of mine already, and before ye

---

[8]*In the 1600's the term father-in-law could also refer to a step-father.*

master shall have anything, I desire they may be thrown overboard, but I give all that I have unto you." Signed, Elizabeth (W) Gillman. (p. 58b)

Mr. Browne entered the court. (p. 58b)

John Harris, indebted to several persons in Accomack Co., left his place of residence which was the house of William Silverthorne. With information that Harris was at Anamestick, it was ordered that Silverthorne have authority to demand Harris' return. If Harris refused, and the local magistrate refused support, then Silverthorne had authority to arrest the magistrate to appear at the next court to give his account of his contempt and rebellion. (p. 58b)

Mr. West exited the court for the following action: (p. 58a)
William Chase acknowledged himself indebted to Jno. West for 350 lbs tobacco. Ordered Chase make payment with court costs. (p. 59a)

At the petition of Col. Edm. Scarburgh, on behalf of the county, it was ordered that attachment be granted against any estate of John Shepheard found in the county for 48 hogsheads of tobacco belonging to the public along with damages. (p. 59a)

At the petition of Col. Edm. Scarburgh, collector for His Majesty on the Eastern Shore of Virginia, attachment was ordered against the estate of John Shepeard and John Mellish and the proceeds of the ship *Royal Oake* and its owners, if such shall be found in Accomack Co., for the sum of 2100 pounds sterling with court charges. (p. 59a)

Mr. Browne exited the court. (p. 59a)

Mr. Robert Pitt had formerly entered his plea in Northampton Co. against the estate of Mr. Gerrard Bucknor. The suit, now in Accomack Co., indicated that the estate of Bucknor owed Pitt for a debt and for what Pitt paid to Mr. Matthews, Nich. Roberts, John Heginbathom and Mr. Benjamin Scarburgh, in all 112 pounds 11 shillings 8 pence sterling. The court had "great cause to suspect some clandestine dealings," for Pitt intercepted letters to the executors and others in England which were to be delivered to Mr. Boys. The court suspected that the claims and proofs offered by Pitt were pretended, and that there was not that much due from Bucknor's estate. Ordered that Pitt be paid from Bucknor's estate all sums according to records providing Pitts 1) notify the executors of Bucknor and have them pay persons who claim money from Pitts, and 2) prove to the executors that Bucknor did not pay the accounts that Pitts now claims. This order would be concluded, if the amounts were for goods and services sent to Virginia. In case the executors refused this order, or couldn't disprove Pitt's claims, then the order was to stand and the money would be used for Pitt's and Bucknor's debts.

Thomas Mathews of St. Katherins near the tower in the county of Midd.?, slopseller[9], swore that in June 1662, Gerrard Bucknor, merchant, and Mr. Robert Pitt bought clothes and other items costing 80 pounds English money, for several servants which were shipped on the *Vincent*. Before leaving on that ship Pitts gave his share of the cost to Bucknor who died. Mathews was forced to ask for the entire amount from Pitts who paid it. Signed by Thomas Mathews. August 1663. Wittnesses: Jno. Denham, John Andrews, John Ayres and Tobias Wolrich, Master of the Chancery.

Francis Holland, servant to Nicholas Roberts ironmonger of Grace Church Street in London, swore that in July 1662, Mr. Gerrard Bucknor and Mr. Robt. Pitt bought nails worth 10 pounds 13 shillings and 4 pence. When Bucknor failed to pay as promised, Pitt paid the debt. Signed by Francis Holland, August 1663. Witness: Jno. Denham, John Andrews, John Ayres and Tobias Wolrich, Master of the Chancery.

Samuell Sikes, servant to John Heginbothom upholsterer of London, made oath that 19 June 1662, Mr. Gerrard Bucknor and Robert Pitt bought 6 pounds 7 shillings 4 pence worth of goods. When Bucknor failed to pay as promised, Pitt was forced to pay. Signed by Samuell Sikes, August 1663. Witnesses: Jno. Denham, John Andrews, John Ayres and Tobias Wolrich, Master of the Chancery. John Andrews and John Ayres made oath that they saw Tobia Wolrich sign.

In a note dated 12 July 1662: Within one month, pay to Mr. Benjamen Scarborough 8 pounds English money. Signed by Robt. Pitt. Accepted by Hen. Jones for his master Gerrard Bucknor.

In a note, Gravesend 21 July 1662: Gerrard Bucknor promised to pay Mr. Robert Pitt in full--7 pounds 11 shillings. Robert Pitt swore in court 16 February 1663, that he saw Bucknor sign his name.

Pitt's accounts showed that Bucknor owed him a total of 112 pounds 11 shillings and 8 pence. (p. 59a-60a)

Deverax Browne had entered his plea against the estate of Mr. Gerrard Bucknor in Northampton Co, and was now presented in Accomack Co. According to the evidence, Bucknor owed Browne, as the attorney for Mr. Thomas Webb and Mr. John Boys, for money paid to Major John Green, Mr. Mathews, Thomas Weekely, and Col. Edm. Scarburgh for tobacco. Money was also due for goods imported by Henry Jones and

---

[9]*Seller of cheap ready-made clothes.*

Robert Pitts. The total of 169 pounds 5 shillings was considered suspicious, for according to Jones, attorney for the executors, Webb and Boys refused to come to account. Explanatory letters sent to the executors and to Webb and Boys from Virginia had been detained. The court delayed judgment upon Browne until he met with the executors and proved accounts and claims relating to goods or servants in Virginia. If the executors refused or couldn't make proof by March 1664, then the amount owed would be confirmed and paid to Browne, on behalf of Boys and Webb, or be used to pay Bucknor's debts. Browne's account listed money due Webb for paying: Major Jno. Greene and Thomas Mathews (goods outward bound on the *Vincent*), Thomas Weekely (to sue the insurers), and Col. Edm. Scarburgh (for tobacco). Money due John Boys for paying: Henry Jones and Robert Pitt (for goods imported).

Robert Pitt was witness to a receipt dated 22 August 1663: Mr. Thomas Webb and Mr. Jno. Boys received 30 pounds from Gerrard Bucknor for freight on the ship *Vincent*. Signed by John Greene. (p. 60b)

On 17 December 1663, Robert Pitt swore that in July 1662, at Gravesend he saw Mr. Gerrard Bucknor give Mr. Webb a note obliging Bucknor to pay Webb 30 odd pounds. Bucknor used four pounds of Webb's for concerns aboard the *Vincent*. There was a difference of 15 pounds between Bucknor and Webb in account. (p. 61a)

Mary Jones claimed 80 pounds sterling due from the estate of Gerrard Bucknor, but Mr. Devorx. Browne protested that the debt was not for goods adventured in Virginia. After Virginia debts were satisfied, there would be little or no money left, so the court could pass no order for Mrs. Jones. She would be paid according to the priority established by the act of assembly. (p. 61a)

In a note dated 26 December 1662, and signed by London merchant taylor Gerrard Bucknor, he promises 160 pounds to Mary Jones. Witnessed by Henry Jones, recorded by Robt. Hutchinson. (p.61a)

Accomack County Court--17 February 1663/64

Present: Capt. Geo. Parker   Mr. Edm. Bowman
             Mr. John West   Mr. Devorx. Browne (p. 61b)

Because Richard Hill had subpoenaed John Levicke and his servant to court, they requested 120 lbs tobacco in compensation. Ordered that Hill pay that and court costs. (p. 61b)

Both parties agreed that William Silverthorne owed Thomas Selby 1722 lbs tobacco. Ordered that Silverthorne pay Selby and court costs. (p. 61b)

Accomack County Court--12 March 1663/64

Present: Capt. Geo. Parker
        Major Jno. Tilney   Mr. Edm. Bowman
        Mr. Jno. West   Mr. Hugh Yeo (p. 61b)

Certificate was granted to Mrs. Dorothy Jordon for 450 acres for transporting:

Jacaminca Bodella	Thomas Glen	William Tompkins
David Edwards	Edw. Spicer	Jane Vina?
Rich. Franklin	Jno. Sturgis	John Yeo (p. 61b)

Mr. Bowman left court for the following action:

The court judged Walter Hargis, servant of Mr. Edmond Bowman, to be 11 years old. (p. 61b)

The court judged Mordica Edwards, servant of John Tompson, to be 15 years old. (p. 61b)

Ordered that Daniell Curtis be released from his bond for good behavior with him paying court costs. (p. 61b)

Certificate was granted to Alexander Addison for 350 acres for transporting:

Samuell Banton	Thomas Cox	Mary Parker
Wm. Branane?	John Jones	(p. 61b)
Peter Clause	Sara Nash	

William Onoughton did not appear in court at the suit of Ralph Dow; ordered that if the sheriff failed to bring Onoughton to court at the next session, the sheriff would be responsible for whatever was due Dow from Onoughton. (p. 62a)

William Onoughton did not appear in court at the suit of Mr. Anto. Hodgkins; ordered that the sheriff bring Onoughton to court at the next session or be himself responsible for whatever was due Hodgkins from Onoughton. (p. 62a)

Samuell Tomlinson, servant of Mr. Devorax Browne, went farther than his master sent him by Mr. Pitt's; ordered that Tomlinson have 28 lashes on his naked shoulders. (p. 62a)

Richard Pim, servant of Luke Denwood, was judged by the court to be 13 years old. (p. 62a)

In the difference between plaintiff Thomas Leatherberry and defendant Ralph Dow, concerning breach of contract, it was ordered with the consent of both parties that Henry White and Charles Rackleffe view the damage. By their report presented to the court, it appeared that Leatherberry sustained no damage, but because Dow did not perform according to the letter of his lease, he was ordered to pay court charges. (p. 62a)

Report of Henry White and Charles Rackleffe who viewed the damage in the case between Thomas Leatherberry and Ralph Dow: concerning the agreement made between Leatherberry and Olister Southland and Ralph Dow, the trees that should have been planted and the fence that should have been repaired were not done according to agreement. Signed 20 February 1663/64, Henry White and Charles Rackleffe.

Report on 12 March 1663/64: There was no damage done to Leatherberry. Signed, Henry White and Charles Rackleffe. (p. 62a)

Certificate granted to Charles Ratcliffe for 400 acres for transporting:

Mary Brangwell	Elizabeth Gunn	John Smock
Wm. Britingham	Edward Hale	Thomas Taylor
Cristian Doset	Charles Ratcliffe	(p. 62a)

Mr. Yeo exited court. (p. 62a)

The suit brought against William Benstone by Mr. Henry Smith for fetching hogs from Smith's plantation was dropped. The jury decided there was no cause for action against Benstone. Smith paid court costs.

Evidence for Smith, 12 March 1663/64:

Affidavit of Robert Hill aged 30 years or upwards: Said that he, in Smith's absence, penned Smith's black and white sow with only an ear tip in March 1662/63, and that William Benstone and his brother viewed her and said they could not be sure it was his sow. But when Hill turned the sow out, they cut three notches in the hair on her back. Hill claimed it was Henry Smith's sow and said that when he heard that Benstone had penned this sow he would have had Benstone choose two men to view it and determine who owned it. Benstone replied that if he came, he would come at his peril. Hill claimed that Benstone had repeatedly taken his hogs off the plantation at Machotanke without permission. The day before Benstone penned the sow, Hill saw Wm. Benstone and his brother on the plantation with a dog and corn; the brother said he was looking for their hogs there. Hill said that Benstone confessed at the last court that he had Smith's sow in his pen three or four hours. Signed, Robt. (H) Hill.

Affidavit of Joseph Newton aged about 18 years, 12 March 1663/64, sworn before Robt. Hutchinson: Said that William Benston told him in November 1663, that in his pen he had the sow with the three notches on her back and only a tip of her ear left. Signed, Joseph Newton.

Affidavit of Edward Low aged about 21 years, and John Higet aged 22 years, 12 March 1663/63: Said that the white sow with black spots and only an ear-tip that was at Henry Smith's plantation on Matchotanck Creek in October 1663 belonged to Henry Smith. When they let her out, they cut three notches in the hair on her back. When William Benston and his brother came to view her, they could not swear it was his sow. At the last court Benston told Smith he had Smith's sow in his pen for three or four hours. Low and Higet said that Benston removed hogs from the Matchotanck plantation without permission in 1663, and that they saw Benston and his brother on the plantation with a dog and basket of corn. Benston's brother told them they were looking for hogs. Signed, Edw. (X in 0) Low and John (H) Higet.

Deposition of James Powell aged about 25 years, 12 March 1663/64: Said that the white sow with black spots and only a tip of an ear that was in the pen on Henry Smith's plantation at Matchotank Creek belonged to Smith. Powell said that William Benston took his hogs off Smith's plantation without permission and confessed at the last court that he had Smith's sow in his pen for three or four hours. James (N) Powell.

Evidence for Wm. Benstone:

Deposition of John Parker aged about 29 years, 12 March 1663/64: Said that Robert Hill asked Parker to tell William Benston that his sow was "blowed with the fly and full of maggots" and that Benston should take measures to save her and take her away. Signed, John Parker.

Deposition of Thomas Leatherberry, 12 March 1663/64: About last July when he was at Mr. Smith's plantation at Matchotank asking for sheep, Smith's overseer, Robert Hill, requested Leatherberry to tell William Benston to fetch home his hogs because they were doing harm. Leatherberry told Benston as requested. Signed, Thomas (T) Leatherberry.

Deposition of William Silverthorne, 12 March 1663/64, before Robt. Hutchinson: Declared that Smith's overseer, Robert Hill, asked him to tell William Benston to fetch away his hogs. Signed, William (WZ) Silverthorne.

Deposition of Francis and Mary Benston, aged about 28 and 26 years, 12 March 1663: Said that a white sow killed by William Benston and now claimed by Henry Smith actually belonged to Wm. Benston. Smith pretended that Benston took this sow and other hogs from Smith's land, but Francis and Mary swore that this sow and other shoats belonging to William Benston came home by themselves.

Signed, Francis Benston and Mary (M) Benston.

Deposition of David Williamson, 12 March 1663/64: He was at Francis Benston's house when Francis and William Benston were coming home from their work. A boy going through the corn field called, "Master, here is William Benston's sow...in the corn field with her shoats." The sow had only a little bit of an ear. Signed, David Williamson.

Deposition of John Renny, 12 March 1663/64: Said that he and Thomas Middleton viewed this sow in Benstone's pen. The sow had only stumps of ears and about three black spots on her. At Benstone's request they searched for any scar on her, but found none. About a week later John, servant to Smith, came to see Renny, who had heard there was likely to be some difference between Smith and Benston about a sow. Renny asked if he knew his master's sow, and John replied that his master's sow had a scar in her foreshoulder and was full of black spots. He knew this because he brought her up in a sloop from Nuswattocks. Signed, John Renny.

William Benston had heard several reports regarding his intention to kill a sow belonging to Henry Smith, so to avoid scandal, Benston requested John Jenkins and Francis Benston to examine the sow before he killed her. They described the location of three black spots on the white sow who had only a small piece of an ear and a short tail. She had no scar. Signed before Robt. Hutchinson 12 March 1663/64, John (II) Jenkins and Francis Benston.

Deposition of Francis Sherwood aged about 30 years, 12 March 1663/64: Said that about last November he talked with Robert Hill who said that William Benstone had taken Mr. Smith's sow, which had a scar under her foreshoulder and a long tail. Signed, Francies (sic) Sherwood.

Deposition of Mary Renny, 12 March 1663/64: Said that she heard Mr. Smith's man say his master's sow had a scar under her foreshoulder as long as his hand which would never be worn away and that she was full of black spots, for he brought the sow up from Nuswattocks. Robert Hill came in and said the sow was full of black spots. Signed, Mary (M) Renny.

Deposition of Amey Fookes aged about 50 years, 12 March 1663/64: Said that about last January she was at Mrs. Anne Toft's house where she talked with Jane, the wife of Robert Hill. Jane said that William Benston had killed Mr. Smith's sow, and she would prove it: "Olester's wife shall swear, and my husband shall swear, and I will swear that it is Mr. Smith's sow." Fookes rebuked her saying, "Jane, you may swear, but you have not the command of other folk's oaths." Jane said, "Nay, they shall, and I will do Benston all the mischief that lies in my power." Signed, Amy (A) Fookes.

Oath of Anne Toft, 12 March 1663/64: What Amy Fookes said is the truth. Signed, Anne Toft.

The verdict: The jury found that Benston had permission to take his hogs from Smith's plantation; there was no cause for action. (p. 62b-64a)

Edward Smith purchased the rights to the land on the north side of Anancock Branch from the Emperor of the Eastern Shore of Virginia called Tappetiapan or by mistake, Debat Abbey. Signed 12 March 1663/64, by Debat (JM) Abbey, Matom (crescent moon) Apy, and Norine (squiggle). Recorded 16 March 1663/64, by Robt. Hutchinson. (p. 64b)

Nathan Bently assigned to John Parker power of attorney to collect all debts due and especially from Mr. Thomas Fookes. Signed 29 November 1663, by Nathan Bently. Witnesses: Richard (R) Prickett and Thomas Fookes. Recorded 8 April 1664, by Robt. Hutchinson. (p. 64b)

Letter to Mr. John Alexander: Edward Hickman, Samuell Calle and John Manington sent greetings and reported receiving Alexander's greetings through Mr. Samuell Stokes. On the ship *Samuell* with Mr. Thomas Sheppard they received 20 hogsheads of poor tobacco and letters of encouragement from "the Coll."[10] for future trade. They did not know how trade was going for Alexander; their trade was so bad this year that they resolved to desist unless things improved. Any goods that Alexander had left, he could send either to Plymouth or Topsham and "charge bills on us" for any additional due. Or he could order what he wanted sent and by whom. They would have sent goods now, but had no order. There was a bill charged for 20 pounds by the Col. payable to Mr. Topley, but it was not paid because they lacked an order from Alexander. They offered the money to Mr. Topley if he would give them a "discharge." They hoped Alexander would be informed of it by Topley, who departed 5 weeks ago. They sent thanks to Alexander's father and offered their services to him. Tobacco this year was worth 3 to 4 1/2 pounds including duties and freight. Signed by Edward Hickman, Samuell Calle, and John Manington. "For Mr. John Alexander, merchant. These present at Potomack in Virginia." Recorded 16 April 1664, by Robt. Hutchinson. (p. 64b-65a)

Accomack County Court, 16 April 1664

Present: Capt. Geo. Parker   Mr. John West
             Major Jno. Tilney   Mr. John Wise (p. 65a)

The case between John Rogers and John Alford was referred to the next

---

[10]*This may be a reference to Col. Edmund Scarburgh.*

court. (p. 65a)

Ordered that John Carrew remain in custody till further orders. (p. 65a)

John Milby complained that John Carew, who lived at Milby's house, had committed "several abuses" against Milby. Ordered that Carew post bond for good behavior, remove his property from Milby's plantation, and stay away from it or forfeit his bond. (p. 65a)

Elizabeth Ward confessed to committing fornication with John Carter. Ordered that the sheriff see that she receive 25 lashes upon her naked shoulders. (p. 65b)

Ordered upon the petition of William Alworth that the sheriff bring to the next court Thomas Church, servant to Mr. Leving Denwood. (p. 65b)

Last February Richard Hill obtained an order for attachment against the estate of Capt. Anto. Fenn for the property of Bridget Neale, which she had given to Hill's wife till they met again. Since Bridget Neale had come into the country as a servant, it was ordered that her goods be secured with her paying court charges. (p. 65b)

The suit brought against Owen Maclamin by Geo. Truet was dropped because Truet failed to enter a complaint. Truet paid court costs. (p. 65b)

Richard Buckland was accused of perjury; ordered that the sheriff take security for his personal appearance at the next court to answer the charges. (p. 65b)

Certificate was granted to George Johnson for 250 acres for transporting:

Audry Angell	Jno. Copeman	Nicholas Rhodes
Anne Beetle	John Humble	(p. 65b)

Certificate was granted to John Wallop, otherwise called Wadlow, for 800 acres for transporting:

John Bill	James Loe	Joane Noseene
Wm. Ellis	Theodorick Longe	Edw. Robinson
Edw. Harlington	Mary Mathews	Jno. Spickwell
Roger Johnson	Hopkin Morris	Mary Upton
Thomas Jones	Wm. Morris	(p. 65b)
Jean Lardois	Owin Neale	

Certificate was granted to Samuell Taylor for 400 acres for transporting:

Ralph Mills	Robert Row	Rich. Whight
Jeffry Norton	Jeb Salzbury	Matthew Williams
Robt. Rathboan	Henry Tomlin	(p. 65b)

Crispiana Penn, servant boy to William Roberts, was judged to be 12 years old. (p. 66a)

William Benston petitioned for relief against Mr. Henry Smith, who had "long detained" Benston, and who refused payment of tobacco owed to Benston. Ordered that Benston be released from imprisonment and that Smith be summoned to appear at the next court to answer for the unlawful proceedings against Benston. (p. 66a)

Mr. John Shepheard, "Supra Cargoe" of the ship *Royal Oake*, was accused on behalf of the public by collector Col. Edm. Scarburgh, and was called to answer the charges. Shepheard appealed to the next court, and it was ordered that he put up security, pay 50% of the damage in case he was condemned, and remain in the sheriff's custody.

Col. Edm. Scarburgh then requested that Shepheard speak and justify himself at this time, for then present were several witnesses who knew much of Shepheard's dealings and of several testimonies printed in a libellous book. Scarburgh maintained that in this "public audience where most of the county were then present" Shepheard should name persons, times, places and circumstances. After many "impertinent speeches" Shepheard answered that it was at Pungotege, but didn't know when. Several dwellers of Pungotege, (Mr. Richard Hill, Mrs. Anne Toft, Anne Francis and Mr. Jno. Fawsett), who had been there at the time were called and asked what they knew of any kind of force regarding Shepheard's printed oath. According to their depositions, Shepheard gave false affidavits in the book. Shepheard denied it and offered as proof the sworn testimony of those that went with him, Mr. Mellish and Mr. Custis. Shepheard refused to name the type of force used, and the court found it strange that unconcerned persons were willing to make oath that not only was there no force, but to the contrary, much good entertainment was given to Shepheard, Mellish and Custis. Lt. Col. Waters, Mr. Jno. Michall, Mr. Rich. Hill, Mr. Isaac Foxcroft and Claus Brett swore that entertainment was given at several houses, and bills of loading were cheerfully signed. No complaints were made by Shepheard at Pungotege, or later at Occahannock or last at Cheriston's, the ship's harbor; some months later there were printed complaints of which no resident knew anything. The court being full of people, everyone was required to speak if they knew anything about the printed oaths of Shepheard, Mellish and

Mountford; none appeared for them, and several testified to the contrary. After this the collector demanded that Shepheard give account of the tobacco loaded into the *Royal Oake*; Shepheard claimed not to know and would not answer how many hogsheads he shipped. He said he gave account to the collector for 340 hogsheads with Scarburgh to pay for 40 hogsheads. After some discourse, Shepheard "did most impudently deny what he had twice before affirmed." The collector then required John Shepheard to present for himself or Edm. Custis any complaints they had against the collector, so he could be put on trial among the people where his actions were known and thus be vindicated of the calumnies printed in the book. Shepheard said he had nothing to say at that time, but admitted the oath in the book was his. (p. 66a-67a)

Deposition of John Alford aged about 28 years, 14 April 1664: Said that when John Milby was a prisoner at Mr. Melling's house, Alford went with Jno. Milby's wife to see Milby, and that words passed between them, but what they were, he didn't know. Signed, Jno. Alford. (p. 67a)

Deposition of Edmond Kelly aged about 22 years, 16 April 1664: About three years ago in James Jones' house in Wickocomoco, Kelly heard Mr. Tho. Thorowgood claim he could please or displease Andrew Peddigree as he wished, for he had a boar of Peddigree's and intended to give it to him when he came from his father. Signed, Edm. (EK) Kelly. (p. 67a)

A jury was summoned to view the corpse of Edw. Whittell, servant to John Renney of Accomack County, who was found hanged in a tobacco house on Renny's home plantation, 8 April 1664. The jury examined the corpse, the place, and the evidence and found that Whittell, "for the want of grace, was guilty of his own death."

Names of the jury:

Thomas Spritiman	Thomas Fowkes
Isacc Foxcroft, Jr.	Miheal (R) Rickett
Charles Scarbrough	George (S) Crumpe
Edw. Revell	Simon ((|)) Miller
Geo. Truett	Robt. (H) Hill
Jno. Alexander	Cristop. (+) Calvert

Deposition of John Croock aged 25 years, sworn before Hugh Yeo, 8 April 1664: He came to the house of John Renny, who was inquiring about a missing servant. The servant was found hanged on a bar in a tobacco house, and Croock, supposing he was not dead, cut him down hoping to save him. Signed, Hans Crooke.

Deposition of Thomas Middleton aged about 21 years, sworn before Hugh Yeo, 8 April 1664: He went to work on the morning of April 8, with his fellow servants, one of which being Edward Whitell, who complained he was not very well. Middleton thought Whittell went into the house. The master came, and missing Whittell, asked where he was. Middleton, making search, found Whittell hanged in the tobacco house. Signed, Tho. (C) Middleton. (p. 67a)

Charles Scarbrough of London sold to Hugh Yeo 400 acres on Pungoteage Creek. Signed 21 September 1663, Charles Scarbro. Witnesses: Wm. Kendall, Fleet Street, London; John Louicke, Mary Hill. Acknowledged in open court by Charles Scarburgh 16 April 1664. Recorded 19 April, by Robt. Hutchinson. (p. 67a)

William Roberts, planter of Accomack, deeded to his daughter Mary Roberts: one mare, four cows, a featherbed, curtains and valence along with furniture. This was to be delivered on the day of his death. Signed 12 November 1663, William (W) Roberts. Witnesses: John Stockly, Alex. (AA) Addison, Henry White. Acknowledged in open court by Roberts, 16 April 1664. (p. 67b)

Priscilla, wife of William Stevens, relinquished all rights to the property sold by her husband to Robert Hutchinson. Signed 6 November 1663, Priscilla (P) Stevens. Witnesses: John Fawset and James Bonwell.
On the same day she and her husband bound themselves to pay Robert Hutchinson 30,000 lbs tobacco on the condition that "their mother," Anne Stevens Wilson, for the rest of her life could use one third of the 700 acres at Matchotanck that they sold Hutchinson. Signed 16 April 1664, by Will. Stevens and Priscilla (P) Stevens. Acknowledged in open court before Geo. Parker, John West, Jno. Tilney, and John Wise. Recorded 19 April by Robt. Hutchinson. (p. 68a, b)

John Wallop was given orders in the name of His Majesty to survey all lands in Accomack county, beginning with the older patents. He had permission to enter any land, and if the owner could not show trees marked for his boundary, Wallop was to determine the property line and record an entry for those lands. The order was dated 22 January 1663/64, and signed by Edm. Scarburgh. Recorded by Robt. Hutchinson, 16 June 1664. (p. 68b)

John Parker, attorney of Nathan Bently, received from John Jenkins for Bently's use, one cow and calf in payment for a bill, for which there is no further claim against John Jenkins. Signed 17 June 1664, John Parker. Witness: Thomas (T) Leatherberry. Recorded 20 June 1664, by Robt. Hutchinson. (p. 68b)

Accomack County Court, 18 July 1664

Present: Capt. Geo. Parker   Mr. Edm. Bowman
               Major Jno. Tilney   Mr. Hugh Yeo
               Mr. Jno. West   Mr. Jno. Wise (p. 69a)

Ordered that Timothy Coe be summoned to next court to give account of the orphans' estate in his custody. (p. 69a)

Mr. Edm. Bowman exited the court for the following:

Mr. Edm. Bowman, Thomas Maddocks' guardian, petitioned, and it was ordered that within ten days the resident on the orphan's land, Henry White, put up security to perform according to agreement and pay court costs. (p. 69a)

Wm. Major presented an account of the estate of Thomas Johnson, Richard Johnson and Elizabeth Johnson, orphans of Col. Thomas Johnson. At Major's request, Mr. Jno. Fawset entered himself as security for the delivery of the orphans' stocks when they came to age. (p. 69a)

David Wheatly behaved insolently in the face of the court; ordered he be committed into the sheriff's custody till further order. (p. 69a)

John Sanderson made complaint against his master John Sturgis for harsh usage, which appeared true to the court. Ordered that John Sturgis post bond with security for his good behavior and pay court charges. If Sanderson grew disobedient and insolent toward his master, then Sturgis could appeal for the delivery of his bond and Sanderson would have to pay court costs. (p. 69a)

Accomack County Court, 19 July 1664

Present: Capt. Geo. Parker   Mr. Hugh Yeo
               Mr. Jno. West   Mr. Jno. Wise
               Mr. Edm. Bowman (p. 69a)

David Wheatly, yesterday committed into the sheriff's custody for insolent behavior to the court, confessed his error and promised to behave better. He was released but had to pay court charges. (p. 69a)

Certificate was granted to John Stockley for 400 acres for transporting:

Eliza. Ashton	Benjamin Hickman	Eliza Stockley
John Bowin	John Moore	John Stockley
Abraham Heath	James Owin	(p. 69b)

Certificate was granted to Richard Kellum for 900 acres for transporting:

Sarah Amsley	Priscilla Fills	John Walpole
Edward Bird	John Kellum	Richard Welch
Robt. Blinkinson	Mary Kine?	Isaac Witson
Sisley Brookes	Henry Moseley	Cristoph.
Dorothy Churchill	Eliza. Phillips	Yeomans
Anne Corbett	John Proctor	(p. 69b)
Danl. Dermon	John Tompson	

Certificate was granted to Henry Smith for 600 acres for transporting:

Jane Angle	David Hamleton	Margret Ray
John Astope	Wm. Hattley	Henry Smith
Eliza. Carter	John Higgs	Philip Smith
Margret Farthee?	Mary James	Tho. Wheeler
		(p. 69b)

Certificate was granted to Thomas Tunnell for 100 acres for transporting Thomas Tunell and Richard Holland. (p. 69b)

Upon his petition John Carey was released from his bond for good behavior and paid court costs. (p. 69b)

Certificate was granted to Samuell Jones for 200 acres for transporting:

Samuell Jones	Samll. Jones, Jr.
Mary Jones	John Jones (p. 69b)

As John Rogers owed John Asford 440 pounds tobacco, it was ordered that Rogers make payment and pay court costs. (p. 69b)

Certificate was granted to George Watson for 300 acres for transporting:

William Beare	William Howe	John Rimington
Mardim Edwards	Elizabeth Peacock	George Watson
		(p. 69b)

Mr. Hugh Yeo exited the court. (p. 70a)

Mr. Jno. Custis, attorney of John Shepheard, entered but could not prove his petition against Henry Smith; the suit was ordered dismissed with Custis paying court charges. (p. 70a)

The suit brought against Henry Smith by John Shepheard was dropped because John Shepheard failed to appear. Shepheard was to pay court costs. (p. 70a)

Capt. William Jones, justice of the peace in Northampton, swore that about
35 or 36 years ago he often sailed to trade with the Indians in Chesepiack Bay and well knew the Pokomoke River which lay a little south of
an unnamed point described in Capt. Smith's map. It was as far south as
a man could see from Watkins Point. Jones affirmed that this river was
then called the Pokomoke River and was never called the Wigtico River
before or since. Jones further stated that at the time he was a married
man and a trader in the Bay of Chesepiack, John Nutwell was a boy
servant to Hugh Hayes and had run away from his master. Jones traded
a hoe to the Indians for Nutwell and brought him home well tied with the
ship's ropes. Sworn in open court 19 July 1664, before Robt. Hutchinson. (p. 70a)

The following persons made oath that they had for a long time known the
River Pokomoke and that the river had been so called "time out of mind"
both by the Indians and the signers. The Pokomoke River was on the
eastern shore of "Chesepiack Bay" in Virginia, south of a small spiral
point on the south side of Anamesecks. The point was as far south as a
man could see on a clear day from a place called Watkins Point
described in Capt. Smith's map. Signed 19 July 1664:

Anto. Hodgkins	Jno. Renny	Edm. Scarburgh
Will. Jones	Edw. Revell	Jno. Wise
Geo. Parker	Charles Scarburgh	(p. 70b)

Henry White bound himself to pay upon demand 40,000 pounds of tobacco
to John Stockley and Alexander Addison. The conditions: John Stockley
and Alexander Addison were security for White's performance of the
agreement by which White held his home plantation. If Stockley and
Addison received no damage by White's nonperformance of the
condition, then the obligation was to be void. Signed 18 July 1664,
Henry White. Witnesses: John Fawsett, John Sturges. Recorded by Robt.
Hutchinson. (p. 71a)

John Williams of Anancock registered his cattle mark: Cropped on both
ears and underbitted on the right with a horseshoe branded on the
buttock. Recorded 4 August 1664, by Robt. Hutchinson. (p. 71a)

Accomack County Court, 16 August 1664

Present:	Capt. Geo. Parker	Mr. Hugh Yeo
	Mr. Jno. West	Mr. Jno. Wise
	Mr. Edm. Bowman (p. 71a)	

In the case between Samuell Showell, plaintiff, and Major Jno. Tilney, defendant, concerning work done by Showell: ordered that Wm. Taylor and Phillip Fisher be appointed to view the work and give a report at the next court. (p. 71a)

Samuell Showell presented an account for work done against Major Jno. Tilney who desired injunction in chancery to the next court, which was granted. (p. 71a)

Major Jno. Tilney entered court. (p. 71a)

In the case between Col. Edm. Scarburgh, plaintiff, and Mr. Charles Scarburgh, defendant, concerning a bill of exchange for 50 pounds sterling which was owed by Charles as his third bill of exchange. He demanded a lawful percentage? and letter, which not appearing, he appealed to the court at James City. Ordered that Charles Scarburgh post security by the next court and pay 50% damage in case he lost the suit. (p. 71a, b)

Mrs. Ann Charlton complained to the court that Mr. Charles Scarburgh had frightened her by several "unhandsome" words and actions, which was acknowledged in part by Scarburgh. Ordered that he be committed into the sheriff's custody and be detained till posting bond with security for his good behavior and paying court charges. (p. 71b)

Mr. Hugh Yeo exited the court. (p. 71b)

Mr. Jno. Shepheard entered action against John Waller, who could not be found. It was ordered that attachment for 792 lbs tobacco proceed against the estate of Waller where the same could be found in the county. (p. 71b)

Mr. John Shepheard entered action against Nehemiah Covington, who could not be found. Ordered that attachment for 450 lbs tobacco proceed against the estate of Covington where the same could be found in the county. (p. 71b)

The court questioned Mr. Charles Scarburgh about whether Col. Edmund Scarburgh had at any time detained his wife from him. Charles answered that she was never detained by Col. Scarburgh or anyone else at Occahannock house when he demanded her. (p. 71b)

Capt. Geo. Parker exited the court for the following:
Mr. Jno. West took the oath of high sheriff of Accomack County. Col.

Edm. Scarburgh and Major Jno. Tilney entered themselves security for his performance of the trust committed to him.

Samuell Jones was sworn undersheriff to Mr. Jno. West. (p. 71b)

Major Tilney and Mr. West exited the court; Col. Edm. Scarburgh and Capt. Parker entered. (p. 71b)

Certificate was granted to John Stockley for 800 acres for transporting:

Florance Allgood	Michael Lewis	Robt. Price
Edward Court	Rebecca	Jno. Smith
Anne Deefe	Malbrooke	Ja. Thornbush
Marth. Ellford	Ja. Morgan	Hartly Wallington
James Hill	Thomas Owin	Rich. Wood
Jno. Hopkins	Jonah Price	(p. 71b)

Certificate was granted to Edward Smith for 1350 acres for transporting:

Charles Amram	Edm. Hilhard?	Mathew Roan
Benjamin Angler?	Roger Isham	Geo. Smith
Robt. Bish	Jostin Markworth	Richard Snow
Jno. Blake	Jeffery Marsh	Tho. Trever
Charles Bugger	Wm. Moningham?	Francis Vincent
Allen Carew	Marmeduke	Francis Weston
Jacob Clackford	Moore	Hen. Whitchurch
Roger Duncomb	John Onslow	Edward Wrath
Paull Emerson	Rich. Overberry	(p. 71b)
Wm. Gresham	Jno. Purback	

Certificate was granted to Charles Rackleff for 200 acres for transporting:

Rich. Holmden	Wm. Thinn	(p. 72a)
Edw. Thurland	Wm. Carlton	

Certificate was granted to Thomas Tunill for 500 acres for transporting:

Abram. Ascough	Rich. Eneling	Thomas Turgis
James Austin	Tho. Rogers	Geo. Westbrooke
Robt. Bickerstasse	Samuell Rouse	(p. 72a)
Geo. Cullen	Jno. Stidolfe	

Certificate was granted to Robert Johnson for 400 acres for transporting:

Ralph Branfield	John Hagward	Edw. Phillips
Nich. Broderick	Edmund Howard	Edward Temple
John Freeman	Richard Lenthall	(p. 72a)

Certificate was granted to Henry Eldrige for 650 acres for transporting:

Charles Browne
Cristoph. Bucle
Henry Chute
Wm. Elliot
Erasmas Gainsford

James Gresham
Wm. Hoskins
John Loyd
Mat. Muschamp
Jno. Owfeild

John Scott
Jno. Vernon
Geo. Woodruffe
(p. 72a)

Certificate was granted to John Renny for 400 acres for transporting:

Geo. Boothby
Wm. Covert
George Garth

Peter Hufey
John Morley
Hen. Pecham

Hen. Petham
Vincent Randhill
(p. 72a)

Certificate was granted to Mary Meridath for 50 acres for transporting John
Heward. (p. 72a)

Certificate was granted to John Trotman for 150 acres for transporting
John Farmington, Thomas Middleton and John Shelley (p. 72a)

Certificate was granted to Charles Ratkliff for 600 acres for transporting:

James Allet
Jno. Aubry
John Baker
John Dawes

George Easy
Peter Guard
William Ire
John Jones

William Sheldon
Tho. Street
Richard West
William Wight
(p. 72a)

Certificate was granted to Southee Littleton for 1200 acres for transporting:

James Austin
Hen. Bill
Ralph Carr
Jno. Charles
Henry Chown
Jno. Churll
James Copping
Tho. Dalma

Tho. Duobe?
Jno. Goringe?
Thomas Gray
Rich. Heath
Edward Holt
Laurance Marsh
Edw. May
John May

Thomas Null?
Stephen Ophish?
Peter Quevell
William Rye
Herbert Springer
Jno. Steward
Robt. Stoller
Anto. Street
(p. 72a)

Certificate was granted to Capt. William Jones for 100 acres for transporting Robert Anderson and Thomas Bickley. (p. 72a)

Certificate was granted to John Dye for 450 acres for transporting:

Jno. Bearcraft
Charles Breet
Walter Duble

George Joy
Richard Longe
Richard Mills

Thomas Seafort
Tho. Stewsby?
Thomas Wild
(p. 72a)

List of tithables in Accomack County in 1664:

Capt Geo. Parker	6		Anto. Longe	1
Jno. Lewis	8		Gausalim van Nitsin	1
Roger Ternan	2		Tho. Tunell	3
Rich. Hill	6		Mr. Southee Littleton	6
Jno. Renny	6		Mr. Geo. Hack	3
James Atkins	1		Wm. Chase	3
Mr. Smith	4		John Brookes	1
Jno. Watts, Cooper	1		Jno. Holden	2
Geo. Trewett	3		Cristop. Calvert	2
Jno. Williams	4		Wm. Darby	1
Teage Andrews	2		Wm. Wilson	1
Francis Sherwood	2		Col. Edm. Scarburgh	27
Francis Benston	3		Mr. Devorx Browne	15
Mr. Jno. Parker	6		Mr. Charlton	1
Mr. Jno. Wise	3		Owin Ocolman	2
Tho. Leatherberry	4		Richard Kellum	7
Walter Taylor	4		Jno. Turnor	2
Jno. Jenkins	1		Jno. Walthom	6
Wm. Silverthorne	1		Susan Richardson	2
Robt. Hutchinson	4		Nath. Bradford	3
James Bonwell	4		Mr. Fawsett	5
John Watts	2		Jno. Wallop	2
John Die	1		Robt. Huitt	8
James Fowkes	1		Alphonso Ball	2
Mr. Hugh Yeo	8		Jno. Drumon	3
Edw. Revell	4		Mr. Bowman	11
Mr. Anto. Hodgkins	4		Wm. White	1
Mr. Jno. Wise	5		Major Jno. Tilney	5
Rich. Prichard	2		Henry Bishopp	5
Mehill Ricketts	4		Edw. Smith	3
Robt. Brase	3		Jonah Jackson	3
Anto. Johnson	3		Geo. Johnson	4
Tho. Newton	5		Henry Browne	1
Tobias Selby	1		James Price	3
John Barnet	1		Timothy Coe	5
Wm. Abram	1		Charles Ratkliff	6
Jno. Alford	4		Henry Smith	5
Tho. Fowkes	4		Thomas Marshall	2
Danll. Ograham	1		Henry Edwards	3
Simon Millard	1		Edm. Kelly	4
George Crump	1		Jno. Smith	2
David Williamson	1		Jno. Sturgis	2

Mrs. Jordan	6	Mr. Denwood	6
Thomas Selby	1	Rich. Cox	1
Thomas Browne	4	Samuell Jones	2
Jno. Paramoore	3	Alexander Adison	5
Henry White	2	Jno. Prittyman	1
Wm. Major	3	Rich. Smith	1
Danll. Etien	1	Edw. Dolby	3
Thomas Bell	1	Wm. Blake	1
Henry Stott	2	Wm. Roberts	6
Jeffry Minshall	3	Tho. Carrell	1
Obedience Johnson	2	Wm. Alworth	1
Jno. Mekittrick	3	Wm. Taylor	4
William Smith	3	Lorence Teage	1
Andrew Fenney	4	Jno. Trotman	1
Edward Moore	3	Jno. Cutting	1
Phillip Fisher	6	Jno. Goring	1
Giles Cope	4	Fulcand Obin	3
Jno. Studson	3	Robt. Watson	2
Ralph Doe	2	Wm. Rodolphus	2
Robt. Hignet	1	Tho. Smith	1
George Brickhouse	2	Edw. Hammon	2
Jno. Hagaman	2	David Wheatly	4
Danll. Quillion	2	total: 424 (p. 72b)	

Accomack County Court--17 October 1664

Present: Col. Edm. Scarburgh   Mr. Edm. Bowman
                Capt. Geo. Parker   Mr. Hugh Yeo
                Major Jno. Tilney   Mr. Jno. Wise (p. 73a)

John Cross owed Mr. John West 1613 lbs tobacco. Ordered that Cross pay the debt and court costs. (p. 73a)

Mr. Isaac Foxcroft owed Richard Hill a "horse colt." Ordered that Foxcroft make payment of the horse and pay court costs. (p. 73a)

Edward Hazard owed Mr. Anto. Hodgkins 460 lbs tobacco and also this year's dues to the "country, county and parish." Ordered that Hazard make payment. (p. 73a)

Upon the request of Richard Buckland, defendant, the case between him and Richard Kellum, plaintiff, was deferred to the next court. (p. 73a)

Robert Brace, defendant, requested and received a deferment to the next court in the case between him and Edward Smally, plaintiff. (p. 73a)

Mr. Wise exited the court for the following:

Robert Brace had contempt for Mr. Wise's warrant, as testified to by Tobius Sellvey and John Smally; it was ordered that Robert Brace stand one hour before the pillory with his fault upon his hat in capital letters, and that he pay for repairing the ducking stool. Brace also paid court charges.

Deposition of Tobius Sellvey aged about 48 years, 17 October 1664: Sellvey went to Robert Brace with a warrant from Mr. Wise. Sellvey read it to Brace, who said he could not and would not go. Sellvey offered to lend him a canoe and a man to transport him, but Brace still refused. Sellvey said, "You may as well go as carry a spade and a hoe on your back." Signed, Tobius Sellvey.

Deposition of John Smally aged about 20 years, 17 October 1664: Said that he went with Tobius Sellvey to carry a warrant to Robert Brace. Smally's testimony was identical with Sellvey's. (p. 73a, b)

John Rogers sued Jonah Jackson over a bull, but not offering proof, the suit was dismissed with Rogers paying court charges.

Deposition of Florance Parker, 17 October 1664: About four years ago there was a difference between John Rogers and Jonah Jackson about a bull calf, but Parker, while not certainly knowing the calf's owner, thought it belonged to Rogers. Signed, Florance Parker. (p. 73b)

John Alford was illegally in possession of land belonging to Mr. Southee Littleton, who requested an order for the return of his land. After considering the pleas on both sides, the court ordered that John Alford "quietly enjoy" the plantation till Christmas so he could harvest his tobacco and corn. If the weather did not permit the full harvest by then, he could still have access to it. Littleton had liberty to come on the plantation to build or clear. (p. 73b)

Capt. Parker exited for the following three actions:

Wm. White, servant to Capt. Geo. Parker claimed his freedom, but the court examined the assignation of his former master, Francis Sherwood, and determined that White came in for the "custom of the country, which is five years" and was ordered to serve out his full term of service. (p. 73b)

Andrew Cross dangerously wounded Capt. Geo. Parker's horse with an ax; ordered that his master, James Bonwell, make satisfaction for the damages and that Cross make satisfaction to his master after his time of indenture was expired. (p. 73b)

Barberry Youres made a motion that she might be free, saying she came in for four years, had served Mr. Browne and was sold to Capt Geo. Parker for three years, which was accomplished. Parker said that he bought her from Browne to complete five years. Because Brown was absent, it was ordered that Barberry return to Parker and serve as formerly, and if it afterward was proved that she had served her lawful time, then Capt. Parker would make satisfaction for the extra time served. (p. 74a)

Mr. Bowman exited court for the following:
Richard Marrinor, servant to Mr. Edm. Bowman, claimed his freedom, having served four years. The court found that Marrinor came in for five years, the "custom of the country." Ordered that Marrinor return to the service of Bowman till five years be complete and then Bowman was to pay Marrinor his corn and clothes according to the custom. (p. 74a)

James Bonwell complained that William Silverthorne had formerly threatened to kill his dog and had now shot him. Ordered that Silverthorne be committed to the sheriff's custody till he posted bond for good behavior and paid court costs. (p. 74a)

Tapatiapon and his great men acknowledged the sale of their land at Matchaprege to Nathaniel Bradford, who gave them permission to plant on it. (p. 74a)

Charles Scarburgh petitioned to be released from his bond for good behavior, which was done after proclamation had been made three time in court. He paid court charges. (p. 74a)

William Major, planter, son of John Major, deceased, relinquished all rights to 200 acres north of Nuswattocks Creek that his father had sold to Stephen Charlton, deceased. Major Jno. Tilney purchased the land from Charlton. Signed 30 April 1663, William Major. Witnesses: Wm. Kendall and John Laurence. Acknowledged 17 October 1664, before Robt. Hutchinson. (p. 74b)

Accomack County Court--18 October 1664
Present: Col. Edm. Scarburgh   Mr. Edm. Bowman

Capt. Geo. Parker   Mr. Hugh Yeo
Mr. Jno. Wise (p. 74b)

Samuell Showell was ordered to pay Major Jno. Tilney all charges upon the "execution," which was determined to be legally served.

At the last court Major Jno. Tilney requested injunction in chancery and now presented his questions and Showell his answers. Tilney offered to pay charges of the suit, which was dismissed. (p. 74b)

Isaac Foxcroft complained that Major Jno. Tilney had blocked the highway, as was also sworn by Jeffery Minshall and John Prittyman. Ordered that Minshall, Prittyman and the surveyor investigate and have the road unblocked if necessary so citizens could have free passage. (p. 74b)

Deposition of Jeffery Minshall, 18 October 1664: The highway by Major Jno. Tilney's little house by the branch was the oldest highway. Signed, Jeffry Minshall.

Deposition of John Prettyman, 18 October 1664: Said the same as Minshall. Signed, John Prettiman. (p. 75a)

Major Jno. Tilney entered the court. (p. 75a)

Certificate was granted to Capt. John Savage for 4200 acres for transporting:

Jno. Abert	Rich. Danny	Francis Hughs
Jno. Andrews	Rich. Dowd	Anne Johnson
Wm. Baldwin	Jno. Draper	Tho. Jollesse
Jno. Beare	John Elliot	Wm. Joyce
Edward Berry	Martha Elmes	Peter Keble
Jno. Beverly	Jno. Ferrers	Jno. Kilving
Eliza. Birken	Jno. Finch	Wm. Kite
Phillip Brace	Tho. Foley	John Larum
Jno. Brad	Stephen Fox	Rich. Lofftis
Jno. Bushell	Henry Frankes	Edw. Mend?
Rich. Callow	Xper Gardner	Paul Methnim
Robt. Candler	Jane Greene	Wm. Morten
Rich. Carwar	Jean Greene	Wm. Muck
Edw. Cary	Rich. Greene	Jno. Nanson
Robt. Challon	James Hall	James Newton
James Charles	Jno. Hancock	Sara Newton
Thomas Chassin	Jno. Harris	Tho. Oriott
Jno. Croft	Jno. Hening	Jeffery Pemell
James Crouch	Jno. Higgens	Edw. Pennell
Anto. Crumpe	Jno. Holt	Phillip Persons

Edm. Pike
Mathew Ray
Tho. Ray
Joan Rivers
Samll. Sanders
Geo. Sands
Walter Savage
June Shaw

James Sheldon
James Sheldon
Robt. Sollers
Tho. Street
Tho. Street
Tho. Taulty
Edw. Tryer
Edw. Vernon

Wm. Wader
Joseph Wash
Tho. Wasson
Edw. Westly
Mary White
Rich. White
Tho. Wild
Charles Yorke
(p. 75a)

Certificate was granted to Arthur Upshott for 300 acres for transporting:
Robt. Booth
Jno. Broughton

John Franklin
Eliza Freeman

Thomas Gething
Richard Sheale
(p. 75a)

Certificate was granted to Arthur Upshott for 200 acres for transporting:
Richard Jefferis
Joan Nosworthy

Henry Reed
Mary Knight

(p. 75a)

Wm. Major and Henry Edwards were appointed to appraise the estate of John Trotman in the possession Nicholas Laurence, who also was to give an account. (p. 75a)

Accepted was William Taylor's offer, to keep the bridge he built in good repair as long as he lives, in exchange for the price of one man's taxes. (p. 75b)

Isaac Foxcroft of Northampton County sold a seven-month-old colt to Anthoney Hodgkins for the use of his daughter Elizabeth Hodgkins. Signed 17 October 1664, by Isaac Foxcroft. Witnesses: Geo. Watson, John (IB) Brookes. Recorded 20 October 1664, by Robt. Hutchinson. (p. 75b)

John Sturgis sold Jno. Tilney a brown and white cow called Sweetlips. Signed 8 June 1664, John Sturges. Witnesses: Rowland Baugh and John Tilney. (p. 75b)

Out of love, John Tilney gave to his godson John Sturgis, son of Jno. Sturgis, the above named cow with the injunction that Jno. Sturgis, Sr., keep the cow and her increase without charge for the child. Signed 8 June 1664, by Jno. Tilney, John Sturges, Rowland Baugh. Recorded 20 October 1664, by Robt. Hutchinson. (p. 75b)

William Smith had sold John Tilney 100 acres at Mackatowses on

Nuswattocks Creek, being part of the patent assigned Smith by John Major. Signed 1 July 1662, William Smith and Sarah (S) Smith. Witnesses: John Storges, John (8) Tatum. On the same day John Tilney assigned his title to this land to Jno Sturgis. Signed, Jno. Tilney and Ann (AT) Tilney. Witnesses: Wm. (N) Blake, Jno. (8) Tatum, William Smith. On 5 December 1662, John Storges and his wife Dorothy assigned this land to Mary Paramore. Signed, John Storges and Dorothy (D) Storges. Recorded 20 October 1664, by Robt. Hutchinson. (p. 76a)

Arthur Upshott, planter of Northampton Co., and his wife Mary sold Edward Hamon of Accomack Co. 700 acres on Occahannock Creek, except for a parcel adjoining William Taylor. Part of the land was in exchange for a parcel that Richard Jacob gave Edward Hamon in his will. Signed 18 October 1664, Arthur (A) Upshor, Mary (T) Upshor. Witnesses: Robt. Watsonn, Henry Stott. Recorded 20 October 1664, by Robt. Hutchinson. (p. 76b)

Gov. Francis Moryson had granted Wm. Thorne 387 acres at Occahanock Creek next to Richard Smith and Rich. Kellam and the main creek. The original patent was dated 21 October 1654, and was renewed 20 November 1662. Signed, Francis Moryson and Tho. Ludwell.
William Thorne assigned the patent to Thomas Bloyes. Signed 10 December 1662, by Winefrit (+) Thorne. Witnesses: Henry Smith and John Nichols. Signed 16 December 1663, by William Thorne. Witnesses: Roger Wolford and Will. Bosman. Recorded 20 October 1664, by Robt. Hutchinson.
On 18 October 1664, Bloyes, for 6600 lbs tobacco, sold the land, housing and fencing to John Fawset. Signed, Thomas Bloyes. Witnesses: Henry Smith, Ed. Boteler. Recorded 20 October 1664, by Robt. Hutchinson. (p. 77a)

Gov. Wm. Berkeley had granted Richard Smith 500 acres on the head of Occahonock Creek bordering Richard Kellum. The original patent was dated 24 March 1650. Signed 3 April 1660, William Berkelry (sic) and Tho. Ludwell. (p. 77b)
Nathaniell Bradford, Sr., currier, and Alice Bradford his wife sold John Fawset and Dermon Selevant 500 acres. Fawset was to have the western half; Selevant was to have the eastern part bordering Robert Richardson. Signed 18 October 1664, Nathaniell Bradford and Alice (O) Bradford. Witnesses: John West and Ed. Boteler. Recorded 20 October 1664, by Robt. Hutchinson. (p. 77b)
Nathaniell Bradford, currier, for considerations accruing to him by the marriage of Alice Smith, daughter of Richard Smith, deceased, granted

to Nathaniell Bradford, Jr., "my heir and the heir of the abovesaid Smith," 800 acres, being part of the 1400 acres purchased by Bradford, Sr. from Col. Edmond Scarburgh, now the home plantation at Matcha-preage. This was given in lieu of 500 acres sold by Bradford to John Fawsett and Dermon Selevant on the north side of the head of Occahon-nock Creek and formerly belonged to Richard Smith. The conditions: if Nathaniell Bradford, Jr. or the heirs of Richard Smith when coming of age, trouble John Fawsett or Dermon Selevant in regards to the possession of the 500 acres, then Fawsett and Selevant should possess the 800 acres. Bradford acknowledged receiving 8000 lbs tobacco, and 4 cows and calves from Fawsett and Selevant. Signed 18 October 1664, Nathaniell Bradford. Witnesses: John West and Ed. Boteler. Recorded 20 October 1664, by Robt. Hutchinson. (p. 77b, 78a)

Accomack County Court--16 November 1664

Present: Capt. Geo. Parker   Mr. Edm. Bowman
             Major Jno. Tilney   Mr. Deverx. Browne
                    Mr. Jno. Wise (p. 78b)

Certificate was granted to Mrs. Dorothy Jordan for 50 acres for transport-ing John Kirke. (p. 78b)

Ralph Jones agreed to transport John Peeck to Nanjemy? for 350 lbs tobacco, but instead brought him to Accomack. Ordered that Peeck pay Jones 200 lbs tobacco along with court charges. (p. 78b)

Nicholas Turnor, who came over with Ralph Jones, could not show proof of his freedom. Ordered that he remain in the sheriff's custody till he could produce proof. (p. 78b)

Robert Brace owed Edward Smally 10 lbs sterling; ordered Brace make payment and pay court costs. (p. 78b)

Col. Edm. Scarburgh entered and Major Jno. Tilney exited the court. (p. 78b)

Denis Selevant owed Major Jno. Tilney 565 lbs tobacco, five barrels of Indian corn and 1300 fencing logs. Ordered that Selevant make payment after 30 days which was allowed for harvest. (p. 78b)

Deposition of John Pye and George Pye aged about 22 years, sworn 3 February 1661/62, before Geo. Parker: Said that Mr. Robert Brace requested John Pye to make a bond to Brace's servant Edward Small to pay him ten pounds at the expiration of his time. Pye did this, and Brace signed it as his act and deed. Signed, Jo. Pye and George Pye. (p. 79a)

The suit brought against Denis Selevant by Thomas Kendall was dropped because there was no cause of action. Kendall paid court costs. (p. 79a)

The difference between Robert Bayley and Mr. Randall Revell was taken into consideration and referred to the court of Northampton County where an original order had been given. (p. 79a)

Mr. Browne exited the court for the following two actions. (p. 79a)

A warrant was ordered for the appearance of Jeffry Minshall at the next court to answer the complaint of Mr. Jno. Fawsett. (p. 79a)

Ordered that Timothy Coe be committed into the sheriff's custody till posting bond for good behavior. He was also to appear at the next court to answer the complaint of Mr. Jno. Fawsett. (p. 79a)

Upon his petition, Wm. Silverthorne's bond for good behavior was released to him, proclamation having been read three times in open court. Silverthorne paid court costs. (p. 79a)

John Devorax stole a gun from an Indian and sold it. Ordered that he be committed into the sheriff's custody until he returned the gun and paid court charges. (p. 79a)

Ordered that Col. Scarburgh be paid out of Jno. Devorax's wages for three coats which were paid to Indians, and also for tobacco expended on goods delivered to Devorax. (p. 79a)

Ordered that Mr. Robert Brace have returned to him his gun that was stolen by his runaway servant and found in the cabin of the King of Kikotank, who affirmed that Jno. Devorax left it there. (p. 79b)

John Devorax had been employed as an interpreter by the county for one year for which he was to receive 1500 lbs tobacco. Because he had behaved "treacherously amongst the Indians to the abuse of His Majesty's subjects and the dishonor of our nation," Jno. Devorax was dismissed as interpreter and forbidden to go among the Indians; if he disobeyed, he risked more severe censure. (p. 79b)

Mr. Browne exited the court. (p. 79b)

Edward Baker, recently of London, being sick, made his will:
- To his son Edward Baker, the sealed gold ring "that I now wear"
- To his bother-in-law, Lt. Col. Wm. Kendall, a gold ring worth twenty shillings
- To Capt. Robert Pitt, a gold ring worth twenty shillings
- Executors of the "goods and chattels that I have now with me in the ship *Mary* of London": Wm. Kendall and Capt. Robert Pitt, commander of the ship. They were to "make the best of his goods" and see that the proceeds be sent to "my loving friends," Mr. George Clark at the sign of the ship and star in Cheapeside, and Mr. Simon Hackett, watchmaker in Cornehill in London, for the use of his children, Edward Baker and Elizabeth Baker. Signed 19 October 1664, Edw. Baker. Witnesses: Devorax Browne, Hn. Jones, Will. Stevens. Proved in court 16 November 1664, recorded the next day by Robt. Hutchinson. (p. 79b)

Accomack County Court--17 November 1664

Present: Capt. Geo. Parker   Mr. Edm. Bowman
              Major Jno. Tilney   Mr. Devorx Browne
                    Mr. Jno. Wise (p. 80a)

Certificate was granted to Edward Moore for 200 acres for transporting:
Edward Chapman   Edward Burgis
Eliza. Moore   Audery Angell (p. 80a)

Certificate was granted to John Evans for 200 acres for transporting:
Mathew Scarbrough   Jno. Anderson
Mary Davis   Olive Adassano (p. 80a)

Col. Edm. Scarburgh entered court. (p. 80a)

Ordered that James Taylor pay 400 lbs tobacco to Mr. Anto. Hodgkins for damages suffered by Hodgkins when Taylor got Hodgkins' "woman servant with child." Taylor was to pay court costs. (in a side note: This order was satisfied 3 Jan. 1664/65, attested by Jno. West, sheriff.) (p. 80a)

Ordered that the court be kept at Mr. Tho. Fookes' house until a court house was erected by the county. (p. 80a)

Ordered that the sheriff, while collecting taxes, be permitted to seize property if necessary to pay the Occahonnock ferryman's wages. (p. 80a)

Col. Scarburgh exited the court for the following three actions:
Ordered that Col. Edm. Scarburgh be paid 3750 lbs tobacco for arms purchased for the county from Capt. Thomas Sprittyman last year. Mr. Fawsett, employed to sell the arms, was to give an account. The sheriff was to collect from several persons for arms sold and delivered. (p. 80a)

Ordered that the county clerk copy in the Accomack records items from Northampton court concerning the estate of Mr. Gerrard Bucknor.
Ordered that a copy of a letter from the executors of Mr. Bucknor's estate be sent to Northampton court. Col. Scarburgh was asked to write Northampton court requesting the bond concerning Mr. Browne, Mr. Pitts and the estate of Mr. Gerrard Bucknor. (p. 80a)

Certificate was granted to Mr. John Dolby for 50 acres for transporting Wm. Shepheard. (p. 80a)

Certificate was granted to Mr. Robert Pitt for 1000 acres for transporting:

Wm. Bayley	Wm. Gunnock	Tho. Sanders
Wm. Clayton	Edward Heath	Anto. Spencer
Thomas Cope	Wm. Knowles	John Tavernor
Rich. Crooke	David Lacy	Tho. Wenham
Jno. Doyley	Mathew Langley	Samps. White
Thomas Dunn	John Norris	Wm. Wright
James Fiens	Jno. Robinson	(p. 80b)

Certificate was granted to Cornelius Watkinson for 450 acres for transporting:

Robert Berry	Joan Hopkins	Richard Prince
Xpher. Browne	Francis Lawley	Henry Vernon
Wm. Child	Robert Leighton	Samuell Wring
		(p. 80b)

Certificate was granted to Richard Hill, Jr., for 450 acres for transporting:

Charles Baldwin	Richard Fowler	Francis Penistone
John Baugh	James Hawley	Richard Taylor
Andrew Clark	William Oakly	Richard Walker
		(p. 80b)

Certificate was granted to Gilbert Henderson for 500 acres for transporting:

Wm. Cartaright	Wm. Chamberlin	John Clark

Robert Compton	Thomas Jones	Thomas Walter
George Crooke	Edward Lenthall	(p. 80b)
Robert Dormer	Timothy Terrill	

Certificate was granted to Mrs. Ann Tofft for 2000 acres for transporting:

Walter Acton	Charles Holloway	Ann Phillips
Abell Barker	Francis Hord	Tho. Settiplace
George Barry	James Jenkins	Henry Silvester
Vincent Barry	Thomas Jones	Francis Smith
Edward Brag	Henry Lee	Francis Tippin
Jno. Charlton	Anto. Libb	Richard Vivers
Thomas Cobb	Richard Lister	Rowland Walter
James Draper	Geo. Ludlow	Jno. Weld
Jno. Draper	Jno. Macken	Tho. Wells
James Dudley	Richard Miller	Thomas Whitmore
Mary Feild	Tho. Moorefeild	Jno. Whittaker
Tho. Fleetwood	Wm. Morton	Richard Wing
Roger Griffin	Jno. Osbald	(p. 80b)
Jno. Harding	Robert Parriot	

Certificate was granted to William Taylor for 600 acres for transporting:

Walter Cane	Francis	Fredrick Thinn
Edw. Faulkner	Markworth	John Wheatly
Phillip Harcourt	Richard Otley?	Jno. White
John Lamb	William Owen	Jno. Wichkem
	Mary Scriven	(p. 80b)

Certificate was granted to Jno. Prittyman for 200 acres for transporting:

Edw. Kinastone	George Weld
Joan Shaw	Thomas Rock (p. 81a)

Certificate was granted to James Gray and Alphanso Ball for 400 acres for transporting:

John Coats	Andrew Hill	Mary Rotherford
Robert Forrest	Arthur Hincks	Edward Walker
Thomas Hayes	Ann Morris	(p. 81a)

Certificate was granted to Jno. Savage for 550 acres for transporting:

Tho. Culpepper	Jno. Heath	Richard Sandis
John Darrell	James Hide	William Sivan
Jno. Eveling	Thomas Lambert	William Swann
Francis Heath	Jno. Marsham	(p. 81a)

Certificate was granted to John Wallop for 200 acres for transporting:

Richard Amhurst	Thomas Hinman
Richard Duck	James Brooke (p. 81a)

Certificate was granted to John Savidge for 100 acres for transporting
Thomas Peake and James Marsh. (p. 81a)

Certificate was granted to John Stockley for 1050 acres for transporting:

James Bane	Tho. Carns	James Orton
Easter Bayley	Peter Heyman	John Palmer
Charles Bishopp	Phillip Hitley	Petter Pett
John Boyes	Henry Hunte	Wm. Radley
Wm. Brent	Rich. Leigh	Herbert Rye
Tho. Brewer	Robert Lewkner	John Smith
Jno. Cane	John Newton	Thomas Thorey
		(p. 81a)

Certificate was granted to Samuell Taylor for 200 acres for transporting:

Francis Clark	Thomas Godffry
Edward Master	Edmond Prince (p. 81a)

Certificate was granted to Tabitha Smart for 1000 acres for transporting:

Robert Barnham	William Fooke	Jno. Parker
John Best	Henry Gilson	Henry Thorne
Wm. Boyce	Rich. Head	Francis Twisman
Tobius Claeve	Jno. Lake	Henry Washington
Jno. Culpepper	Richard Masters	Robert Wivell
George Curtis	George May	Jno. Woodyer
Tho. Flude	Phillip Packett	(p. 81a)

Certificate was granted to Teague Miscall and Wm. Onoughton for 400
acres for transporting:

Edward Browne	Henry Porter	William Turnor
Robert Carr	Mary Scroope	John Turvil
John Danvers	Thomas Smith	(p. 81a)

Major Tilney exited the court for the following action:
Certificate was granted to Major Jno. Tilney for 600 acres for transporting:

Anto. Bateman	Edw. Fellmoore	Herbert Kendall
Arnold Brams	Robert Heath	John Locton
Geo. Buraham	Wm. Hugeson	Wm. Meridath
John Dimock	Martha Jones	Henry Stone
		(p. 81b)

Certificate was granted to Nicholas Hudson for 200 acres for transporting:

Robert Blayes
Anne Waterson

Richard Ward
Ann Bryan (p. 81b)

Certificate was granted to John Townsend for 100 acres for transporting Humphery Brookes and Elizabeth Moore. (p. 81b)

Certificate was granted to Col. Edm. Scarburgh for 7150 acres for transporting:

Xper. Alanson	Henry Corton	Tho. Grabb
Geo. Alosse	Thomas Crispe	Anto. Hall
James Ash	Henry Crooker	Thomas Hall
Samuell Ash	Jno. Curle	Tho. Hardres
Jno. Awbry	Norton Curtis	Jno. Hawkins
Nich. Banister	James Danenant	Tho. Hawlis
Henry Banton	Jeffry Daniell	Robt. Heywood
Francis Barrell	Jno. Danvers	Bernard Hide
Wm. Batten	Morris Diggs	Robt. Holt
Jno. Batting	Jno. Erule	Richard How
Laurence Bele	Jno. Estcourt	George Hutton
Tho. Bennet	Richard Estrovel?	Benjamin Ifford
Tho. Biddulph	Sisley Evans	Samuell Ire
Henry Bigland	Jno. Eveling	Jno. Jarnis
Walter Bokeland	Giles Eyre	Jno. Jordan
Wm. Boreman	John Eyres	George Joyce
Rich. Bowle	Francis Fane	Thomas Joyce
Jno. Bowles	Edw. Finch	Jno. Kent
Jno. Bowles	Wm. Fisher	Wm. Kent
Jno. Boyle	Wm. Fiske	Tho. Lambert
Walter Bracy	Jno. Fitz	Wm. Leonard
Stephen Brett	Henry Ford	James Lewis
Tho. Broadneck	Anto. Foull	Alexander Light
Wm. Browne	Rich. Foull	Agnes Loe
Rich Brownelow	Jno. Foyle	Maxamillion Loe
Wm. Brownker	Walter Francklin	Rich. Long
Wm. Buggnit	Ralph Freck	Jno. Longe
Isaac Burges	Edw. Gerford	Jeremy Looce?
Henry Burwell	Anto. Gibbon	George Low
Ralph Buskin	Wm. Glauvill	Wm. Low
Wm. Calley	Simon Glurst	Wm. Madox
Alexander Cole	Edw. Goddard	Rich. Manley
Thomas Cole	Amy Goodrich	Tho. Manley
Jno. Collins	Thomas Gore	Edw. Manning

Jno. Manum
Jno. Mauden
Jno. Metten?
Sara Mountfort
Jno. Needham
John Nevell
Geo. Newman
Edw. Nicholas
Jno. Nordell
Edw. Notley
Robert Oliver
Jno. Palmer
Walter Parker
Wm. Paunet
Jno. Person
Thomas Peston
Tho. Petchell
Robt. Phillips
Rowland Plott
Jno. Ploydon

Tho. Polehill
Edw. Poole
Gilbert Raleigh
Mary Rivers
Samuell Rye
Wm. Sadler
Jno. Scott
Jno. Selyard
Edw. Seymor
Edw. Seymor
Phillip Sherrard
Robt. Snowton
Richard South
Tho. Stewkley
Joseph Stockman
Ja. Stonehouse
Wm. Street
Edm. Sutton
Michael Swanson
Jno. Talbott

James Thinn
Nich. Tooke
Jno. Tooker
Edw. Tope
Jno. Trouts
Henry Trucher
John Underhill
Jno. Verier
Henry Wallis
Tho. Wanke
Jno. Warner
Edmond Webb
Jeffry Wells
Anne White
Wm. Willis
Edw. Wyatt
Wm. Yorke
(p. 81b, 82a)

Letter dated 5 August 1664, to the court from near relatives regarding the estate of Gerrard Bucknor, who died suddenly and left "a troublesome estate." After praising the court, they allowed money to Robert Pitt, Mary Jones and Mr. Webb, the receipts going to their attorney Henry Jones and his kinsman/assistant Thomas Hedges. Signed by Ra. Allen and T. Buckner, recorded 21 November 1664, by Robt. Hutchinson. (p. 82a, b)

Ralph Allen and Tho. Buckner, both of London, assigned power of attorney to Henry Jones of London and his kinsman Tho. Hedges regarding the estate of Gerrard Bucknor, "late of the city of London, merchant in the country of Virginia or elsewhere." Sealed and delivered in the presence of Devorax Browne, Thomas Hedges and Thomas Webb. Recorded 21 November 1664, by Robt. Hutchinson. (p. 82b)

Ralph Allen merchant of London and Thomas Buckner gentleman of Chiswick, executors Gerrard Buckner's estate, sent a letter dated 9 June 16 1664, acknowledging a debt of 70 pounds sterling owed to Robert Pitt from Buckner's estate. Sealed and delivered in the presence of Mary Jones, John Wiltt, William (WN) Newby. Presented to Accomack court 16 November 1664, and proved by the oaths of Mrs. Mary Jones and John Wiett. (p. 83a)

Ralph Allen of London and Thomas Buckner of Chiswick in Midd. County acknowledged that Gerrard Buckner's estate was indebted to Mary Jones for 90 pounds sterling. Signed 3 June 1664, witnessed by Richard Clement, Robert Pitt, John Wiltt and William (WN) Newby. Sworn 16 November 1664, by Mr. Robt. Pitt and John Wiett. (p. 83a, b)

Ralph Allen and Thomas Buckner acknowledged that Gerrard Buckner's estate was indebted to Thomas Webb for 50 pounds sterling. Signed 10 August 1664, in the presence of Henry Jones and Devorax Browne, presented to the court 16 November 1664. (p. 83b, 84a)

Col. Edm. Scarburgh, Lt. Col. Wm. Kendall, Capt. Wm. Jones, Capt. Wm. Andrews, Mr. Jno. Custis and Mr. Wm. Spencer were present at the 2 March 1662/63, session of the Northampton County court where John Alexander, Robert Pitts, Mr. Jno. Boice, Mr. Thomas Webb and Mary Jones made claims on the estate of Gerrard Buckner, most of which at the time was floating aboard a ship. The court proposed that Devorax Browne, agent for Thomas Webb, and Mr. Robert Pitts, agent for Mr. John Bogs, give bond and be accountable for the tobacco aboard the ship *Vincent*. Copied by Robt. Hutchinson. (p. 84a, b)

Accomack County Court--16 December 1664

Present: Capt. Geo. Parker   Mr. Devorax Browne
          Major Jno. Tilney   Mr. Hugh Yeo
               Mr. John Wise (p. 84b)

Henry Smith owed Mr. Jno. Shepheard 130 lbs tobacco. Ordered that Smith pay Shepheard and court costs. (p. 84b)

Col. Edm. Scarburgh entered court. (p. 85a)

Upon the action of Thomas Harmonson, attachment for 450 lbs tobacco was made against the estate of John King, who could not be found in the county. (p. 85a)

Jeffery Minshall "committed the sin of drunkenness" and was fined 50 lbs tobacco and court costs. (p. 85a)

Timothy Coe was cleared from his bond for good behavior and paid court costs. (p. 85a)

The case between Wm. Onoughton and Elizabeth Die was referred to the next court at Elizabeth's request. (p. 85a)

James Stevens, servant to Robert Huitt, was judged to be 14 years of age. (p. 85a)

Mr. Tho. Harmonson complained that John Goring had not performed as bargained on the plantation where Goring lived. Ordered that Goring uphold the bargain expressed by David Williamson and Ralph Dow in their depositions and pay court costs. (p. 85a)

Deposition of David Williamson aged about 35 years, 16 December 1664: Mr. Harmonson and John Goring requested Williamson to go to Ralph Dowe's house to witness their bargain. The conditions were that Goring was to have the land for one year, paying quit rents, providing a new covering and weatherboarding for the house, and repairing fences. Goring was to release to Mr. Fisher one room in the house if Fisher sold the land. Signed, David Williamson.

Deposition of Ralph Dow: Dow agreed with the deposition of David Williamson. Signed, Ralph (R) Dow. (p. 85a)

Major Tilney exited the court for the following action:

Major Jno. Tilney informed the court that he had cleared a highway at his plantation at Matchepungo, but that Mr. Isaac Foxcroft had complained that it was inconvenient and requested that it be changed. Ordered that Charles Rackleife and a surveyor determine the most convenient route for the neighborhood. (p. 85b)

Ordered that Mr. Jno. Fawset pay John Drumon 50 lbs tobacco for his attendance at court, being summoned against Jeffry Minshall. (p. 85b)

In his lifetime, Thomas Clyfton owned 200 acres by right of patent, half of which he sold. As Clyfton died intestate, a jury found that his land lapsed to His Majesty. Ordered that after Alexander Addison, John Wallop and Major Tilney divided the land, Col. John Stringer have first choice on behalf of His Majesty. (p. 85b)

Col. Edm. Scarburgh left the court for the following two actions:

Mr. Henry Jones and Mr. Thomas Hedges, attorneys of Mr. Ralph Allen and Mr. Thomas Buckner (executors of Gerrard Buckner's estate) were possessed of Buckner's estate. Jones and Hedges defended the estate against several claims including those of Col. Edm. Scarburgh and Mr. Jno. Alexander, supported by the testimony of Mr. Robert Pitt, Mr. Devorax Browne, Mr. Thomas Webb, and Mr. Henry Jones. After discussing the price of tobacco, the court awarded Scarburgh and Alexander 178 pounds 16 shillings sterling and court costs. (Side note: 19 January 1664/65, this order was satisfied in part by the seizure of 93 pounds 7 shillings 8 pence sterling, sheriff John West.) (p. 85b 86a)

In the case between Col. Edm Scarburgh and the attorneys of Mr. Buckner's estate, a letter from Mr. Thomas Webb claimed that Scarburgh received goods from Mr. Buckner and wondered why Scarburgh would ask for anything out of the estate. Scarburgh requested proof from the attorneys, who had none. Described were actions by Scarburgh, Mr. Devorax Browne, and Mr. Robert Pitt, who was accused of advising the executors of the estate to give letters of attorney and let it lie till Col. Scarburgh was dead, and then recover the money. This was denied by Pitts. (p. 85b, 86a)

Ordered that the estate of Mr. Gerrard Buckner pay 70 pounds sterling to Mr. Robert Pitts. (side note: the order was satisfied 21 February 1664/65.) (p. 86b)

Mr. Deverax Browne exited the court for the following two actions:

Ordered that Mr. Henry Jones and Mr. Thomas Hedges, attorneys for the executors of Buckner's estate (Ralph Allen and Thomas Buckner) make payment of 50 pounds sterling to Mr. Thomas Webb, whose agent was Mr. Deveorax Browne. (side note: order satisfied 23 February 1664/65.) (p. 86b)

Mr. Devorax Browne argued for Mr. Thomas Webb's debt due from the estate of Mr. Gerrard Buckner. It was alleged by Henry Smith that Mr. Webb had included with his claim 61 pounds 5 shillings as money delivered to Mr. Pitts for Col. Scarburgh, but Webb was willing to take 50 pounds. (p. 86b)

Ordered that Mr. Henry Jones and Mr. Thomas Hedges, attorneys for executors of Mr. Gerrard Buckner (Mr. Ralph Allen and Mr. Thomas Buckner) pay 90 pounds sterling to Mrs. Mary Jones. (side note: partially satisfied by seizures 17 April 1664, 19 February 1666/67, and 16 July 1667.) (p. 87a)

Ordered that the following persons appear at the next court to answer charges of fornication:
- Elizabeth, servant of Mr. West, and Patrick, West's former servant
- Thomas Taylor and Mary Brangwell, Charles Rackleife's servants
- Elizabeth, servant of Robert Brace. (p. 87a)

The court was charged with not ordering the vestry to appoint men to go in procession, for not building a prison and for not providing weights and measures. (p. 87a)

Ordered that the sheriff seize fines imposed on the following persons for being delinquent in providing powder and shot. If anyone had a reasonable account, he could be referred to the Col. of the regiment who could acquit him or return him to the sheriff:

| Hen. Bishopp | 4 | Henry Browne | 1 |
| Geo. Brickhouse | 1 | Mr. Devorax Browne | 12 |

Timothy Coe	5	Simon Miller	1
Owin Colleman	2	Jeffry Minshall	2
Giles Cope	3	Jno. Paramore	3
Hugh Cornelius	1	Daniell Quillion	1
George Crump	1	Wm. Roberts	6
Wm. Darby	1	Tho. Smith	1
Thomas Davis	1	Edw. Smith	2
Leving Denwood	5	Wm. Smith	3
Ralph Dow	1	Jno. Smith	2
Henry Edwards	3	Henry Stott	1
Edw. Hamon	2	Jno. Sturgis	1
Rich. Hill, junior	1	Wm. Taylor	3
Jno. Hudson	3	James Taylor	3
Henry Hudson	1	Abram Taylor	1
Robt. Huett	3	Mr. Jno. West	7
Samuell Jones	2	Henry White	1
Tho. Marshall	2	Wm. White	1
Bartho. Meeres	1	Jno. Willis	1
John Mikett	2	(p. 87a)	

Ordered that Timothy Coe appear at the next court. (p. 87a)

Ordered that the sheriff summon the grand jury to the next court to have their oaths administered. (p. 87b)

Several persons were absent at muster; ordered that they be fined 20 lbs tobacco apiece. If anyone gave a reasonable account he would be referred to the Col. who could acquit him or return him to the sheriff.
Persons delinquent at a muster held 15 April 1664:

William Blake	John Holden	Mr. Henry Smith
Robert Brace	Edward Martin	Robert Watson
Thomas Carrell	Jno. Prittyman	Henry White
Timothy Coe	Davis Selevant	(p. 87b)
Robert Hignet	Thomas Smith	

Persons present but with no arms:

Edward Hamon	John White (p. 87b)

Persons delinquent at August muster 1664:

Geo. Brickhouse	Edw. Dunston	Rich. Hill, Jr.
Wm. Britaine	Owin Edmonds	Henry Hudson
James Camwell	John Eyres	Daniell Isham
Japhet Cooke	Edm. Furland	Danill Meccery
Richard Cox	Jno. Goring	Fulcot Obin
Morgan Dowell	Jno. Hagaman	Jno. Prittyman

Danll. Quillion   Samuell Taylor   (p. 87b)
William Redolphus   Henry White

Accomack County Court--16 January 1664/65

Present: Col. Edm. Scarburgh   Mr. Devorax Browne
            Capt. Geo. Parker   Mr. Hugh Yeo
            Major Jno. Tilney   Mr. John Wise (p. 87b)

Thomas Allum, servant of George Brickhouse, was judged to be 13 years of age. (p. 87b)

Richard Buckland, declaring that he had set up a house for the "entertainment of inhabitants or strangers" requested a court order that debts owed to him might be collected along with the public funds. Ordered that the sheriff be empowered to receive his dues after the public dues were satisfied. (p. 87b)

John Major petitioned the court for his freedom. After reviewing the deposition of Mr. Hack, the court ordered that John Major return to his present master, Robert Richardson, until 14 December 1665, and then to receive his dues and be free. (p. 87b, 88a)

Deposition of George Hack aged about 40 years, 16 January 1664/65: Said that he sold John Major to William Smith for thirteen years. Signed, G. Hack. (p. 88a)

Col. Edm. Scarburgh accused all the surveyors of the highways of delinquency. (p. 88a)

Certificate was granted to William Smith for 150 acres for transporting:
John Farmor   Thomas Harrison   Richard Turner
                                           (p. 88a)

Certificate was granted to Robert Richardson for 350 acres for transporting:
Tobius Bull   Eliza. Passell   Katharin Stubbs
Sebbella Bullock   Sara Passell   (p. 88a)
Wm. Fetherstone   Robert Richardson

Mr. Yeo exited the court for the following action:
Ordered that Timothy Coe, for his "obstinate and perverse behavior as a grand juryman" both to the court and others, be fined 500 lbs tobacco and court costs. (p. 88a)

Accomack County Court--17 January 1664/65

Col. Scarburgh and Mr. Browne exited the court for the following action:
John Wallop swore that John Paramore hired him to survey 300 acres.
  Ordered that Paramore pay John Wallop and court costs. (p. 88a)

Mr. Anto. Hodgkins was presented as foreman of the new grand jury, but
  pleading in the name of Governor Wm. Berkely, was dismissed from that
  office. (p. 88a)

John Drumon was to continue as constable by his consent. (p. 88b)

Phillip Fisher was to continue as constable by his consent. (p. 88b)

Ordered that the surveyors for the highways for the following year be:
  - George Truet in the place of Edward Revell
  - Nathaniell Bradford in the place of Wm. Taylor
  - Timothy Coe in the place of Charles Rackleff
Ordered that the "high road" from Mr. Dolby's house to Pokomoke and
  Assateage be cleared 40 feet wide or else 10 feet wide clear of all logs
  and boughs overhead, with small pines, branches and foliage cut 100 feet
  on each side of the path; a main road should be made down into every
  neck, and the private ways from house to house should be cleared 10 feet
  wide.
Ordered that Mr. Anto. Hodgkins be supervisor over the surveyors,
  appointing their limits; also that the constable and one or two of the
  grand jury view all the highways and return an account of how they
  found them. (p. 88b)

Mr. Browne exited the court for the following two actions:
Cristopher Thompson acknowledged writing letters that "scandalized and
  defamed" Mr. Devorax Browne, but because only "ill language" was
  involved, his behavior was recorded by the court and he was ordered to
  pay court costs.
The case of Devorax Browne and Cristopher Thompson was referred to the
  next court at the request of Mr. Devorax Browne. (p. 88b)

John Mickeele? petitioned against James Kaine, who had settled at
  Monoakin to avoid process against him. Because other debtors had also
  escaped to Manoakin and Anamessick, Col. Scarburgh was requested to
  write the conditions and be sent to Kaine and also Edward Hazard. (p.
  88b)

Major Tilney exited the court for the following action:

Thomas Smith was sued by Danll. Quillion for neglecting to confirm 400 acres. It appeared by the deposition of Major Jno. Tilney that Smith was to give assurance to Quillion, and as Quillion had not received his patent from Col. Scarburgh, it was ordered that Smith perform according to agreement. (p. 88b)

Devorax Browne petitioned the court and declared that he became bound in behalf of his brother Mr. Thomas Webb for the concerns of Mr. Gerrard Buckner's estate only to secure what was due to Webb. Granted that Browne, on behalf of his brother, be satisfied out of what was currently in the hands of Mr. Browne or Mr. Thomas Webb. (p. 89a)

Col. Edm. Scarburgh and Mr. Yeo exited the court.

Lt. Col. Wm. Kendall told Edm. Scarburgh that Mr. Thomas Buckner, in a letter to Kendall, spoke of Scarburgh's concerns. For a "declaration of truth and illustration of justice" the following was recorded: In the letter Mr. Thomas Buckner, in reference to the estate of his kinsman Gerrard Buckner, said that by Col. Edm. Scarburgh's order Gerrard and Mr. Thomas Webb were possesed with tobacco when Buckner died, and that Webb sold the tobacco for 6 pence per pound, which was a good price considering the tobacco was decayed. Scarburgh declared this to be untrue; he had never heard of Mr. Gerrard Buckner until the arrival of the ship *Vincent*, Buckner dying before its departure. Scarburgh, who never ordered Mr. Webb to dispose of his goods, felt injured and complained that Webb and Buckner, pretending orders from Mr. Pitts, took Scarburgh's goods shipped in John Alexander's name and detained out of customs due on the *Golden Faulcon* what they pleased for freight, customs, excise and Virginia customs, and then "tossed and tumbled my goods from one to another." Scarburgh also held accountable Mr. Bogs, who bought some of the goods at 6 pence per pound, it being an old trick to make one colleague a buyer so all could profit. Scarburgh thought there was no good dealing, the thing being low and unworthy with "considerable persons" negotiating with such noise and ending in a "stink." Out of pocket about 40 pounds, Scarburgh claimed he was also forced to loose 50% of what his tobacco sold for elsewhere that year, which would not have happened if he had not, out of modesty, "restrained the truth." This was affirmed by Bogs and Buckner's letter obtained in London from the governor after they presented him some of Scarburgh's tobacco. It stated that Scarburgh's tobacco was most excellent and good, equal to, if not better than, the best of that kind from Virginia. Yet Scarburgh was content with the court's decision and annexed this complaint as a record of the "wrongs which Mr. Tho.

Buckner would seem to extenuate." Signed 16 January 1664/64, Edm.
Scarburgh. Recorded by Rbt. Hutchinson. (p. 89a, b)

Deposition of Major Jno. Tilney, 17 January 1664/65: Said that while at
Tilney's house, Thomas Smith promised to pay for the land Daniell
Quillion had sold him. Signed, Jno. Tilney. (p. 90a)

Col. Scarburgh entered court. (p. 90a)

Robert Hignet, alias Higason, admitted transporting sixteen head of cattle
out of the county without certificate. Ordered that he be fined 16,000 lbs
tobacco and pay court costs. (p. 90a)

John Allford admitted transporting seven head of cattle out of the county
without certificate. Ordered that he be fined 7000 lbs tobacco and pay
court costs. (p. 90a)

Mr. George Hack and Danll. Maccery admitted transporting eleven head of
cattle out of the county without certificate. Ordered that they be fined
11,000 lbs tobacco and pay court costs. (p. 90a)

Elizabeth Leveret confessed to stealing a pig from John Barnet. Ordered
that she have twenty lashes upon her naked shoulders and pay the cost
of Barnet's suit. (p. 90a)

Upon the complaint of Mr. Jno. West and the examination of Mr. Anto.
Hodgkins, it appeared to the court that William Chase had abused Jno.
West, the high sheriff, with "base and scurrilous" language. Ordered that
Chase be committed into the sheriff's custody, post bond for good
behavior and appear at the next court for further action. (p. 90a)

Thomas Taylor and Mary Brangwell were presented for fornication. As
Charles Rackleff agreed to pay both their fines and court costs, they
were acquitted from corporal punishment. (p. 90a, b)

James Taylor committed fornication with Dorothy Younge; Charles
Rackleiff was engaged to pay his fine with court costs, which was
ordered put in the court records. (p. 90b)

Elizabeth Leveret was presented for fornication. Ordered that she appear at
the next court to receive the punishment the court thought fit. (p. 90b)

John Johnson committed fornication and appeared incorrigible to the court.

Ordered that he be committed to "Bridewell"[11] to be employed in work there till the further pleasure of the court. (p. 90b)

Accomack County Court--16 February 1664/65

Present: Col. Edm. Scarburgh   Mr. Edm. Bowman
             Major Jno. Tilney   Mr. Hugh Yeo
                    Mr. Jno. Wise (p. 90b)

Cristopher Tompson owed Mr. Browne 22 lbs tobacco. However, if Tompson, at the next court, could prove by the deposition of Mr. Ryding that the musical instrument (value: 350 lbs tobacco) in his possession (and claimed by Mr. Browne) was given to him by Mr. Anscum, then Browne would have to pay 328 lbs tobacco to Tompson with court costs. If Tompson failed to prove his allegation, he would have to pay Browne 22 lbs tobacco and court costs. (p.90b)

Thomas Marshall was brought to court for disposing of tobacco without a certificate. He pleaded ignorance and was acquitted but paid court costs. (p. 91a)

Col. Scarburgh exited the court. (p. 91a)

Jno. Pott, servant of John Watts, was judged to be 15 years old. (p. 91a)

Thomas Clark, servant of Robt. Huitt, was judged to be 12 years old. (p. 91a)

Jno. Loyd, servant of Henry Edwards, was judged to be 14 years old. (p. 91a)

Robert Mountfort, servant of John Smith, was judged to be 16 years old. (p. 91a)

Col. Scarburgh and Mr. Devorx. Browne entered the court. (p. 91a)

Elizabeth Leverett had committed fornication with James Boyd. Ordered that the sheriff give her 30 lashes on her bare back. (p. 91a)

---

[11]*Bridewell was a house of correction in London. The term was also loosely used to mean a jail or prison.*

The goods in the custody of Mr. Anto. Hodgkins, and claimed by Mr. Brace, were ordered delivered to the sheriff till the next court. (p. 91a)

Ordered that John Devorax, when he came into the county, be summoned to the next court. (p. 91a)

John Paramore was security for the appearance in court of Daniel Hardhead, alias Barber, but since Hardhead/Barber was sick, Paramore was continued as security for the next court. (p. 91a)

The suit brought against Mrs. Dorothy Jordan by John Paramore was dropped at the suit of Mrs. Jordan because Paramore failed to enter a complaint. Paramore paid court costs. (p. 91a)

Thomas Tunnill and Richard Johnson posted security to "hold the parish harmless" from supporting an illegitimate child born to Mary Vincent. (p. 91b)

William Chase, bound over to this court to answer for a misdemeanor against High Sheriff Mr. Jno. West, promised better behavior and was dismissed, paying court costs. (p. 91b)

Mr. Edm. Bowman left court for the following two actions: (p. 91b)
John Cross owed Mihill Ricketts 1086 lbs tobacco. Ordered that Cross make payment, but he requested the case be referred to the next court, which was granted. (p. 91b)

Capt. Edm. Bowman, assignee of Lt. Col. Thomas Lambert, obtained on 16 February 1663/64, an order of attachment for 2171 lbs tobacco against the estate of Capt. John Belgrave, which was in the custody of John Walthom. Ordered that the attachment proceed with court charges. (Side note: 29 March 1665, order issued for 1100 lbs tobacco in the hands of Jno. Walthom was satisfied 3 April 1665.) (p. 91b)

Major Tilney and Mr. Hugh Yeo exited the court. (p. 91b)

Mr. James Jolly allowed tobacco to be transported without certificate; he pleaded ignorance of the law and was acquitted, but paid court costs.
Ordered that the county clerk take bond from James Jolly for last year's public dues for himself and family according to country, county and parish laws. (p. 91b)

William Alworth was granted his request to keep the ferry at Occahannock and have his customers pay him. (p. 92a)

The jury of inquest for the year 1665:

Alphonso Ball	Edward Revell	Thomas Tunnell
James Bonwell	Robt. Richardson	John Walthom
Hen. Edwards*	Thomas Selby	Cornelius
Mr. Jno. Fawset	Tobius Selby	Watkinson
Jonah Jackson*	Fran. Sherwood*	Robert Watson
John Jenkins	Edward Smith	Henry White
Tho. Leatherberry	William Smith	Jno. Williams
Wm. Major	Hen. Stott*	(p. 92a)
Jeffery Minshall	Jno. Tompson*	

All were sworn in the January court except for starred names, who were
sworn in the February court. (p. 92a)

Col. Scarburgh exited the court for the following:
Col. Scarburgh had ages determined by the court for the following servants:
William Davis, 15 years; Jno. Devenish, 13 years; and Wm. Gardner,
9 years old. (p. 92a)

Accomack County Court--17 February 1664/65

Present: Col. Edm. Scarburgh   Mr. Hugh Yeo
            Capt. Edm. Bowman   Mr. Jno. Wise (p. 92a)

Richard Bayley and Mary his wife requested that the will of Mr. Henry
Jones be recorded and probation read. The court considered that Mrs.
Eliza. Bowman and Mr. George Watson, the only witnesses to the will,
also got legacies, and were therefore not competent witnesses. The will
was recorded and probated, but not legally approved. The court,
considering the perishable nature of tobacco and at the request of the
petitioners, asked Capt. Edm. Bowman to enter into the estate of Jones
and all others in his trust and take inventory with the court clerk.
Bowman was to dispose of Jones' tobacco as he saw fit and otherwise
administer the estate, provided that he first gave bond for double the
value of all the goods. (p. 92a, b)

Browne Henricks[12] and Diana, wife of Lambert Groten, were apprehended

---

[12]Browne Henricks was identified as a runaway at the court held 17
April 1665.

at Assatege by the Indians and Richard Bundick, the Indians being given 50 arms length of white shell bead wampum called Roanoke for each person. Ordered that Bundick, for his pains in bringing them in, be paid the equivalent of 500 lbs tobacco from Browne Henricks' goods, which were to be appraised by Mr. George Watson and Edward Revell. (p. 92b)

Susanna Johnson, wife of John Johnson, Negro, petitioned the court to release Johnson. Ordered that if John Johnson would post security to "save the parish harmless" from supporting the illegitimate child born to Hanah Leach, pay all damages and charges, provide a nurse for the child, and post bond for his good behavior, then he would be released from Bridewell.[13] (p. 92b)

George Watson and Edw. Revell were appointed to appraise the things presented to the court belonging to Browne Henricks, and found that his goods amounted to 337 lbs tobacco. Since Richard Bundick was awarded 500 lbs tobacco for his pains in apprehending Browne Henricks and Diana wife of Lambert Groten, and since Henricks had paid only part, it was ordered that he stand indebted to Richard Bundick for 163 lbs tobacco and pay court charges. (p. 92b, 93a)

Accomack County Court--13 March 1664/65

Present: Capt. Geo. Parker   Mr. Hugh Yeo
                Capt. Edm. Bowman   Mr. Jno. Wise (p. 93a)

Major Jno. Tilney entered the court after the following:
Certificate was granted to Major Jno. Tilney for 100 acres for transporting Jewell Mezeck and James Regnolds. (p. 93a)

Certificate was granted to Mr. Henry Smith for 500 acres for transporting:

Richard Barnes	Mary Lewis	Arthur Robins
Anne Frowin	Edward Ludlow	John Willmot
Isaac Hillier	Anne Ostipe	(p. 93a)
Alice Hunt	James Powell	

William Brookes, servant of James Hinderson, was judged to be over 16

---

[13]*Bridewell was a house of correction in London. The term was also loosely used to mean jail or prison.*

years of age. (p. 93a)

Ordered that the case between John Parmore and Mrs. Jordan be suspended
till the next court, Paramore being sick and Mr. Watson (appearing for
Mrs. Jordon) not having recorded his letter of attorney. (p. 93a)

Ordered that John Goring pay Mr. Henry Smith 250 lbs tobacco and pay
court costs. (p. 93a)

Accomack County Court--14 March 1664/65

Col. Edm. Scarburgh entered the court after the following action:
Lt. Col. Wm. Kendall examined the complaint of Charles Scarbrough that
his wife was being kept from him, and after some discussion, Scarbrough
was content to let his wife remain at her mother's house till his business
with Col. Scarburgh was finished. (p. 93b)

Certificate was granted to Richard Bayley for 800 acres for transporting:

Mathew Carter	Roger Jones	James Warren
Edm. Elmsman	John Moore	James Whally
Humphey Gorland	Edw. Ragnor	James White
Arthur Grimes	Wm. Ray	Lewis Wilford
Tho. Hartcoate	Jno. Walbrooke	(p. 93b)
Mathew Johnson	Tho. Warmer	

Certificate was granted to John Wallop for 300 acres for transporting:

William Burford	Edw. Martington	Thomas Stany
Walter Gillton	Ralph Massey	Roger Wye
		(p. 93b)

Certificate was granted to Samuell Taylor for 150 acres for transporting:

Richard Gray	James Luellyn	William Orton
		(p. 93b)

Certificate was granted to Charles Rackliffe for 600 acres for transporting:

Nehemiah	Rowland Nurse	Michaell Worrell
Carlington	John Ross	Edward Wrath
Edgar Jones	James Roxford	Lewis Wright
Roger Lasingby	John Smith	(p. 93b)
Owin Laugherne	Robt. Wont	

The suit brought against Cristopher Calvert by William How was dropped
because How failed to enter a complaint. How paid court costs. (p. 93b)

John Die and his wife failed to appear in court to answer the complaint of William Ebourne. Ordered that a special warrant be issued for their appearance at the next court. (p. 93b, 94a)

John Devorax pretended that he "found" several things belonging to Robert Brace, but did not make publication of the fact as required by law. As Devorax was suspected to be guilty of small theft, it was ordered that the sheriff see that he have 30 lashes upon his naked shoulders and pay court costs.

Robert Brace made complaint of several items lost, some of which were discovered in the possession of John Devorax, who pretended but could not prove that he found them. Ordered that the sheriff deliver the goods to Brace, and when Devorax was thought able, then to make satisfaction for the loss and damage sustained by Brace, who was to bring an accounting to the next court. (p. 94a)

Col. Edm. Scarburgh disbursed 50 arms length of white shell bead wampum called Roanoke, two matchcoats [fur mantles], and 250 lbs tobacco for the use of the county while bringing in John Devorax. Ordered that Scarburgh be paid out of next year's levies, and if Devorax ever became able, he was to repay the county. (p. 94a)

Morris Mathews provided security for the good behavior of John Johnson, Negro, for saving the parish from supporting the illegitimate child of Johnson and Hanah Leach, and for court costs. (p. 94a)

Major Jno. Tilney exited the court for the following:

Col. Edm. Scarburgh brought a complaint against Charles Scarborough for felonious actions. Charles cast himself on the mercy of the court with tears in his eyes, desiring their favor and clemency. The court judged him to be somewhat distracted, and Col. Scarburgh did not pursue his complaint. Ordered, that until the governor's pleasure was known, Charles remain the sheriff's prisoner and not be released till he posted security for his good behavior and appearance at the next court. (p. 94a)

Accomack County Court--17 April 1665

Present: Capt. Geo. Parker   Capt. Edm. Bowman
              Major Jno. Tilney   Mr. John Wise (p. 94b)

Mr. John West requested to be released from supporting the illegitimate child born to Elizabeth Furnis and Patrick Haies as he had been doing.

Ordered that the parish take care of the child. (p. 94b)

Col. Edm. Scarburgh entered the court. (p. 94b)

The suit brought against Mrs. Dorothy Jordan by John Paramore about his claim of land was dropped because Paramore failed to prove his bill of complaint. Paramore paid court costs. (p. 94b)

Elizabeth Alford, having recently lost her husband Ambross Alford, requested relief until she could return to her former home. Ordered that the church warden and vestry in office on her arrival here be financially responsible for maintaining her and her children till they could be transported. (p. 94b)

Since Alexander Massey originally transported Ambross Alford, his wife, and children to this country, and since Ambross was dead and his wife Elizabeth wished to be transported to the place from whence she came, it was ordered that Alexander Massey transport them and pay court costs. (p. 94b)

Hugh Yeo entered court. (p. 94b)

James Wingfield complained that the sheriff, on the order of George Watson, seized the horse which Wingfield bought from Capt. Wm. Jones as proved by a bill of sale. Ordered that the sheriff return the horse and that Wingfield be left to his own remedy for recovering damages and court costs. (p. 95a)

John Barret, who recently died leaving only a small estate, owed Mr. Browne 820 lbs tobacco. Ordered that James Armitage be servant, and that Mr. Browne receive the estate for payment of the debt and be accountable for the rest for payment to creditors. Mr. Littleton and Thomas Tunnell were appointed to appraise the estate. (p. 95a)

The case between Cornelius Watkinson and John Savage was referred to William Taylor and Samuell Showell, who were to audit the account in question and give a report to the next court. (p. 95a)

Browne Henricks, apprehended as a runaway and brought in by the Indians, had been committed to Bridewell.[14] The court "commiserating his

---

[14]*Bridewell was a house of correction in London. The term was used loosely for jail or prison.*

distress" released him with Major Jno. Tilney becoming security for paying all charges associated with Henrick. (p. 95a)

Capt. Parker and Mr. Wise exited the court. (p. 95a)

Certificate was granted to Robert Hutchinson for 1200 acres for transporting:

Jno. Blackborne	George Jenkins	Thomas Pittman
Grace Danour	James Lipscomb	Lenord Power
Geo. Evelling	Gatrill Littleton	Anne Ridge
Jane Evelling	Henry Lurton	Mary Ridge
Mountjoy Evelling	Hugh Meeres	Rowland Rolly
Rebecca Evelling	Ellinor Meridath	Susan Tessero
Rowland Hudson	Frances Pittman	Dorcas Woodford
Robt. Hutchinson	Joseph Pittman	Robt. Woodford
		(p. 95a)

Capt. Bowman exited and Capt. Parker entered the court. (p. 95a)

Jane Pitts, servant to Hugh Everet, declared that she came into the country agreeing to serve only three years, but was willing to serve Capt. Edm. Bowman for four years providing he not dispose of her to anyone else. At the next court she was to bring her indenture. (p. 95a, b)

Capt. Bowman entered the court. (p. 95b)

Jane Merideth, hired servant to Edward Hamon, died without relatives in this country and left her 5 year-old daughter named Ann Meridath in the custody of Hamon. He was willing to save the parish from supporting the child provided he could keep her till she reached age 21. Ordered that Hamon, after posting security, could keep the child and provide for her. (p. 95b)

Ordered that attachment proceed against the estate of John Alford to determine what is due to Mr. John West.

Col. Scarburgh exited the court for the following action:

Ordered that attachment proceed against the estate of John Alford to determine what is due to Col. Edm. Scarburgh. (p. 95b)

Thomas Tunnell claimed that John Barret owed him 141 lbs tobacco and an additional 100 lbs tobacco for trouble in tending him in his sickness. Ordered that Tunnell be second in line for payment. (p. 95b)

Ordered that John Pick and his wife be summoned to the next court to answer things objected against them. (p. 95b)

John Die was suspected to be guilty of hog stealing, but as there was no positive proof, it was ordered that he post security for his good behavior and pay court costs.

Deposition of William Ebourne aged about 32 years, 17 April 1665: Said that the hog's ear brought by his wife to Col. Edm. Scarburgh's house was the same ear that Ebourne found in Jno. Die's house. Signed, William (X) Ebourne.

Deposition of Mary Bell aged about 42 years, 17 April 1665: During a search for goods lost by William Ebourne and Bell, the hog's ear was found at John Die's house. Die's child said, "That is my father's mark." Signed, Mary (M) Bell.

The jury considered the ear of a hog found in John Die's house and could find "no matter of fact." The jury:

Alphonsoe Balle	Robt. Richardson	John (|-|-|)
Henry (0) Bishopp	Fran. Sherwood	Tompson
John Fawsett	Edw. Smith	Tho. (TT) Tunnell
Wm. Major	Jno. Smith	(p. 95b, 96a)
Jeffery Minshall	Wm. Smith	

Elizabeth, the wife of John Die, upon the complaint of William Ebourne and Mary Bell, was found guilty of several small thefts. Ordered that she be brought in by the sheriff and receive 30 lashes upon her bare back.

Deposition of Margret Ebourne aged 25 years, 17 April 1665: Said that the edging? and the lace on the cap presented to the court was stolen from her by Elizabeth Die. Signed, Margret (M) Ebourne.

Deposition of Mary Bell aged 42 years, 17 April 1665: Said the green stockings, the lawn apron, the Holland handkerchief with buttons, the small piece of licin? and the three or four yards of ribbon presented to the court are the goods taken from her. Signed, Mary (M) Bell.

The jury considered the goods belonging to Mary Bell and William Abram (sic) that were found in the possession of Elizabeth Die by Constable Thomas Leatherberry, who had been asked to search for items with these particular marks by Mary Bell and Margret Abourne. The following jury found Elizabeth Die to be guilty:

Alphonsoe Balle	Robt. Richardson	John (|-|-|)
Henry (0) Bishopp	Fran. Sherwood	Tompson
John Fawsett	Edw. Smith	Tho. (TT) Tunnell
Wm. Major	Jno. Smith	
Jeffery Minshall	Wm. Smith	

Since Elizabeth Die had taken several articles from William Ebourne, ordered that the sheriff deliver the goods to Ebourne with Die paying court costs.

As Elizabeth Die had taken articles from Mary Bell, ordered that the sheriff deliver the goods to Bell with Die paying court costs. (p. 96a, b)

Mr. Wise entered the court. (p. 96b)

Ordered that Robert Hutchinson, clerk of the court, take an inventory of Dr. Geo. Hack's estate before the next court. Mrs. Anna Hack was to give him notice. Mr. Anto. Hodgkins, Mr. Mihill Rickets, Mr. Thomas Fookes, and Mr. Edw. Revell were requested to appraise the estate. (p. 96b)

Ordered that Charles Scarborough stand before the pillory one hour with "A SCANDALOUS PERSON" written in capital letters.

Charles Scarborough, upon the complaint of Col. Edm. Scarburgh, was found guilty of small theft. Ordered that he be whipped when the court saw fit.

Charles Scarborough was found guilty by the following jury:

Alphonsoe Balles	Robt. Richardson	John (| - | - |)
Henry (0) Bishopp	Francis Sherwood	Tompson
Mr. John Fawsett	Edw. Smith	Tho. (TT) Tunnell
Wm. Major	John Smith	(p. 97a)
Jeffery Minshall	William Smith	

Capt. Geo. Parker exited the court for the following actions:

Capt. Geo. Parker was sworn high sheriff.

John Parker was sworn undersheriff to his brother Capt. George Parker.

Col. Scarburgh and Mr. West entered themselves security for Capt. George Parker's performance in his office.

Capt. Parker demanded a prison for security of prisoners committed to his charge. (p. 97a)

Ordered that the following persons be summoned to the next court:
- Mr. Anto. Hodgkins for breaking the Sabbath
- Jno. Goffling and Anne Durum, servants to Mary Paramore, for fornication
- Hanah Leach, servant to Mrs. Ann Toft, for fornication with a Negro
- Elizabeth Leveret, servant to Robt. Brace, who admitted lying to Tobias Sellvey. (p. 97a)

Col. Scarburgh exited and Mr. West entered the court. (p. 97a)

Ordered that Charles Scarborough pay 50 pounds sterling to Col. Scarburgh and pay court costs. (p. 97a)

Accomack County Court--16 June 1665

Present: Major Jno. Tilney   Mr. Hugh Yeo
             Mr. Jno. West   Mr. Jno. Wise (p. 97b)

Henry White, as proved by the oaths of William Major and Obedience Johnson, engaged Japhet Cooke to make 20 hogsheads, which was not done. Ordered that Cooke perform the work and pay the cost of the suit.

Deposition of William Major, 16 June 1665: In April he heard Henry White speak to Japhet Cooke about setting up some casks. Cooke agreed to come in May to hew the timber. There had been some previous "squabbling" between them regarding a conversation with Thomas Tunnell. Signed, William Major.

Deposition of Obedience Johnson aged about 20 years, 16 June 1665: Said the same as William Major. Signed, Obedience Johnson. (p. 97b)

Ordered that John Cross pay Arthur Upshott 350 lbs tobacco and pay court costs. (p. 97b)

Nathaniell Bradford complained that Alphonso Balls had ridden his horse without permission. Ball confessed that at the request of Bartholomew Meeres' wife, he rode before her to Tobius Sellvey to obtain help for Bartholomew, who was very sick. The court believed that Ball mistakenly committed the trespass, so ordered him to pay 100 lbs tobacco and court costs.

Deposition of Robert Atkins aged about 21 years: Said that after Alphansoe Balls and the wife of Bartholomew Meeres used the horse, she took the horse to the tanner's old plantation on a Friday and gave it to Atkins, the tanner's servant. On Saturday Atkins fetched the horse and carried to his master's house at Matchapreage two tables, a grindstone and three hides and then turned the horse loose in the woods. On the following Friday Atkins was sent down into Matchapungo Neck to look for the horse, where he found him looking well. His master saw the horse when he got home and sent Atkins to Occahonnock to his old plantation for hides. After spending the night, Atkins caught the horse and carried eight hides home. The horse did not falter in the least and ate corn before being released in the woods. Toward the end of the next week, Atkins searched for the horse and found him dead. Signed, Robt. (O) Atkins.

Richard Hill, Jr., was found guilty of riding Nathaniel Bradford's horse without permission, however, by the testimony of Edward Hitching he committed the offense mistakenly. Ordered that Hill pay Bradford 100 lbs tobacco and pay court costs.

The wife of Bartholomew Meeres confessed that during her husband's sickness she rode a horse belonging to Nathaniel Bradford. Bartholomew Meeres took the guilt, so it was ordered that he pay Bradford 500 lbs tobacco for the trespass and pay court costs. (p. 97b, 98a)

Elizabeth Leveret came to Tobius Sellvey, a grand juryman, and confessed that she had twice perjured herself. The sheriff was ordered to see that she received 21 lashes upon her bare back. (p. 98a)

Certificate was granted to John Fawset for 300 acres for transporting:

George Canneck	Wm. Landers	Henry Merrell
Mary Gilman	Anne March	Eliza. Moulton
		(p. 98a)

Certificate was granted to Robert Drake for 1000 acres for transporting:

Thomas Banes	Edward Gill	Elizabeth Starkey
Abram. Bermudion	Richard Harris	Moses Stone
Christian Boures	Wm. Houlder	Indyan Tom
Geo. Brigg	Grace Lais	James Walker
Robt. Carver	Robt. Lawson	Thomas White
Suger Coleman	Anne Oxden	Thomas Wright
Anne Deacon	Richard Spades	(p. 98b)

Accomack County Court--16 August 1665

Present:	Col. Edm. Scarburgh	Capt. Edm. Bowman
	Major Jno. Tilney	Mr. Hugh Yeo
	Mr. Jno. West	Mr. Jno. Wise (p. 98b)

Ordered that Denis Selevant pay George Crumpe 1400 lbs tobacco and pay court costs. (p. 98b)

The case between Teage Andrews and Rody Patrick concerning defamation, being trivial, was dismissed. Patrick paid court charges. (p. 98b)

The case between Robert Bayley, plaintiff, and Jno. Rogers, defendant, concerning defamation was dismissed for lack of cause. Robert Bayly paid the cost of the suit. (p. 98b)

Ordered that John Pick, for his misbehavior, post bond for his good behavior and pay court costs. (p. 98b)

Bartholomew Meeres' petition to be released from his bond for good behavior was granted after proclamation was made three times with no objection. Meeres paid court costs. (p. 98b)

Robert Bayley had often insolently sought to defame the court of Northampton by "scandalizing the just issue of the law." Ordered that Bayley stand with his hands in the pillory one hour with his fault, written in capital letters, pinned to his back: FOR CALUMNIATING THE COURT OF NORTHAMPTON. The sheriff was to detain him till he posted bond for good behavior and paid court charges. (p. 98b, 99a)

Elizabeth Die, formerly ordered to receive 30 lashes on her bare back, came to court to receive punishment, but petitioned the court's favor because of her sickly condition. Ordered that her punishment be suspended till the court thought fit. (p. 98a)

Ordered that John Carew be fined 1000 lbs tobacco for not tending corn. He paid court charges. (p. 99a)

Because many offenses committed in the county should be properly prosecuted by an attorney general, the court appointed Mr. Jno. Fawset to that position. (p. 99a)

Major Tilney exited the court for the following action:
For his obstinate and surly behavior to justice of the peace Major Jno. Tilney, Phillip Fisher was ordered removed from his office of constable. He was replaced by Wm. Smith, with the oath given by Major Jno. Tilney. (p. 99a)

Accomack County Court--16 September 1665

Present: Major Jno. Tilney   Capt. Edm. Bowman
             Capt. Jno. West   Mr. Jno. Wise (p. 99a)

Thomas Fowkes complained against Jno. Picke for scandalous words and for removing Fowkes' logs. Picke promised to restore the logs and expressed sorrow for the scandalous words. Ordered that the suit be dismissed with Picke paying court charges. (p. 99a)

At the request of Jno. Picke, the case of Isaac Heman, plaintiff, and Jno. Picke defendant, was referred to the next court. (p. 99a)

Col. Edm. Scarburgh entered the court. (p. 99a)

In the case of Mr. Isaac Foxcroft, plaintiff, and William Alworth, defendant, Foxcroft lacked clear evidence to prove his charge, but it was acknowledged by Alworth and others that they had reported uncertain scandals, so it was ordered that all persons take care of their own expenses for appearing at court. Foxcroft paid the cost of the suit.

In the case of Mr. George Watson, plaintiff, and William Alworth, defendant, it appeared that Watson "unnecessarily moved in an impertinent cause." Ordered that Watson pay the cost of the suit.

In the difference between Mr. Isaac Foxcroft and Mr. Geo. Watson, plaintiffs, and Wm. Alworth, defendant, for scurrilous words, it was ordered that persons subpoenaing others take care of their own charges.

Deposition of Mikall Huit aged about 45 years: At Col. Edm. Scarburgh's house Huit heard William Alworth say, "There was a Bare belonging to Occahannock Creek that was foul of a woman, and there was nine men to rescue her." Huit asked what woman it was, and Alworth answered, "Mrs. Foxcroft." Huit then asked who the "Bare" was, and Alworth "made very strange that I did not hear of it, and said it was Mr. Watson." Then Alworth "spoke it a great deal plainer and said that he [Watson] lay with her at William Taylor's, and there was nine men to part them." Huit asked who the nine men were, but Alworth did not name them; he said Huit would hear it at court. Mrs. Scarburgh asked who was going to court, and Alworth replied, "Watson and Foxcroft both, unless the Cuckold would put his horns in his pocket."[15] Signed, Mikall (u) Huit

Deposition of Mary Hill aged 40 years, 16 September 1665: Said that William Alworth was called into Col. Scarburgh's house at Occahannock and asked if he had heard any more about Mr. Geo. Watson and Mr. Foxcroft's wife. He said no more than formerly which was, "Nine men hear Mr. Watson lie with Mrs. Foxcroft." Signed, Mary Hill. (p. 99b)

Order was entered at the suit of Mr. Thomas Fowke against the sheriff for the non-appearance of Dorothy Longo. (p. 100a)

---

[15]*Men whose wives were unfaithful were known as cuckolds, who were reputed to wear horns. Alworth was saying that if Mr. Foxcroft took off his horns, i.e. sought to cover up the affair, he would stay away from court.*

Ann Durrum, servant to the estate of John Robinson, was presented to the court for fornication. Capt. Jno. Custis, on behalf of Robinson's orphans, requested that she serve an additional two years, which was granted.

Ann Durrum committed fornication with John Gofling, and as Capt. Jno. Custis agreed to pay the fine of 500 lbs tobacco, she was acquitted from corporal punishment.

John Gofling, servant to the estate of John Robinson, committed fornication with Ann Durum, and as Capt. Jno. Custis agreed to pay the fine of 500 lbs tobacco, he was acquitted from corporal punishment.

Upon the motion of Capt. Jno. Custis, it was ordered that the parish take care of the illegitimate child recently born to Ann Durum. (p. 100a)

Ordered that the sheriff take John Carew into custody until he posted bond for good behavior toward Fenlow Mackwilliam and all loyal citizens. Carew paid court costs. (p. 100a)

John Studson, who recently died, had owned cattle that were now in the possession of Mary Paramore. The cattle derived from a heifer and cow calf given to Studson by John Robinson, deceased, on the condition that the cattle return to Robinson if Studson were to die in his minority without issue. Capt. Jno. Custis, on behalf of Robinson's orphans, petitioned the court for the return of the cattle. Ordered that Mary Paramore deliver the cattle and pay court costs.

The Northampton County deed of gift, signed 11 November 1653, by John Robinson, planter, specified the following:
- to his son John Robinson, Jr.: one red cow called Husse, one black heifer, one pied cow calf, to have forever
- to his son Wm. Robinson: one pied heifer, to have forever
- to John Studson, son of John Studson, deceased: one pregnant red heifer, one brown cow calf, to have under the same conditions as Mary.
- to Mary Studson, daughter of John Studson, deceased: one pregnant red and white cow, to have forever unless she died in her minority or without issue, then the cattle and their increase would return to John Robinson, Sr., or his heirs. Witnessed by Thomas Johnson and Alphonsus Ball. Recorded by Edm. Mathews. (p. 100a, b)

The sheriff complained of uncivil behavior by Phillip Fisher, who pleaded ignorance, was discharged, and paid court costs. (p. 100b)

John Williams complained that he "goeth in danger of his life" by the evil behavior of William Onoughton. Ordered that the sheriff take Onoughton into custody till he posted a bond for keeping the peace. (p. 100b)

Hanah Leach committed fornication with John Johnson, Negro. Col. Scarburgh agreed to pay her fine of 1000 lbs tobacco, so it was ordered she be acquitted from corporal punishment. (p. 100b)

Certificate was granted to John Williams for 500 acres for transporting:

William Beverly	James Cotten	Francis Taylor
Hen. Blundell	Oliver Osborn	Thomas Winch
Lodwick Browne	Samuell Palmer	(p. 101a)
Francis Bruse	John Roll	

Certificate was granted to Robert Houston for 500 acres for transporting:

Hen. Baniton	Richard How	John Ventris
Robert Crumpton	Thomas Kent	Thomas Wanklin
James Eveling	John Low	(p. 101a)
Wm. Grubb	Mary Pithouse	

Certificate was granted to Bartholomew Meeres for 300 acres for transporting:

Edm. Croffts	Alice Gifford	James Penring
Jno. Duckett	David Lucas	Sara Powell
		(p. 101a)

Certificate was granted to Dermon Selevant for 200 acres for transporting:

Thomas Gabell	Thomas Gibbs	(p. 101a)
Richard Archer	Edwin Malet	

At the court held 16 January 1664/65, Timothy Coe, a juryman, was ordered to pay 500 lbs tobacco for his "obstinate and perverse behavior." Coe pleaded ignorance and asked that his fine be remitted. Ordered that the payment be suspended, but if Coe ever incurred another fine, he would be liable for both fines. (p. 101a)

Tobius Sellvey declared that he had given medical treatment to several people in the county and requested that his dues might be collected by the sheriff along with the public dues. Ordered that the sheriff collect all such proven debts. (p. 101a)

Edward Revell, attorney for Mr. Randall Revell, requested renewal of the order against William Silverthorne dated 29 April 1661. Ordered that Silverthorne pay 7118 lbs tobacco and court costs.

The original order was copied along with the arbitrators, Col. Scarburgh and Lt. Col. Kendall, and those present at court: Col. Edm. Scarburgh, Mr. Wm. Jones, Major Jno. Tilney, Mr. Jno. Robins, Lt. Col. Jno.

Stringer, Capt. Wm. Andrews, and Capt. Geo. Parker. It was recorded in Northampton Court by Will. Mellinge. (p. 101b)

Robert Bayly presented a paper against Mr. Randall Revell, calling it a "petition and declaration." The court found it to be neither "sense nor English," and asked Bayly what he wanted to say. He wanted to prosecute Revell for a controversy formerly judged in Northampton Court where Bayly "did scandal the court of Northampton" and requested new process in Accomack, which was done 16 November 1664. But Mr. Revell produced writing dated 17 July 1660, that cleared the Northampton Court of error and condemned Bayly of "insolence and false imputations" for which he was censured. Now Bayly was again "vehemently" urging the controversy "more out of rage than right," so the case was dismissed with Bayly paying the cost of the suit. (p. 101b)

At the last court for "misdemeanor and small thefts," William Browne was committed into the sheriff's custody as if in Bridewell[16] to be whipped and worked until this court for further order. Ordered that Browne be continued as before till the next court. (p. 102a)

List of tithables in Accomack County, 1665:

Col. Edm. Scarburgh	33	Edw. Revell	3
Mr. Robt. Pitt	5	Jno. Watts, tailor	3
Jno. Anderson	3	Wm. Silverthorne	1
Mr. Jolly	6	Jno. Renny	4
Geo. Johnson	4	Alexander Massy	2
Mr. Anto. Hodgkins	5	Richard Hill	6
Robt. Hutchinson	5	Jno. Wallop	2
Francis Sherwood	2	Wm. Custis	4
Mr. Tho. Fowke	5	Tho. Leatherberry	6
Rich. Bundick	2	James Fookes	4
Jno. Jenkins	1	Jno. Lewis	6
Geo. Truitt	3	Tho. Ryly/Roger Turner	2
David Willisome	3	Wm. Willson	1
Francis Benston	2	Danll. Ograham	1
Wm. Benston	1	Wm. Darby	1
Jno. Williams	5	James Bonwell	4
Jno. Watts, cooper	2	Mr. Hugh Yeo	9
Jno. Parker	5	Capt. Edm. Bowman	5
Tege Anderson	3	Abram Taylor	2

---

[16]*Bridewell was a house of correction in London.*

Jno. Eyres	4	Wm. Major	3
Richard Bayly	6	Wm. Taylor	5
Robt. Huett	6	Henry Smith	9
Wm. Dine	2	Rich. Hill, Jr.	1
Wm. White	1	Obedience Johnson	3
Tho. Hall	3	Alphonsoe Balls	1
Dermond Correne	1	Robt. Richardson	2
Andrew Finne	2	Jno. Walthom	5
Owen Collona	3	Nath. Bradford	5
Mr. Browne	15	Alexander Addison	5
Jno. Drumon	3	Richard Kellum	7
Wm. Ebourne	2	Stephen Barnes	1
Jno. Barnet	1	Mrs. Jordan	8
Tobius Sellvey	4	Jno. Savage	1
Robt. Brace	2	Jno. Fawsett	6
Richard Johnson	1	Joseph Harrison	1
Mihill Ricketts	4	Jno. Paramore	3
Thomas Tunnell	3	Geo. Hamling	2
Mr. Littleton	6	Dermon Selevant	3
Jno. Mickeele	3	Edw. Hiching	1
Jno. Holding	1	Jno. Turner	3
Wm. Houton	1	Jno. Willis	1
Richard Cox	1	Peter Seuorne?	1
Mrs. Hack	6	Samll. Showell	1
Xper Calvert	2	Barth. Meeres	1
Wm. Chase	4	Mary Paramore	3
Jno. Brookes	1	Henry Edwards	4
Richard Buckland	1	Mr. Jno. West	8
Anto. Longo	1	Jno. Prittyman	1
Walter Taylor	7	Ralph Dow	2
Mr. Jno. Wise	7	Hen. Stott	2
Edw. Moore	4	Jeffry Minshall	3
Hen. Bishopp	5	Thomas Browne	3
Edward Smith	3	Henry White	2
Thomas Marshall	2	Edm. Kelly	4
Jno. Smith	3	Tho. Carwell	1
James Comwell	1	Thomas Bell	2
Henry Browne	1	Danll. Etion	2
Thomas Selbyey	1	Jno. Goring	1
Wm. Alworth	1	Benjamin Lawrance	1
Samuell Jones	2	Nich. Laurance	1
Charles Rackleff	5	Timothy Coe	3
Thomas Allygood	1	Fulcot Obin	1

Wm. Roberts	7	Jno. Haggaman	2
Robt. Watson	1	Phillip Fisher	4
Jno. Pepper	1	Charles Russell	1
Wm. Blake	1	Jno. Tompson	2
Liverig Denwood	5	Wm. Smith	3
Jonah Jackson	3	Edward Dunston	2
Edward Hamon	3	John Evans	2
Geo. Brickhouse	4	Edward Dolby	2
Donack Denis	1	Major Jno. Tilney	11
Richard Smith	1	total: 468 (p. 102a, b)	

Accomack County Court--16 November 1665

Present: Col. Edm. Scarburgh   Capt. Edm. Bowman
Major Jno. Tilney   Mr. Hugh Yeo
Capt. Jno. West   Mr. Jno. Wise (p. 102b)

George Chilton was committed to the sheriff's custody till further order for insolency and contempt of Mr. Jno. West's warrant. (p. 102b)

Cornelius Watkinson, Phillip Howard and William Darby were arrested by Mr. Jno. Fawsett for performing a play called "The Bear and the Cub" on 7 August 1665. The court suspended action till next court and ordered that Watkinson, Howard and Darby appear in costume and reenact the play. Watkinson and Howard were to be held until they posted security to perform the order.

Ordered that the sheriff arrest "the body of William Darby" for his appearance at the next court to answer for being an actor in the play called "The Bear and the Cub." (p. 102b)

Isaac Heman complained that John Pike illegally detained him in his service. The court found that Heman was bound to serve two years, expiring next September first. Ordered that Pike keep Heman employed to learn carpentry and to give him adequate meat, drink, apparel and lodging during the service.

Deposition of Grace Lambert aged about 63 years, 16 September 1665: Robert Davis, while staying at Lambert's house, said that Isaac Heman, his servant, was free in twelve months last April?, which was before John Pike came to the house. Signed, Grace (crescent) Lambert.

John Walthoum testified the same. Signed, John Walthoum.

David James testified the same. Signed, David (X) James. (p. 102b, 103a)

Isaac Foxcroft, sued by Mr. West, did not appear in court. Order was entered against the sheriff for the non-appearance of Mr. Foxcroft. (p. 103a)

The court denied the request of John Carew that his bond be released. Ordered that it be continued. (p. 103a)

John Williams complained that he "goeth in danger of his life" by the evil behavior of William Onoughton. Ordered that Onoughton remain in custody till he posted a bond for keeping the peace and paid court costs.

Deposition of William Silverthorne, 16 November 1665: Last September as he was coming home from the muster, he saw William Onoughton load his gun in a trembling and shaking condition in the path between Mr. Fowkes and Mrs. Hodgkins' house. Silverthorne asked why he loaded the gun, and Onoughton replied that he had his enemies before and behind and would rather kill than be killed. Silverthorne then said, "Let me have your gun, and you shall have mine." Onoughton refused and added, "There are those that go in the name of an Englishman, but I am not afraid of them." They parted, but afterward Onoughton came to Silverthorne's house and said he had shot his gun at Mrs. Hodgkin's house and had loaded it again. Signed, William (WS) Silverthorne.

Deposition of Hanah Snoswell, 16 November 1665: Said that William Norton (sic) [*Hanah's deposition, like Silverthorne's, refers to William Onoughton*] took her sharp pointed Dutch knife and went to Goodman Williams. When he came home he returned the knife and said he had done no harm with it, for "I went through the corn field because they should not see me before I was upon them, but the dogs betrayed me and I missed of my purpose." Signed, Hanah (X) Snoswell. (p. 103a)

On 16 August 1665, Morris Mathews entered into a good behavior bond for 8000 lbs tobacco with John Pike as security. This was forfeited, so judgment was ordered against Pike and Mathews for 8000 lbs tobacco. (p. 103a, b)

The suit brought against Dorothy Longo by Thomas Fowke for scandalous words was dropped because the court failed to find a cause for action. Fowke paid court costs. (p. 103b)

Capt. Geo. Parker complained that William Onoughton damaged a horse named Dunn when Parker lent it to Col. Scarburgh. James Bonwell and Robert Hill were appointed to evaluate the damage to the horse and give an account at the next court so Onoughton could make payment. (p. 103b)

Thomas Leatherberry, John Watts and Mary Paramore complained that Mr. Charles Scarburgh's land at Pungotege was not laid out; ordered that John Wallop survey Scarburgh's land as well as the land between the main Anancock Creek and John Williams and George Truet. (p. 103b)

Mr. West left the court for the following action:
Ordered that Mr. Jno. Fawsett and Thomas Leatherberry examine the account between Mr. Jno. West and Wm. Onoughton and give their report of trespass to the next court. (p. 103b)

Mr. Yeo exited the court for the following two cases. (p. 103b)
Ruth, the wife of Richard Bundick, assigned her illegitimate child John to Mrs. Dorothy Jordan and her daughter Elizabeth. The court assented, binding the child according to law.
In a letter to "Good Mistress Jordan," Ruth Bundick apologized for not being in court, but her husband would be there to dispose of her child. It was her desire that Mrs. Jordan and her daughter should have the child to serve them according to the custom of Virginia, having been informed of their tenderness to him. She thanked them for their kindness and gave them her love and "best respect." Signed Ruth Bundick, the letter was presented to the court by Richard Bundick 16 November 1665, and recorded by Robt. Hutchinson. (p. 103b)

Fenlow MackWilliam, who formerly posted bond for John Carew's good behavior, requested to be discharged. Proclamation was made three times with no objection. Ordered that MackWilliam be discharged and pay court costs.
Ordered that [John Carew] be kept in custody until posting bond for his good behavior with other security in the place of Fenlow MackWilliam and paying court costs. (p. 104a)

Ordered that William Onoughton, for breaking out of prison and taking a cutlass and other things from Capt. Parker, have 30 lashes upon his bare back.
Ordered that William Onoughton, for insolent behavior to Capt. Parker, post security for good behavior and pay court costs. (p. 104a)

Ordered that the list of John Allford's cattle presented by William Chase be recorded and that Chase be paid. (p. 104a)

Major Tilney left court for the following two actions:
Robert Walby petitioned the court for freedom from his master Major Jno. Tilney. Walby had entered the country without indenture and had served

five years according to law. Walby was declared free. Tilney was ordered to pay Walby corn and clothes according to the custom, 100 lbs tobacco for extra service, and court costs. (p. 104a)

John Rickords, servant to Mrs. Ann Hack, declared that on October third he was free. He brought in witnesses who confessed they were not present at the assigning of Rickords, but pretended to hear at other times. Further proof being demanded, Rickords produced a canceled indenture wherein the words stating his time of service were obliterated and changed. Ordered that Rickords serve according to the custom of the country with Mrs. Hack paying court costs and Ricords reimbursing her after his term of service. (p. 104a)

Accomack County Court--17 November 1665

Present: Col. Edm. Scarburgh   Capt. Edm. Bowman
          Major Jno. Tilney   Mr. Hugh Yeo
              Mr. Jno. Wise (p. 104a)

Mr. John Fawsett and Thomas Leatherberry reported that William Onoughton "damnified and committed trespass" against Mr. John West. Ordered that Onoughton pay 1500 lbs tobacco to Mr. Jno. West and pay court costs.

Fawsett and Leatherberry in reporting damage done to Capt. Jno. West, found that Wm. Onoughton neglected 32 day's work for which 800 lbs tobacco was allowed West.

Onoughton contracted to look after Capt. West's cattle and hogs, but contrary to his obligation, he willfully killed 23 pigs at different times. Capt. West was allowed 700 lbs tobacco for his damages in destroyed stock. The other stock committed to Onoughton's care were referred to the court for consideration. Signed 16 November 1665, by John Fawsett and Thomas (T) Leatherberry. (p. 104a, b)

Mr. West entered court. (p. 104b)

Ordered that the sheriff take William Jones into custody and see that he be given 29 lashes on his bare back for incorrigible behavior. (p. 104b)

Major Tilney exited the court for the following action:

Major Jno. Tilney requested, on behalf of the orphan Richard Hinman, for another guardian in place of Timothy Coe. Hinman chose Major Tilney as guardian and accused Coe of prejudice toward both orphan and estate.

If the accusation was proven at trial, Coe would have to make payment;
if proven false, Hinman would have to return to Coe as his guardian. (p.
104b)

Mr. West exited the court for the following action:
George Chilton disobeyed Mr. West's warrant, and for his contempt of the
court, it was ordered that Chilton stand upon the pillory one hour with
his fault on his back in "great" letters: "FOR CONTEMNING AU-
THORITY." He was to post bond for good behavior and pay court costs.
(p. 104b)

Ordered that William Browne be delivered to Col. Scarburgh to be whipped
and worked as a prisoner to pay for the trespass committed against
Scarburgh. The payment due to the sheriff for Browne's imprisonment,
whipping and working would be satisfied by Browne's labor. (p. 104b)

Richard Kellum, appointed constable in the place of Jno. Walthoum,
requested to be released. Ordered that Kellum be discharged.
Ordered that John Walthoum be restored to his office as constable and to
be sworn before Capt. Bowman or another of the justices.
Ordered that the court clerk make a copy of the constable's oath for John
Walthoum to be sworn. (p. 105a)

Certificate was granted to Germon Gillit for 200 acres for transporting:
| Germon Gillit | Thomas Gillit |
| Sarah Gillit | Germon Gillit (p. 105a) |

Major Tilney exited the court for the following action:
Ordered that William Roberts pay Major Jno. Tilney 300 lbs tobacco for
his attendance as coroner for the illegitimate child of Roberts' servant,
who in turn was to pay by serving beyond her time of servitude. If
Roberts refused to pay, then the servant was to serve Tilney directly and
then serve her master afterwards. (p. 105a)

Ordered that the sheriff seize no more than 2000 lbs tobacco this year from
Morris Mathews as part of the forfeited security for John Pike. Half was
for the levy, and half for Mr. John Fawsett, the attorney for Accomack.
(p. 105a)

In the August court John Carew was fined 1000 lbs tobacco for not tending
his corn. Ordered that 500 lbs tobacco be seized by the sheriff this year;
the rest to be seized next year. (p. 105a)

Ordered that Mr. James Jolly's debt of 882 lbs tobacco due to Accomack
County be paid to Robert Hutchinson in partial payment for writing and
attendance on the commissioners of Virginia and Maryland. (p. 105a)

Certificate was granted to William Alworth for 400 acres for transporting:

Robert Bedford	Edward Games	Alice Robins
Robert Buse	James Herbert	Rebecca
Oliver Evans	John Risly	Wallingford
		(p. 105a)

Certificate was granted to Elizabeth Rackleff for 600 acres for transporting:

James Beecher	William Hudly	Samll. Mountagne
Francis Boteter	Henry Kerling	Thomas Roles
John Burgoin	Wm. Luke	Francis Roterdam
Thomas Dyer	James Monax	Walter Vaux
		(p. 105b)

Certificate was granted to Richard Robinson for 150 acres for transporting
Thomas Joy, John Nordell, and Edward Lewis. (p. 105b)

Certificate was granted to James Taylor for 200 acres for transporting:

George Lore	William Howlis	(p. 105b)
John Foyle	Jane Southby	

Certificate was granted to Nicholas Laylor for 200 acres for transporting:

William Winn	Thomas Carne	(p. 105b)
Martha Estcourt	Jane Vaughan	

Certificate was granted to Robert Johnson for 200 acres for transporting:

John Vann	John Otaway	(p. 105b)
James Dalston	Thomas Rowse	

Certificate was granted to John Wallop, alias Wadelow, for 450 acres for
transporting:

Walter Booth	Richard Hemstead	Lewis Price
William Bussy	John Hemsteed	Eliza Stetford
George Harris	Robert Minthard	Mary White
		(p. 105b)

Certificate was granted to Thomas Davis for 400 acres for transporting:

John Armiger	William Dines	Stephen Tompson
John Browne	Roger Nepair	Wm. Warde
John Chester	William Suazy	(p. 105b)

Certificate was granted to John Davis for 400 acres for transporting:

Henry Coker	John Pleydell	Jonah Wallis
Thomas Gore	Robert Spencer	John Wingatt
John Harvey	William Sundon	(p. 105b)

Certificate was granted to James Hinderson for 400 acres for transporting:

John Aubry	John Long	Edward Top
James Collini	John Parce?	Eliza. White
Florence Evans	Alice Stewkly	(p. 105b)

Deposition of Hanah Snowswell, 16 November 1665: Said that William Onoughton beat her in the cornfield. She fell under his feet, and he said when she was not able to work, she should be freed, as Parker's horse was. Signed, Hanah (x) Snowswell. (p. 106a)

Accomack County Court--18 December 1665

Present: Col. Edm. Scarburgh   Mr. Hugh Yeo
             Major Jno. Tilney   Mr. Jno. Wise
                 Capt. Jno. West (p. 106a)

Ordered that Nicholas Laurance pay the cost of his being brought to court, and that the case be continued till his wife appeared before the court to answer the objections the court had against her. (p. 106a)

On 17 December 1663, Henry White obtained an order that Thomas Leatherberry and Arthur Upshott (guardian to the orphans of Alexander Mattocks) should show the bounds of their land so White could survey his 500 acres. Ordered that Leatherberry and Upshott show their bounds before the next court or pay damages. (p. 106a)

In the difference between Mr. John Fawsett and Mr. John Shephard, it was ordered that the accounts between them be balanced and that they share the charges of the suit. (p. 106a)

Ordered that Elizabeth Dunston become the administrator of her husband's estate, with her giving security.
Ordered that Mr. Devorax Browne be paid first out the estate of Edward Dunston - 830 lbs tobacco. (p. 106a)

Thomas Summers made oath to the will of Mr. Lyving Denwood, and it was recorded. (p. 106a)

John Rowles formerly provided security for the bond of Morris Mathews,
but now requested to be released. Proclamation was made three times
with no objection, so Rowles was discharged, paying court costs.
Ordered that Morris Mathews be taken into custody till he posted bond with
other security in the place of John Rowles. (p. 106a)

William Onoughton, who posted bond for keeping the peace at the
complaint of John Williams, petitioned to have his bond returned.
Williams declared that his fear was over, so the bond was delivered to
William Onoughton, who paid court costs. (p. 106b)

Summoned to court at the suit of John Williams, Denis Selevant did not
appear. As Francis Sherwood was bail for Selevant's appearance,
judgment was entered against Sherwood for 850 lbs tobacco and the
mauling of 1000 logs and court charges. (p. 106b)

Ordered that the case between George Johnson and Elizabeth Die be
referred to the next court and that she bring her evidence. (p. 106b)

Col. Scarburgh left the court for the following action:
Col. Scarburgh sued the estate of Mr. James Jolly, who could not be found.
Ordered that attachment for 1200 lbs of pork and court costs proceed
against Jolly's estate if it could be found in the county. (p. 106b)

Ordered that Mr. Wise be appointed instead of Mr. Hodgkins to finish the
appraisal of Mrs. Hack's estate before the next court. (p. 106b)

Ordered that Christopher Calvert be fined 50 lbs tobacco for drunkenness
and pay court costs.
Ordered that John Avery be fined 50 lbs tobacco for drunkenness and pay
court costs.
Ordered that William How be fined 50 lbs tobacco for drunkenness and pay
court costs. (p. 106b)

The case between Major John Tilney and Timothy Coe was referred to the
next court. Because Tilney wished to enlarge on his charges, ordered that
he bring in his declaration so Coe could have a copy. (p. 106b)

Mr. West had on hand 850 lbs tobacco, the remainder of fines paid by
delinquents at musters. Ordered that 400 lbs tobacco be paid for a drum
and the rest be paid to Mr. Fawsett, clerk of the regiment. (p. 107a)

Ordered that the church wardens of Accomack parish provide for Anne

Browne, the wife of William Browne, until six weeks after her delivery; then she was to work for her livelihood. (p. 107a)

Ordered that Edward Martin be summoned to the next court to show why he should not pay charges accruing upon the information given by him against Cornelius Watkinson, Phillip Howard and William Darby. (p. 107a)

Three courts ago, John Carew posted bond for good behavior. He now requested to be released. Proclamation was read three times without objection so his bond was delivered to him with court costs. (p. 107a)

Elizabeth Rackleff was granted a letter of administration for her husband's estate, with her putting up security.
Ordered that the estate of Charles Rackleff be inventoried by the clerk of the court and that Mr. John Fawsett, Alexander Addison, John Walthoum, and Ralph Dow appraise the estate before the next court and give an account to the court.
Charles Rackleff formerly agreed to pay James Taylor's fine for fornication. Widow Rackleff now requested payment from Taylor. Ordered that Taylor pay 500 lbs tobacco and all costs of the suit. (p. 107a)

Certificate was granted to John Davis for 300 acres for transporting:

Richard Holt	William Orly	Miles Seyes
Edward Jarvis	John Pile	Richard Warcop
		(p. 107a)

Certificate was granted to Henry White for 500 acres for transporting:

Humphry Alston	Morgan Evans	Jane Summers
Henry Charnock	Joan Gwyn	William Thorp
George Darby	Jeffry Hall	(p. 107a)
Sammuell Dier	Lewis Hedman	

Certificate was granted to Charles Rackleff for 500 acres for transporting:

John Anderson	James Dancomb	George Spiggott
Walter Carey	John Denton	Edward White
Thomas Chaney	Thomas Geety	(p. 107b)
Richard Crawly	Walter Neale	

Certificate was granted to Tobius Selvey for 600 acres for transporting:

Rowland Ash	Jeffry Daniell	Sisly Okely
Thomas Bassett	Barbery Fisher	Joan Ramsy
Alexander Clerk	Giles Maning	Walter Strickland

Edward Tooker   Henry Trechard   William Vaughan
                                                   (p. 107b)

Certificate was granted to John Williams for 300 acres for transporting:
  Thomas Halsey   Edward Hite   Jaspher Rowles
  Robert Hillton   James Moore   John Somervill
                                                   (p. 107b)

Ordered that high sheriff Capt. Parker take into his custody the estate of
  Alexander Wilson, deceased, and that it be sold at auction on 22
  December, and that the clerk take inventory for the court. (p. 107b)

Ordered that the surveyors bring in their accusations of persons not clearing
  their highways. (p. 107b)

Ordered that the following persons be summoned to appear at the next
  court:
  For Sabbath breaking:
  - Capt. Bowman for having his servant fetch a hide on Sabbath
  - Wm. Taylor, informed on by Major Jno. Tilney
  For fornication:
  - Jno. Truman and Anne Beale
  - Deborah Eldredge
  - Alice Johnson, servant to Wm. Roberts for having an illegitimate child
  by a Negro belonging to Tho. Browne
  - Jno. Rickards and Eliza. his wife, servants to Mr. Hack
  - Anne Dix by her own confession with Wm. Jones, deferred till delivery
  - Rich. Francklin with Jane his wife
  - Richard Shale with Jane Hatch, servants to Mr. Upshore
  - Jno. Ticke and Phillice his wife
  - Danll. Ograham and Mary Turner, twice
  - Wm. Jones and Ruth Bundick
  - Wonne Mackelanny and Ellinor his wife
  - Francis and Mary and? AbChurch, Porky Jone and Bowin, Porky Jone
  and Wm. the Croockneck Sawyer, Short Arst Nan and the Joyner,
  servants to Col. Edm. Scarburgh
  - Peter and Lidia, servants to Mr. Browne, twice. (p. 107b)

The grand jury, who requested to be released, was appointed to choose
  their replacements and present them at the next court. (p. 108a)

For accommodating the court, Mr. Thomas Fowke was paid out of fines the
  same amount given to Mr. Hodgkins for entertainment. (p. 108a)

Accomack County Court--16 January 1665/66

Present: Col. Edm. Scarburgh   Mr. Hugh Yeo
             Major Jno. Tilney   Mr. Jno. Wise
                     Capt. Jno. West (p. 108a)

Robert Huit was prosecuted at His Majesty's suit concerning four hides
brought to Col. Scarburgh's house at Occahonnock. Two hides were
without ears [whose marks would determine ownership], as testified by
Major Jno. Tilney and Capt. West, and because Huit requested four men
to view the hides, it was ordered that the hides be brought to the next
court and that Huit post "very good security" for his appearance there.

Note to "Mr. Attorney" signed by Jno. Tilney and John West, 14 January
1665/66: While they were at Col. Scarburgh's house, Robert Huit's wife
brought four hides to sell, two of which had no ears. This was contrary
to law and gave just cause to suspect Huit's behavior. Both men offered
to give further information upon request.

Robert Huit, suspected of killing other men's cattle, was bound over to the
next court. Ordered that he be placed in custody till he posted bond with
security for his good behavior and paid court costs. (p. 108a)

Major Tilney left the court for the following action:

Major Jno. Tilney exhibited several articles in behalf of Richard Hinman
against Timothy Coe, who in his defence presented his account of
Hinman's estate. In case of objections, the articles were left as proof. It
was uncertain whether Coe lost Hinman's sheep through neglect;
Hinman's plantation was to be viewed by Phillip Fisher and Henry
White, who were to report any waste or damage caused by Coe. Tilney
was declared guardian to Richard Hinman, whose estate, now in the
hands of others, was to be delivered up on demand. (p. 108a)

Jane Hatch confessed committing fornication with Richard Shale. Because
her present master, Mr. Upshore, agreed to pay her fine and court
charges, she was acquitted from corporal punishment. (p. 109b)

Robert Bayley requested to be released from his bond for good behavior.
Proclamation was read three times with no objection, so his bond was
ordered released with him paying court costs. (p. 109b)

Richard Turner alleged that he had served several masters seven years and
requested his freedom. Because his present master, William Smith,
claimed that there was an indenture for Turner to serve a longer time,
Smith was given two months to find it. If no indenture was found, Smith

was to free Turner, giving him corn and clothes, and also to pay him for any service that he had performed past his due time. (p. 109b)

The Indians of Pokomoke complained against John Williams for intruding on their land. Evidence presented by Robert Houston and Roger Hotson, indicated that the Indian who was recognized as the owner by the Indian King of Pokomoke had sold the land to Williams. Ordered that Williams pay the Indian according to his agreement, not to put cattle or hogs on the land this year and not to incite the Indians by planting in their fields. (p. 109b)

Accomack County Court--17 January 1665/66

Present: Col. Edm. Scarburgh   Mr. Hugh Yeo
            Major Jno. Tilney   Mr. John Wise
               Capt. John West (p. 109b)

According to the testimony of Mrs. Leatherberry and Sarah Dowlis, Thomas Roberts had spoken "several scandalous words" against the government. Ordered that he have 39 lashes upon his bare back.

Deposition of Ellinor Leatherberry and Sarah Dowlis: They said that Thomas the sawyer raised a discourse saying that the laws were unjust, unconscionable and unreasonable. He said that William Jones was likely to die from the punishment he received. If it had been administered in England, those responsible would have been hanged. He could not tell how they would answer for it, and often mentioned the Colonel's name [undoubtedly Col. Edm. Scarburgh] in connection with the abuses done to Jones. He further said that men abused their servants and were more dissolute than their servants were. In the discourse concerning William Jones, Mrs. Leatherberry cited Exodus 20:20, 21 [which in part says that God's "fear may be before your faces that ye sin not"], but he replied, "Fie, fie upon it. Those were abominable sayings." He said, "Four men whipped Wm. Jones by the Colonel's order as long as they were able to stand. They stood up for the laws of the country, but they that followed the prosecution of them deserved death." More abominable things were spoken but "through long discourse is a great deal forgotten." (p. 110a)

Timothy Coe, surveyor, presented Mr. Isaac Foxcroft for not clearing his highways. Ordered that he pay 500 lbs tobacco and court costs. (p. 110a)

Timothy Coe, surveyor, presented John Prittyman for not clearing his highways. Ordered that he pay 500 lbs tobacco and court costs. (p. 110a)

Capt. West left the court for the following action:

Mr. James Jolly admitted owing Capt Jno. West 490 lbs tobacco. Ordered that he pay it and court charges.

Col. Scarburgh left the court for the following action:

Last court at the suit of Col. Scarburgh, attachment was issued for 1200 lbs of pork against Mr. James Jolly, who admitted the debt. Ordered that he pay it and court costs. (Side note: order was satisfied 21 July 1666, by sheriff Capt. Parker.) (p. 110a)

Edward Martin was questioned concerning information given to Mr. Fawset about a play called "The Bear and the Cub." Several persons were brought into court and charges made, but the court found them not guilty of fault and suspended the payment of court charges. Upon the oath of Fawsett, it appears that the charges and "trouble of that suit" arose from information provided by Edward Martin. Ordered that Martin pay all costs of the suit. (p. 110a, b)

Thomas Smith behaved insolently toward the commands of Major Jno. Tilney as a magistrate. Ordered that Smith be taken into custody till he posted a bond for his good behavior and paid court costs.

A note to the court signed by Jno. Tilney, 16 January 1665/66: About six or eight days ago Tilney went to Thomas Smith's house and there found William Jones, who Tilney understood to be a servant belonging to someone in Northampton County. Tilney said Smith was breaking the law by entertaining a person with no certificate and immediately charged Smith to take him to the nearest constable. Smith refused to go. (p. 110b)

In the case between Thomas Leatherberry and John Watts, planter: Ordered that each have their land surveyed, and if necessary the surveyor should question the "most ancient and known persons...to inform him of the names of places and of Undiman's Branch." If their patents adjoined, the land would be divided proportionally. (p. 110b)

Mr. John Fawset and Mr. George Watson were appointed to examine the accounts in the case of Henry Eldridge and Richard Pricket and give a report. (p. 110b)

Several evidences were examined concerning the death of John Manington, servant of Thomas Leatherberry. The court had Leatherberry taken into custody until he posted bond with security for his good behavior and for his appearance at court. The evidence was to be transmitted to the governor.

Deposition of Thomas Roberts aged 30 years and John Dickeson aged about
24 years, 17 January 1665/66: Said that they worked at Thomas Leatherberry's from the last of August till 10 December, and while there they
saw great abuses done to Leatherberry's servant, John Manington. He
was beaten with unlawful sticks by Leatherberry and the other servants,
and especially by a woman servant who "often bitterly swore by the
blood of God that she would be the death of him." She said, "I know I
shall be hanged for thee," and swore that she would scald him if he did
not leave the fire. The morning that Roberts and Dickeson left, which
was 10 December and two or three days before the servant died, a
servant called Anthony was beating him with a bull's pizzell[17] at the
mill where he was grinding. That same day, as Roberts and Dickeson
were going to John Parker's to work, they met Leatherbery about a mile
from his house with a stick under his arm driving John Manington before
him. Roberts and Dickeson asked if the servant had run away, but
Leatherberry answered, "No. I have given him a drench,[18] and now I
am walking of him." At another time Roberts and Dickeson heard the
servants and Cornelius Watkinson brag about how each of them had
whipped him a spell. Signed, Thomas (26) Roberts and John (O)
Dickeson.

Deposition of William Crabtree aged about 30 years, 17 January 1665/66:
Crabtree was sent to get walnuts on Monday morning, and going up the
hill by the bridge between his master's and Thomas Leatherberry's, he
met Leatherberry coming up the hill driving his man before him.
Crabtree asked if Leatherberry was going to Col. Scarburgh with his
man, but Leatherberry said, he had given him a drench and was now
walking him. When Leatherberry came back, Crabtree heard him say to
his servant, "Hup, go. Are you hot?" The servant answered, "Master, I
am hot." Leatherberry said, "If you are not hot, I will make you hot."
Signed, William (T) Crabtree.

Deposition of Katherin Parker aged about 20 years, 17 January 1665/66:
Said that she was sent on an errand to Thomas Leatherberry's the 13th
or 14th of December. There she saw John Manington drinking at a pail
of water and a woman servant of Leatherberry's beating him with a
loblolly pine stick and calling him rogue. Katherine, seeing her using
him so badly in the condition he was in, asked her why she did it. She
replied, "Hang him, if he would have worked, he had not come to this."
This was the day before John Manington died. Signed, Katherin (KO)

---

[17]*A whip made from the penis of a bull.*

[18]*A purging drink, often forced down the throat.*

Parker.

Deposition of Henry Mitchell aged about 24 years, 17 January 1665/66: While he was at Thomas Leatherberry's house sitting in the chimney corner, Thomas Leatherberry's late deceased servant John was standing in the chimney corner eating. Coming from where he stood, John stumbled at the andiron and fell with his arm in a kettle of wort [beer in the making], and his arm catching the handle, he pulled the wort down on himself. While he was down, the woman servant struck him with a loblolly pine stick, but Mitchell thought it not hard enough to do him harm. The woman asked John why he did not get up. Signed, Henry (M) Mitchell.

Deposition of Howell Glading aged about 34 years, 17 January 1665/66: Said that he was at Pungoteage when John Manington, servant of Mr. Leatherberry died. Glading said he knew nothing about the cause of death. Signed, Howell (* in a circle) Glading.

Deposition of John Jenkins aged about 50 years, 17 January 1665/66: Said that a little before the last court Mr. Leatherberry asked Jenkins and his wife to come to his house where he had a dead servant named John Manington lying on a mat in the outward room and covered with a rug. Leatherberry uncovered him and Jenkins saw that Manington was dressed in a clean shirt and decently washed with a clean cloth to tie up his jaws. Leatherberry lifted the front of his shirt and Jenkins could see no marks of blows, but as a servant was shrouding him, Jenkins saw what looked like a stripe on his ribs on the right side. Jenkins did not see the back, but saw that his right leg was scalded and saw that blood had run from his leg onto the ground. Jenkins said that Manington "went with all his limbs to the grave" which was about five or six feet deep. Signed, John (II) Jenkins

Deposition of Cornelius Watkinson aged about 23 years, 17 January 1665/66: About three days before last court, Watkinson was at the house of Mr. Leatherberry, who had a dead servant named Jno. Manington. Watkinson saw Anthony and other servants stripping him and the woman servant washing him, but saw no hurt on his body other than a scald and scurvy. Signed, Cornelius Watkinson.

Deposition of Peter Inskipp aged about 21 years, 17 January 1665/66: Said that he was at work at Mr. Leatherberry's house when John Manington died. He saw Anthony and other servants of Leatherberry strip him, and the woman servant washed him, tied up his jaws and put on a clean shirt. He saw no marks of blows on him, but Manington had scurvy and had been scalded. Signed, Peter Inskipp. (p. 110b-112a)

The court reversed their order concerning Thomas Roberts. Earlier in the day it was ordered that he have 39 lashes, but upon further consideration, the court thought fit that his punishment be suspended. (p. 112a)

Certificate was granted to James Jolly for 500 acres for transporting:

Edward Chicking	James Jolly	William Jones
Thomas Cobb	Eliza. Jolly, his wife	William
Elizabeth	Eliza. Jolly, his	Xper. Wright
John	daughter	(p. 112a)

John Renny was appointed surveyor of the highways from Pokomoke River to the south side of Deep Creek on the Bay Side and to Mattomkin Bridge on the Seaboard Side.

James Bonwell was appointed surveyor of the highways from the south side of Deep Creek to the bridge at Pungoteage between Edward Revell and Mrs. Hodgkins, and on the Sea Side from Mattomkin Bridge to Mr. Wm. Custis' house.

Alphonso Ball was appointed surveyor of the highways from the bridge at Pungoteage between Edward Revell and Mrs. Hodgkins and on the Bay Side to the head of Occahannock and on the Sea Side from Mr. Wm. Custis' house to John Turner's house.

Henry Bishopp was appointed surveyor of the highways from the head of Occahanock on the Bay Side and from John Turnor's on the Sea Side and through to the end of the county. (p. 112a, b)

According to an act of the Assembly, the highways should be cleared 40 feet wide, but several landowners were unable to do it. Ordered that a cart way ten feet wide be cleared both on the highway and down into every neck and that the small pines and brush be cleared for 50 feet on each side of the path. All branch roads should be made passable for cart and horse. If the cost was too great for a land owner, then the neighborhood was to join together to complete it; if the cost was too much for them, then the county would defray the cost of bridges. If the surveyors failed to report on negligent landowners within three months, they would be fined 500 lbs tobacco for each delinquent landowner. (p. 112b)

Ordered that at next court John Drumon be sworn as constable from Pokomoke to the south side of Deepe Creek on the Bay Side and to Mattomkin Bridge on the Bay Side.

John Williams was sworn as constable from the south side of Deepe Creek to the bridge at Pungotege between Edward Revell and Mrs. Hodgkins on the Bay Side and from Mattomkin Bridge to Mr. Wm. Custis' house on the Sea Side. At Williams' request it was granted that John Watts, planter, be the substitute in Williams' absence.

Ordered that John Walthoum go to Capt. Jno. West to be sworn as constable from the bridge at Pungoteage between Edward Revell and Mrs. Hodgkins to the head of Occahonnock on the Bay Side and from Mr. Wm. Custis' house to John Turnor's on the Sea Side.

Ordered that John Stott be constable from the head of Occahonnock on the Bay Side and from John Turnor's house on the Sea Side down through to the end of the county. (p. 112b)

Ordered that Mr. John Fawset, Alexander Addison, Jno. Walthoum and Ralph Dow, appraisers of the estate of Charles Racklef, be sworn by the next magistrate, perform the order next February 6, and have the court clerk present to take down the inventory. (p. 112b, 113a)

Anne Beadle was to be whipped for fornication, but Capt. Parker was contracted to pay 500 lbs tobacco; ordered she be acquitted from corporal punishment. (p. 113a)

Francis Sherwood, security of Denis Selevant's appearance, had judgment entered against him at the suit of John Williams for 850 lbs tobacco and the mauling of 1000 logs plus court costs. Sherwood was granted his request to have till the next court to produce Selevant, and a letter was to be sent to the next magistrate in Northampton County for Selevant's return. (p. 113a)

Col. Scarburgh exited the court for the following:

Col. Edm. Scarburgh complained that William Price burned Scarburgh's barn and also fathered the illegitimate child of Scarburgh's servant, Porky Jane, who died giving birth. Ordered that after Price's term of servitude was expired, he was to make satisfaction by service to Scarburgh; setting the amount of additional time was suspended because Price and his confederates had formerly conspired and attempted to run away, and might attempt "more desperate devices" if they knew of further punishment. Therefore, open censure was delayed for Price, Hugh Bowin (for getting syphilis from a prostitute), and Thomas, commonly called Snudge. Price and Snudge carried a coal of fire to light their tobacco and threw it in the straw where they were standing at the barn door; at "noon-day" the barn and all the corn in it was burned while Price and Snudge stood by. The deserved censure was delayed, but their actions were recorded so the offenders could not claim that no complaint was made. (p. 113a)

Abchurch, Wm. Price (sawyer), Hugh Bowin, John Blocksam, Anne Carpenter and Mary Scadding, who by confession and trial were guilty of fornication, sought mercy and requested that their master Col. Edm.

Scarburgh pay their fines and court charges. They were therefore acquitted of corporal punishment and ordered to serve Col. Scarburgh for their fines, court charges, and the care of their illegitimate children in addition to the year and a half additional servitude required by law. (p. 113a, b)

At the next court the following persons were to take the oath of a juryman: Phillip Fisher, Giles Cope, Bartholomew Meeres, John Eyres, John Watts (cooper), Jno. Turner, Dorman Selevant, Edward Dolby, Thomas Marshall, Luke Denwood and John Holden. (p. 113b)

Accomack County Court--16 February 1665/66
Present: Col. Edm. Scarburgh   Capt. Edm. Bowman
               Major Jno. Tilney   Mr. John Wise
                    Capt. Jno. West (p. 113b)

Ordered that Mrs. Hack pay 1700 lbs tobacco to Mr. Jno. Dolby, who, at the governor's command, accommodated at his house the commissioners examining the complaint of her deceased husband. (p. 113b)

Mr. Devorax Browne entered the court. (p. 113b)

The case against Robert Hewitt for goods feloniously taken for Mr. Jarvis was suspended till the next court.
The jury was to view the four hides brought to Col. Scarburgh's house by Robert Hewitt's wife to see if the ears missing from two hides were eaten off by dogs or cut off. A report was to be made at the next court. (p. 113b)

Mr. Browne left the court for the following action:
Japhet Cook was contracted by Mr. Devorax Browne to set up 50 hogsheads for tobacco by the end of last October, but failed to do so. Ordered that Cook pay 20 lbs tobacco per month (after November) for every unfinished hogshead. (p. 113b)

Ordered that the case between Jno. Rogers and Robert Bayley be dismissed with Rogers paying court costs. (p. 113b)

Ralph Dow, who had charge of William Jones, took 600 lbs tobacco from Cristopher Scanly? in payment for work done by Jones. Ordered that Dow pay that amount to Jones when the court thought fit. (p. 113b, 114a)

Col. Scarburgh left the court for the following two actions:

The case of Edward Revell, plaintiff, and Mr. Charles Scarburgh, defendant, for trespass, was dismissed with Revell paying court costs.

Even though the suit was dropped, the court recorded the following: Scarburgh said that Revell had no land where he claimed and proved his patent to be older than Revell's. Also, Scarburgh's bounds were set by a jury on 30 July 1663. Revell pleaded that one jury member was missing, and while it was affirmed that there was a substitute, only the foreman's signature appeared. It was therefore ordered that the former jury again be impanelled with open positions filled and with Mr. John Wallop the foreman instead of Thomas Parker. During a dry time next summer when springs and branches were distinguishable, they were to determine the main branch of Pungotege and consequently the land in question. (p. 114a)

Capt. Bowman and Mr. Browne left the court. (p. 114a)

Ordered that George Watson be paid 9000 lbs tobacco out of the estate of Mr. Henry Jones, deceased. Capt. Edm. Bowman, the assignee of Mr. Jones, having already paid part, was ordered to pay 2514 lbs tobacco out of the estate. (p. 114a)

Capt. Bowman entered the court. (p. 114a)

Ordered that Robert Hewitt post bond for his good behavior, being convicted of a felonious act.

Robert Hewitt was convicted by a jury and by the complaints of several persons suffering losses. Ordered that he be fined 2000 lbs tobacco and pay court costs.

The jury found that the ears of two of the four hides were willfully removed thus preventing identification. The names of the jury:

Alexander (AA) Addison	Tobius Selvey
Richard Bally	Francis Sherwood
Henry (7 in circle) Bishopp	John Smith
Phillip Fisher	Walter (^) Taylor
Robt. Richardson	William (WT) Taylor
Cha. Scarburgh	John Walthoum (p. 114a, b)

Ordered the case between John Cox, plaintiff, and Mrs. Hack, defendant, be referred to the next court and John White to be present. (p. 114b)

Thomas Roberts, servant to David Williamson, entered suit against Ellinor, the wife of Thomas Leatherberry and Sarah Dowlis, servant to Leatherberry. The court found the cause neither legal or reasonable and ordered that the suit be dropped with Roberts paying court costs. (p. 114b)

At the request of Teage Andrews, the case between him and Mr. James Fookes, for Andrews' entertainment of Fookes' son, was referred to the next court. (p. 114b)

Ralph Dow petitioned to be discharged concerning the completion and repair of the Otterdam Bridge. Upon the testimony of Henry Bishopp and Timothy Coe, the present and past surveyors, that the job was sufficiently done, ordered that Dow be relieved of further trouble concerning the bridge. (p. 114b)

Ordered that William Onoughton be released from his bond for good behavior, proclamation being made with no objection. Onoughton paid court charges. (p. 114b)

William Jones was willing to live with Mr. Brookes, who was willing to keep him. Ordered that Brookes furnish Jones with "necessaries according to the value of his labor and no more." (p. 115a)

Certificate was granted to Alexander Williams for 450 acres for transporting:

Ann Corker	Wm. Hopton	Hugh Owin
David Gosse	Edward Lingen	Herbert Price
John Holt	Thomas Other	James Rye (p. 115a)

Certificate was granted to David Williamson for 3000 acres for transporting:

Jno. Algernall	Francis Butler	Edw. Feild
Edw. Ames	Edward Cason	Jno. Fetherly
Jno. Arris	Tho. Cawly	Ralph Freeman
Tho. Ashton	Wm. Cecill	Ralph Freeman (sic)
Edw. Atkins	Cha. Chamberlin	James Grimston
Robt. Austin	Tho. Colston	Edw. Haines
Robt. Barnard	Francis Compton	Jno. Hales
Robt. Barnard (sic)	Hen. Coningsby	Wm. Hales
Henry Bercher	Albane Cox	Erasmus Harby
Jno. Berkeby	Tho. Dockwray	Jno. Hewet
Wm. Bladwell	Ralph Dorkby	Jno. Heydon
George Blumly	Jno. Dorkway	Rich. Jenings
Henry Blunt	Rich. Elmes	Jno. Jesson
Edw. Briscoe	John Farrar	Jno. Jesson (sic)

Rich. Jones
Joshua Lomax
Landers Mead
Maurice Rawdon
Robert Sadler
Anto. Smith
Edm. Smith

Edw. Smith
Arthur Sparkes
Tho. Stanly
Jno. Stone
Laurance Thorch
Jasper Trice
Lionell Waldon

Jno. Watts
Rich. Weaver
Henry Williams
James Willmott
(p. 115a)

Certificate was granted to David Williamson for 3000 acres for transporting:

Ja. Alablaster
Xper. Allanson
Robt. Apreece
Rich. Ashley
Maurice Bigg
Thomas Blois
John Boyes
Roger Bradshaw
Tho. Brealer
Tho. Brett
Jno. Bristoll
James Brooke
Francis Burton
Jno. Cason
Albernill Cecill
Tobias Cleer
Jno. Coltropp
Richard Combs
Thomas Cotten
Geo. Curtis

Jacob Eaton
Wm. Flud
Thomas Fortree
Anto. Foule
Tho. Hardress
Jno. Heron
Robt. Lowkner
Rich. Manly
Jno. Marsh
Wm. Marston
Jno. Mason
Edw. Master
Rich. Masters
Geo. May
Geo. Middleton
Rich. Nayler
James Newman
Jno. Nowell
Robt. Oliver
Thomas Oxton

Robt. Paine
James Pashly
Tho. Peale
Nich. Pedley
Peter Pett
Henry Pettis
Harbert Randall
Wm. Rooke
Jno. Sacker
Robt. Sadler
Jno. Smith
Jeremy Standford
Fortree Stephson
Francis Thirsten
Nich. Toke
Ja. Trouts
Robt. Watson
James West
Edw. Wyatt
Jno. Zouch
(p. 115a)

Certificate was granted to Cristopher Thompson for 500 acres for transporting:

Rich. Allen
Stephen Brent
Robt. Buidlos
Edward Fleetwood

Robt. Fowler
Jno. Molinex
Jno. Salmon
Edward Stanly

Ja. Thorbane
Jno. Verier
(p. 115b)

Certificate was granted to Mrs. Anne Toft for 7250 acres for transporting:

Jno. Annisly
Anto. Archer
Rich. Armhurst

Ralph Ashton
Ralph Ashton (sic)
Robt. Austin

Wm. Bankes
Anto. Bateman
Wm. Batten

Jno. Birom
Ja. Blathurst
Wm. Bois
Luke Bollings
Wm. Boreman
Geo. Bourn
Jno. Boys
Arnold Braens
Rich. Brownlow
Jno. Buckhurst
Tho. Buggions
Robt. Burnham
Oliver Buttler
Jno. Byrom
Tho. Carns
Robt. Cat
Francis Clerke
Tho. Collier
Tho. Crisp
Ja. Culpepper
Jno. Culpepper
Jno. Curtis
Tho. Cutbert
Jno. Dalliston
Jno. Darrell
Edw. Derming
Jno. Ducken
Rich. Duke
Rich. Earle
Jno. Entwis
Jno. Eveling
Nich. Feather
Wm. Fisse
Rich. Fleet
Edw. Flinch
Tho. Flud
Tho. Flute
Walter Franklin
Hen. Gilborn
Jno. Girling
Tho. Godfrey
Mark Gresham
Edw. Hales

Jno. Hallsteed
Rich. Hardness
Robt. Hayes
Jno. Head
Jno. Heath
Robt. Heath
Edw. Helmer
Robt. Heywood
Tho. Hide
Bernard Hide
Ja. Hinman
Robt. Hobb
Tho. Hobb
James Hodgkins
Jno. Horsman
Wm. Hugeson
George Hutton
Robt. Ireland
Robt. Jones
Herbert Kendall
Roger Kenion
Tho. Kirland
Tho. Lake
Steph. Lamard
Thomas Lambert
Geo. Lands
Wm. Leech
Rich. Leige
Ja. Leight
Jno. Leight
Wm. Leonard
Thomas Long
Tho. Lovelace
Edw. Master
John Menns
Jno. Meridath
Hump. Miller
Edw. Monins?
Nich. Mosely
Jno. Munn
Geo. Newman
Toby Nordes?
Jno. Norton

Tho. Norton
Tho. Notres
Cutbert Ogle
Hen. Palmer
Jno. Parker
Phillip Parker
Tho. Payton
Edm. Peirce
Tho. Peirce
Rich. Penington
Wm. Pierpoint
Jno. Polehill
Hen. Porter
Davis Pothell
Jno. Prests?
Jno. Radly
Laurance Ranstom
Robt. Rawley
Jno. Reinalds
Alex. Rigby
Jno. Rigby
Jno. Righell
Jeffry Rishton
Jno. Rivers
Rich. Sandis
Jno. Scott
Jno. Seliard
Tho. Seth
Jno. Seyliard
Wm. Sivan
Wm. Sivan
Henry Slayter
Richard Standish
Tho. Stiles
Tho. Strangford
Francis Suane?
Thomas Subin?
Nich. Townly
Jno. Tuffton
Roger Twisden
Walter Vane
Francis Vincent
Wm. Wall

Jno. Walpoole   Jno. Wieth?   Alex. Wood
Hen. Washby   Wm. Wild   (p. 115b)
Nath. West   Jno. Willis

Certificate was granted to Col. Edm. Scarburgh for 3000 acres for transporting:

Samll. Abdy	Reynold Cornwall	Tho. Peale
Jno. Ashburnham	Thomas Cowles	Thomas Pitt
Tho. Awbry	Jno. Dansey	Jno. Rodd
Jno. Barnaby	Jno. Dimock	Thomas Rodd
Jno. Baskerfeild	Edw. Freeman	Edw. Rothwell
Giles Bennet	Tho. Geers	Jno. Rudhall
Jno. Best	Arthur Gomond	James Scadamore
Jno. Birch	Jno. Graham	James Sheffeild
Tho. Blany	Humphry Gregory	Henry Smith
Jno. Bramstone	Wm. Hall	Hen. Thornhill
William Bridges	Henry Harley	Jno. Tomkin
Tho. Broadnax	Edw. Herbert	Timo. Veynall
Anto. Browne	Jno. Hoaden	Nich. Wallnim
Ralph Buskin	Rich. Hopton	Tho. Welcomb
Tho. Carpenter	Wm. Howorth	Tho. Whittington
Tho. Carver	Rich. Hulse	Rich. Wigmore
Job Charlton	Andrew Jennet	Jno. Wilson
Jno. Cocks	Jno. Kidley	Robt. Wiseman
Robert Colldron	Edw. Noell	Wm. Woolley
Tho. Coningsby	Tho. Nurse	Thomas Wright
		(p. 116a)

Capt. Edmond Bowman sued Mr. George Watson for tobacco due the estate of Mr. Henry Jones, but Watson claimed that he had tobacco due him. Both parties agreed to ask the judgment of the court. It was ordered to be recorded that Watson's account was due him and that it was reasonable that Watson be paid a customary salary for services done in posting the books.

Robt. Hutchinson recorded the account of Geo. Watson in which he processed goods and tobacco worth 143,005 lbs tobacco and received 9000 lbs tobacco in wages. (p. 116a)

The jury of inquest for the year 1666:
Sworn in January:

Mr. William Custis, foreman	James Fookes	John Brooke
	Andrew Finney	William Abourn
Richard Bayley	Thomas Browne	Robt. Houston

Richard Buckland	Wm. Chase	John Watts, Senior
Obedience Johnson	Wm. Roberts	
Sworn in February:		
Phillip Fisher	Jno. Watts, Junior	Tho. Marshall
Giles Cope	John Turnor	Jno. Holding
Barth. Meeres	Dermon Selevan	Edw. Hamon
Jno. Eyres	Edward Dolby	(p. 116b)

Accomack County Court--16 March 1665/66

Present: Col. Edm. Scarburgh   Capt. Edm. Bowman
           Major Jno. Tilney   Mr. Hugh Yeo
           Capt. Jno. West   Mr. John Wise (p. 116b)

Names of the jury impaneled:
Mr. Jno. Smith, foreman

Wm. Abourn	Rich. Buckland	John Renny
Teage Anderson	Timothy Coe	Francis Sherwood
Rich. Bayley	James Fookes	Jno. Walthum
John Brookes	Rich. Kellum	(p. 116b)

William Browne had several hogs around Hunting Creek. Ordered that the sheriff take them into custody and dispose of them to defray the cost of Browne's wife's delivery. Any remainder was to be used for the good of Browne's children. (p. 116b)

Mr. Browne entered the court. (p. 116b)

Thomas Smith was taken into custody till his trial for enticing Nicholas Cooper, servant of Phillip Fisher, to run away. (p. 116b)

Mrs. Jordan entered process against John Kirke, who was not to be found in the county. Ordered that Mrs. Jordan keep Kirke's tobacco till the next court, and give him notice to appear there; if he did not appear, she would receive what was owed to her out of his estate. (p. 116b)

For 13 days, Teage Andrews illegally "entertained" Thomas Fookes, son of Mr. James Fookes. Ordered that Andrews pay Mr. Fookes 30 lbs tobacco for each day and pay court costs.
Ordered that Teage Andrews be taken into custody till he posted bond for his good behavior and paid court costs. (p. 117a)

Francis Sherwood, who had provided security for the appearance of Denis Selevant, personally brought Selevant to court. Sherwood asked and was granted release from the judgment of Jno. Williams against him as security for Selevant.

Denis Selevant was taken into custody until night to answer the suit of Jno. Williams. (p. 117a)

At the last court Richard Turnor sued for freedom from his master, William Smith, and was to be set free if Smith did not produce Turnor's indenture. The indenture showed that Turnor must serve till 25 December 1667. Ordered that Turnor complete that time and make good his loss of time and all court charges. (p. 117a)

Mr. Yeo exited the court for the following action:

Certificate was granted to Mr. Hugh Yeo for 500 acres for transporting:

Margery Acres	Xper. Mathews	Tho. Wingood
Wm. Chapman	Richard Southerne	William Yeo
Richard Gibbs	Katherin Tompson	(p. 117a)
Michall Harrison	Mary Turnor	

Morris Mathews was released from his bond for good behavior, proclamation being read three times without objection. He also paid court costs. (p. 117a)

The court determined the ages of two servants of Col. Scarburgh: Andrew Stopp was judged to be 10 years old and William Lichfeild to be 11. (p. 117a)

Judgment was entered against the sheriff for the non-appearance of Jenkin Price, who had been sued by Mr. John Fawset for 1132 lbs tobacco. (p. 117a, b)

The suit brought against John Andrews by Thomas Davis was dropped because Andrews failed to enter a complaint. Andrews paid court costs. (p. 117b)

Thomas Smith, posting very good security, was given till the next court to answer the charges against him. (p. 117b)

The case between Richard Cox and Mrs. Hack was dismissed with Cox paying court costs. (p. 117b)

Certificate was granted to Henry Bishopp for 2200 acres for transporting:

Lewis Aleberry
Jno. Ashenhurst
Abram. Atkins
Oliver Atkins
James Austin
Henry Banister
John Barrell
Jno. Blacklitch
Arthur Brockley
Tho. Challcott
Oliver Chichester
Edward Crome
Robt. Davell
Tho. Feilding
John Ford

Geo. Forge
Ralph Golsborrog
Peter Heyman
Joan Hill
Rich. Houghton
John Kett
Rich. Kirkby
Jno. Knatchbull
Rowland Light
Constantine Lor
William Maddox
Wm. Man
Tho. Manley
Robt. Marry
Godfry Martin

Henry Matson
Edward Mosely
Jno. Samon
James Simons
Edw. South
Jno. Spencer
Wm. Stockes
James Upton
Robt. Ware
Jeffry Wells
James Whiting
Roger Willis
Robt. Wivell
Geo. Woodyer
(p. 117b)

Certificate was granted to Mr. Thomas Ryding for 250 acres for transporting:

Michaell Lingsly
Henry Moore

Jno. Moorefeild
Thomas Trury

Sara Whittaker
(p. 117b)

Certificate was granted to John Pike for 400 acres for transporting:

Mathew Gross
James Hollings
James Huntly

Aldred Roberts
Henry Rouse
Robert Smith

Jonah Wallbrooke
James Yeamans
(p. 117b)

Certificate was granted to Laurance Robinson for 400 acres for transporting:

Mary Gibbons
Mathew Gosling
Rebecca Moore

Martha Morris
Thomas Mouse
Edward Rice

Thomas Stanby
Owin Williams
(p. 117b)

Certificate was granted to Samuell Taylor for 200 acres for transporting:

Thomas Algate
John Croiden

Oliver Crow
John Gill (p. 118a)

Certificate was granted to Thomas Selby for 1000 acres for transporting:

James Ashton
Jeffry Ballcott
Miles Frost
Mathew Gore
Thomas Hoard
Miles Lackland

Joan Limes
Henry Maslin
Thomas May
Rowland Mercer
Owin Morris
Alice Oakeland

Ja. Ouldcastle
Arthur Ren
Tho. Roxford
Sara Shelling
Robt. Shipp
Jean Taylor

Robert Weaver   Timothy White   (p. 118a)

Certificate was granted to John Wallop for 650 acres for transporting:

Jno. Cottswell	Robert Horton	Jean Stanly
Roger Draper	John Hubard	Jeames Wheatly
John Golding	Edward Long	Abraham Willet
Margret Hall	Thomas Mackrell	(p. 118a)
Edgar Hallsey	Luke Roe	

Mr. Jno. Fawsett, Alexander Addison, Jno. Walthum and Ralph Dow were appointed in February court to appraise the estate of Charles Rackliff, deceased, but Eliza. Rackliff, his widow, did not allow the inventory to proceed. Ordered that the appraisers go to Rackliff's house on April 5, to appraise the estate with the court clerk present to take inventory. If Eliza. Rackliff refused to obey, the attorney would proceed against her as wrongfully possessing an estate and to bear the costs of delay and court charges. (p. 118a)

Ordered that the county attorney proceed against all persons entering the estate of any deceased person without legal permission. (p. 118a)

Henry White sued Thomas Leatherberry and Arthur Upshott, overseer and guardian for Alexander Mattocks, for not showing the bounds of the Leatherberry and Mattocks land. Since the court formerly ordered this, and since the court had often "censured the neglects" of the these parties, the court ordered that Henry White survey on the land adjoining Leatherberry and Mattocks, and if any problems ensued for lack of knowing the marked trees, then Leatherberry and Upshott would pay all damages, costs of delay and court costs. (p. 118a, b)

Major Jno. Tilney exhibited articles on behalf of Richard Hinman against Timothy Coe, Hinman's former guardian. Ordered that the accounts be audited with the charges of the suit to be paid from the orphan's estate and Coe to pay for his own defense. (p. 118b)

Accomack County Court--16 April 1666

Capt. Robert Pitt took the oaths of commissioner and of allegiance by Col. Scarburgh. Major Tilney, "in distaste" withdrew from the court with Mr. Browne and Mr. Yeo declaring against it. (p. 118b)

William Berkeley in a letter signed 4 April 1666, expressed it to be his will that Capt. Robert Pitt be a commissioner of Accomack County, and that Capt. Parker continue as sheriff for the year. (p. 118b)

Accomack County Court--16 April 1666

Present: Col. Edm. Scarburgh   Mr. Devorx. Browne
              Capt. Jno. West   Mr. Hugh Yeo
              Capt. Robt. Pitt   Mr. Jno. Wise (p. 118b)

The names of the jury:

Alphanso Ball	Jno. Jenkins	Derman Selevant
Francis Benston	Samuell Jones	Jno. Watts, Sr.
Thomas Browne	Barth. Meeres	Jno. Williams
Wm. Chase	Robt. Richardson	David Williamson
		(p. 118b)

Major Tilney entered the court. (p. 118b)

The court considered the case of Thomas Smith and found that he was falsely accused. He was acquitted and could legally seek compensation from those who unjustly troubled him. (p. 118b, 119a)

Examination of Nicholas Cooper aged about 20 years, before Robt. Hutchinson, 16 March 1665/66: Last Friday night one hour before sunset, Cooper met Thomas Smith on the orchard side of a plantation of Major Jno. Tilney's. Smith asked Cooper to go with him to "James Citty, where I should never see the face of my master again." Cooper accepted, and Smith told him to get what food and clothes he could and to meet him at Ellias Hartree's plantation and from there to go to Mr. Foxcroft's and take his boat. Signed, Nicholas (O) Cooper.

Deposition of John Bagwell aged about 25 years, sworn before William Waters, 22 March 1665/66: On Friday, the ninth of March, about an hour before sunset, Thomas Smith came to Bagwell's present house smoked his pipe, stayed awhile and inquired the way to Robert Haies house, where he eventually went. Signed, John Bagwell.

Deposition of Ann, the wife of John Bagwell, aged about 19 years, sworn before William Waters, 22 March 1665/66: Said that all her husband said was true. Signed, Ann (0) Bagwell.

Deposition of Joan, the wife of Robt. Haies, aged about 30 years, sworn before William Waters, 22 March 1665/66: On Friday the ninth, about sunset, Thomas Smith came to her house and asked for her husband. She invited him in to sit and wait for her husband, who did not return home that night as expected. Without seeing Robt. Haies, Smith went away toward Magetty Bay the next morning. Signed, Joan (W) Haies.

Deposition of Mary Gunter aged about 30 years, sworn before Willi. Spencer, 21 March 1665/66: Said that Thomas Smith on the 13th day of this month came to her house near night and asked for lodging. She asked where he came from, and he said from below, from Bagwell's where he spent the night. Signed, Mary (M) Gunter.

Lettice Simons, sworn before Willi. Spencer, 21 March 1665/66: Said the same as Mary Gunter. Signed, Lettice (O) Simons.

Richard Willdgows, sworn before Willi. Spencer, 21 March 1665/66: Willdgows, who slept by Smith, said the same as Mary Gunter. Signed, Richard (R) Willdgows. (p.119a, b)

Anne Hack asked to be released from her late husband's fine for transporting eleven cattle. With the governor recommending pity, the court ordered that the judgment be obliterated and that it be in full force against the principal, John Meccary.

Letter to Gov. Wm. Berkeley from Ann Hack, widow: Said that George Hack, when he was alive, let a poor man named Danll. Maccary have a sloop which was used to transport eleven cattle without a certificate from Maccary's plantation at Craddock in Accomack. Her husband and Maccary were jointly fined 11,000 lbs tobacco, the order being passed a little before her husband's death, and now likely to be charged to Ann, who was unable to pay. Maccary had moved up the bay, and Ann and her children would be ruined. She nor the estate was liable, the cattle belonging to Maccary and shipped in the presence of his neighbors. She begged the governor's consideration to care for the widow and the fatherless.

William Berkeley sent the above letter to the commissioners with a note to have compassion on the "poor widow and her children." The commissioners would do the governor a favor by doing so. (p. 119b, 120a)

Attorney Jno. Fawset complained that Alphanso Ball was illegally possessing the estate of John Die; Ball requested to be allowed till the next court to make probation of John Die's will, or be prosecuted for possessing it. (p. 120a)

Mr. Browne exited the court. (p. 120a)

John Renny had for several courts been security for the appearance of James Jolly; the sheriff acknowledged that Jolly was present, so it was ordered that Renny receive his bond and pay court costs. (p. 120a)

Thomas Fowke passed a promissory note for 750 lbs tobacco to Jno.

Tronally, but the note could not be found. Since Fowke acknowledged the note, it was ordered that he give Tranally another and pay court costs. (p. 120a)

A note from the governor stated that he desired Capt. Parker to continue as sheriff for 1666.

Exit Major Tilney.

On the 16th of April 1666, the governor's pleasure was read in court for continuing Capt. Parker as sheriff. "Major Tilney immediately taking offence at the Honorable Governor's desire, rose up from the court in an abrupt manner and said he would not sit any longer." Signed by Edm. Scarburgh, Jno. West, Jno. Wise, Robt. Pitt, Geo. Parker. (p. 120a)

Soon after the former proceeding, the commissioners and "other persons of quality" were at dinner along with Major Tilney, who fell to "strange and abusive words to Capt. Parker." Reprimanded by Mr. Wise, Tilney turned on him, giving him similar or worse affronts, and then also to Mr. West. Col. Scarburgh then reprimanded Tilney, who used "many ill words" to the Colonel, and continued his behavior, even when requested and commanded in the king's name to stop. Tilney persisted in the worst of words which could be attested by many, including the following: Geo. Parker, Edm. Scarburgh, Jno. West, Jno. Wise, Robt. Pitt. (p. 120b)

Thomas Smith posted bond for good behavior last January. Ordered it be delivered to him, proclamation being read three times with no objection. Smith paid court costs. (p. 120b)

Capt. West left court for the following:

Henry White and Henry Bishopp were appointed to assess the condition of the plantation and housing that belonged to Richard Teage, and to inquire about the condition it was in when Teage died. Mr. Fawsett was to see that the report and Teage's will were brought to the next court. (p. 120b)

Mr. Fawsett entered himself security to pay all damages awarded against him in the difference between him and Jenkin Price. (p. 120b)

Last March Thomas Smith posted bond for his appearance at this court; since he appeared and cleared himself of the charge, it was ordered that his bond be delivered to him, with him paying court costs. (p. 120b)

Mr. John Fawsett entered action against Jenkin Price at the last court for 1132 lbs tobacco and had evidence to prove the debt, but Price did not appear. Order was entered against the sheriff, who had till this court to produce Price. Fawsett, however, did not think Price would come and did not bring the proof. Ordered that the case be suspended till the next court with Price giving security or to remain in custody. (p. 120b, 121a)

Ordered that the vestry of Accomack and part of Hunger's Parish divide the parish into precincts where the neighbors would join in and see that the [boundary] marks were renewed. They should appoint days before 3 June to go in procession; whoever was delinquent was to be fined. (p. 121a)

Henry Bishop, surveyor of the highways, complained that his area was so large that he could not manage it. Ordered that William Major be appointed surveyor from the head of Occahanock down on the Bay Side to the end of the county. (p. 121a)

The suit brought against Cornelius Watkinson by Howell Glading was dropped because Glading failed to enter a complaint. Glading paid court costs. (p. 121a)

James Jolly acknowledged owing Richard Buckland 690 lbs tobacco. Ordered that he pay it and court costs. (p. 121a)

Certificate was granted to John Paramore for 1500 acres for transporting:

Jno., a Scott	Mary Goodrigg	Rowland Meeres
James Allington	George Greene	Susan Poole
Eliza. Bankes	Wm. Greene	Timothy Rice
Eliza. Bright	James Harlow	Mary Ringsby
Jno. Carpenter	Owen Heuland	John Seabourne
John Clark	Arthur Hickman	Mark Tomlin
Tho. Eastfeild	John Horrod	John Waller
James Enfeild	Mary Jones	Timothy Ware
Mathew Frith	Rowland Larke	John White
James Garland	Peter Martin	Luke White
		(p. 121a)

Certificate was granted to Lt. Col. Wm. Waters for 2000 acres for transporting:

Wm. Barlington	Timo. Forrest	Hen. Morecraft
Tho. Chester	James Gunter	Owin Morgan
Thomas Cowley	Humphry Hooke	Jno. Muddiford
Stephen Cromwell	Tho. Illford	Lewis Northgate
Martha East	Edw. Inglesby	Thomas Oake
Evan Ellis	Wm. Islingham	Tho. Oakeland
James Farar	Michaell Long	Abram. Oglesby

Jno. Oldis
Alice Ouldfeild
Edm. Reninger
Edgar Roxberry
Jno. Short
Jean Smith
Jno. Smithfeild

Robt. Taylor
Morris Thomas
Eliza. Thurkettle
Eliza. Upton
Richard Watkins
Tho. Wells
Nicholas Wharton

Mary White
Lewis Whittaker
Timothy Williams
Francis
   Willoughby
James Worrell
   (p. 121b)

Certificate was granted to Mr. Jno. Robins for 2000 acres for transporting:

Jeffry Baldwin
Jane Bifort
Rebecca Billingly
Arthur Bishopp
Isaac Blades
Thomas Blake
Mathew Blore
Edward Brookes
Mary Cadger
Mathew Coome
Miles Courtney
John Fourd
Edw. Goslin
James Griffin

Roger Holt
Robt. Jones
Wm. Lee
Thomas Lewis
Lettice Long
Rowland Maldin
Rice Martin
Henry Morgan
Jane Morris
Lewis Morris
Richard North
Jno. Oughtred
James Roe
Laurance Roe

Thomas Rosse
Jeffry Rouse
Michaell Roxsby
Joan Shalling
John Strong
Henry Swart
Henry Tomlin
Jno. Upton
Guido Valence
Robt. Willington
Jno. Wood
Mary Wrath
   (p. 121b)

Ann Dix, servant to Mrs. Charlton, was accused of fornication by Richard
Bayly, a grand jury man. Ordered that she be summoned to the next
court to answer the charges. (p. 121b)

In front of Capt. Jno. West and Mr. Jno. Wise, Howell Glading admitted
owing 500 lbs tobacco to Capt. Wm. Jones. Recorded by Robt.
Hutchinson. (p. 121b)

Accomack County Court--26 June 1666
Held at the house of Col. Edm. Scarburgh

Present: Col. Edm. Scarburgh   Mr. Hugh Yeo
             Capt. Jno. West   Mr. Jno. Wise (p. 122a)

Major Jno. Tilney complained that his hired servant, Daniell Clainey,
assaulted him and was stubborn and incorrigible. Part of this appeared
to be true, so it was ordered that Clainey be taken into custody and kept
to work till the next court when he would be tried. Tilney was to

produce all his evidence so the court could proceed to judgment. (p. 122a)

Col. Scarburgh exited and Major Jno. Tilney entered court. (p. 122a)

Col. Edmund Scarburgh and Mr. Charles Scarburgh swore that they were present at Pungotege with Mrs. Ann Toft and Robert Risdon, master of the catch *Virginia Merchant* also known as *Providence of Garnsey*, which was fully loaded and bound for the sea. They witnessed the bill of loading signed by Risdon dated last 15 January and the settling of all accounts between Mrs. Ann Toft and Risdon, who also signed a discharge to Mrs. Toft and Edm. Scarburgh for wages paid to Risdon and a servant. Risdon was discharged from all former accounts except for Ann Toft's interest in the catch and the obligation of going on the voyage and returning. Signed by Edm. Scarburgh and Cha. Scarburgh, who both made oath on 26 June 1666; recorded by Robt. Hutchinson. (p. 122a)

Accomack County Court--16 July 1666

Present: Major Jno. Tilney   Capt. Edm. Bowman
               Capt. Jno. West   Mr. John Wise (p. 122a)

The names of the jury impaneled:

Richard Bayley	Timothy Coe	Robt. Richardson
Thomas Browne	Danll. Foxcroft	Tobius Sellvey
Rich. Buckland	Tho. Leatherberry	Mr. Jno. Shepherd
William Chase	Edward Moore	John Williams
		(p. 122a, b)

John Trueman was released from his bond for good behavior made last January, it being proclaimed three times without objection. Trueman paid court costs. (p. 122b)

Jeffry Minshall with Thomas Smith contracted with Col. Edm. Scarburgh, Mr. Devorax Browne and Capt. Edm. Bowman for certain sums of tobacco. Minshall required security from Smith. Ordered that he give Minshall a counter bond and pay court charges. (p. 122b)

Mr. James Fookes admitted owing Denis Selevant 700 lbs tobacco. Ordered that Fooks give security for paying the tobacco after the next crop and pay court costs. (p. 122b)

The case between Mr. Fawset, plaintiff, and Wm. Stevens, the attorney of Jenkin Price, defendant, was dismissed because Fawset had no lawful power to sue; he paid court costs. (p. 122b)

Ordered that Richard Buckland be fined for swearing in the face of the court. (p. 122b)

Order was entered against the sheriff for the non-appearance of Mr. Henry Smith at the suit of Mr. Wallop. (p. 122b)

The suit brought against John Groves by Mr. Jolly was dropped at the request of John Renny, who was security for Groves' appearance. Jolly failed to enter a complaint and paid court costs. (p. 122b)

Certificate was granted to Richard Kellum for 350 acres for transporting:

Wm. Ashby	John Hutchinson	Richard Wyer
Robert Browne	Nich. Taylor	(p. 122b)
Jone Burt	Robert Wapull	

Col. Edm. Scarburgh, plaintiff, complained against David Williamson, defendant, who had contracted with Scarburgh last April first to provide four sawyers to work at Gargaphie until they had hewed 10,000 feet of good planks and boards. Williamson failed to do this, and Scarburgh was suing and wanted a jury to view the damages. Ordered that a jury be impaneled and go to Gargaphie on Thursday the 19th of July, and give a report at the next court.

Deposition of Cornelius Watkinson aged about 24 years, 16 July 1666: Said that at the last court David Williamson asked him to hew timber at Gargaphie, which Watkinson offered to do for 30 lbs tobacco per day. Williamson refused. Signed, Cornelius Watkinson.

Deposition of John Rowles aged about 24 years, 16 July 1666: Said that David Williamson at the last court (16 April) asked him to hew timber at Gargaphie, but refused to pay the requested 30 lbs tobacco per day. Signed, John Rowles. (p. 123a)

It was formerly ordered that men be appointed to give notice to workers to assist Thomas Bowles, millwright, around his mill dam. Ordered that the following give the notice:
- George Johnson to give notice from Hunting Creek to Pokomoke, after himself being notified by Thomas Bowles
- John Drumond for Hunting Creek and Deep Creek
- James Bonwell for Cheroonessick and Anancock Creek
- Edward Revell for Pungotege Creek

- Mr. Southy Littleton for Nandue?
- Robert Hewet for Craddock
- Mr. Fawset for Occahannock
- Timothy Coe for Nuswattocks
- Henry Stott for the Sea Side from the lower end of the county to Henry Bishopp's house
- Jno. Smith from Henry Bishopp's to Wm. Custis' house
- Mr. Wm. Custis from his house upward on the Sea Side. (p. 123a)

Accomack County Court--18 September 1666

Present: Major Jno. Tilney   Capt. Edm. Bowman
             Capt. Jno. West   Mr. Jno. Wise (p. 123b)

Certificate was granted to Mr. Jno. Robins for 1800 acres for transporting:

Andrew (Irishman)	James (Negro)	Xper. Nutter
Stephen Avis	Johannack (Negro)	Paull (Negro)
Black Jack (Negro)	Jone (Negro)	Peter (Negro)
Wm. Clemance	Jno. King (Negro)	Philassa (Negro)
Congo (Negro)	Wm. Line	Wm. Pladget
Cosongo (Negro)	Little Tony (Negro)	Robin (Negro)
Donath (Irishman)	Long James (Negro)	Jno. Robins
Wm. Fennell	John Margritts	Richard Robins
Jone Francklin	Ann Miles	Wm. Savidge
Dick Frigot	Alice Mitchell	Daniell Selby
Great Tony (Negro)	Samuell Mitchell	Jno. Simonds
Hanah (Negro)	Cornelius Morris	Jno. Wotter
		(p. 123b)

The names of the jury impanelled:

Alexander Addison	Robt. Houston	Peter Walker
Rich. Bayley	Mr. Jno. Renny	Jno. Walthom
Nath. Bradford	Samll. Showell	Henry White
James Fookes	John Smith	Jno. Williams
		(p. 123b)

John Pike acknowledged owing Nicholas Wise 434 lbs tobacco. Ordered that Pike pay it to Mr. Jno. Fawset, attorney for Nicholas Wise. Pike also paid court costs. (p. 123b)

Jno. Lacock, master of the ship *Daniell*, received from Robert Houlston (sic) a hogshead of tobacco weighing 479 lbs to be exchanged for five gallons of rum at 30 lbs/gallon and sugar at 4 lbs/gallon to make up the difference. Ordered that Lacock pay Houston and court costs. (p. 123b)

Ordered that Mr. Jno. Fawset and Alexander Addison audit the accounts between Mr. James Fookes and Denis Selevant and give a report. (p. 123b)

Col. Edm. Scarburgh entered the court. (p. 123b)

Mr. Fawset, attorney for the county, accused George Hamling of possessing the estate of William Rodolphus without probate. Hamling pleaded ignorance and the case was dismissed with Hamling paying court costs. (p. 123b)

Roger Barker, prosecuted for entertaining runaways, was in part found guilty. Ordered that Roger Barker be taken into custody until posting bond for good behavior and paying the cost of the suit. (p. 124a)

Thomas Ordell halted an auction contrary to law, as testified by James Atkinson. Ordered that Thomas Ordell be taken into custody until posting bond for his good behavior and paying court costs. (p. 124a)

It was ordered that William Chase should be paid a heifer for looking after the cattle of John Allford. Chase gave an account of 13 cattle, with two running wild at Mr. Littleton's bay side, one at Mrs. Hack's, and a ewe at Mr. Wise's.
Mr. Wise testified that John Alford assigned a steer to Mr. Tho. Fowke. Ordered that Wm. Chase deliver it to Fowke. (p. 124a)

Col. Edm. Scarburgh exited the court for the following action:
Col. Edm. Scarburgh prosecuted James Jolly for intrusion on his land at Pokomoke, presenting a patent bearing the date 16 September 1664. Jolly admitted it. Ordered that the sheriff evict Jolly, who was to pay court costs. (p. 124a)

Major Tilney exited the court for the following action:
Major Jno. Tilney prosecuted Daniell Clansy for abusive behavior and laying violent hands on Tilney, as testified by John Deekes and Robert Blades. Ordered that Daniell Clansy remain in custody, have 20 lashes on his bare back, post bond for good behavior and pay court costs.
Deposition of John Deekes aged about 60 years: Said that he was at Major Tilney's house on June 15 or 16 when he heard Daniell Clansie say he had struck Major Tilney and would strike him again, saying many

abusive, uncivil words and threats. Clansie said, "If the best man in the country should strike him, [I] would strike him again, excepting the Governor." Clansie acknowledged his intention to strike Robert Blades with his hoe, "very much threatening the said Blades." Sworn before Will. Jones and Jno. Dicke, 7 July 1666. Signed, John (O) Deekes.

Deposition of Robert Blades aged about 21 years, sworn before Edmond Bowman, 14 July 1666: Said that Daniell Clansic, a hired servant of "my Master Tilney," was at work when Tilney asked him to do better work. Clansie replied that he would make it worse since Tilney found fault with it. Tilney said, "You rogue, as I pay you wages for your work, I will make you make better." Clansie replied, "No more rogue than yourself." Tilney accused Clansie of striking him; Clansie admitted it and said he would do it again. As Clansie repeated his remark about the governor, Blades saw that he had "fast hold of my master's collar," and Tilney commanded Blades to grab him. Clansy struck Blades in the face with his fist and tried to hit both Tilney and Blades with a hoe. He tried to get his knife out of his pocket, but was prevented by Tilney "striking up his heels." Clansy threatened both men, heaping abusive words on Tilney. Signed, Robert Blades. (p. 124b)

Instead of Alphanso Ball, deceased, Peter Walker was named surveyor for the highways from the bridge at Pungotege between Edward Revell and Mrs. Hodgkins to Occahannock on the Bay Side, and from Mr. Wm. Custis' house to Jno. Turnor's house on the Sea Side. (p. 124b)

George Hamling, who married the widow of William Rodolphus, petitioned the court for administration of Rodolphus' estate. Ordered that it be granted if Hamling put in security. Also ordered that an inventory be made by the county clerk before the next court. (p. 124b)

Ordered that the sheriff summon Mr. Henry Smith, Wm. Taylor, Jno. Shepherd and Ralph Dow, appraisers of the estate of Wm. Rodolphus, to be sworn before Capt. Edm. Bowman. They were to meet October 9 at Hamling's house to appraise the estate. (p. 124b)

Capt. Jno. West sued John Watts for recovery of 800 acres of land that was sold conditionally. There was a collateral agreement for Watts' resigning the land. Ordered that Capt. Edm. Bowman, Mr. Jno. Wise and Phillip Fisher evaluate the work done by Watts on West's land and compare it to the value of using the land and timber. West was to repay tobacco received from Watts. They were to share the cost of the suit.

Deposition of Phillip Fisher aged about 29 years, sworn before Edm. Bowman 18 September 1666: Said that about last June he was at Capt.

Bowman's house with Capt. Jno. West and John Watts who discussed the land Watts had bought. West wanted payment, but Watts said he had no tobacco or security, and wished he "had never meddled with the land." He added that if Capt. West would pay back his tobacco and a year's pay for work on the land, he would give it back. West said he would pay him, but expected rent for the time Watts lived on it. Watts refused the rent and thinking he deserved something more, said he would let Capt. Bowman and Fisher determine it. West did not agree and requested Watts to live by the agreement or leave the land. Signed, Phillip Fisher. (p. 125a)

The case between Capt. Jno. West and Mr. Jno. Parker was deferred to the next court so West could produce evidence. (p. 125a)

Capt. West entered the court. (p. 125a)

Letter of administration for the estate of John Die, deceased, was granted to Laurance Robinson, who gave security. The court clerk was ordered to take inventory on 2 October 1666.
Appointed appraisers to the estate of John Die, deceased: Mr. Richard Hill, Wm. Custis, Geo. Truet and Francis Benston. Before the appraisal they would be sworn by a magistrate. (p. 125a)

Robert Hewet requested the return of his bond; it was proclaimed three times with no objection. Ordered it be returned with him paying court charges. (p. 125a)

Thomas Benthall sued Capt. Wm. Jones for 1810 lbs tobacco. Benthall let the issue be decided by the oath of Jones, who swore that he owed Benthall nothing. The case was dismissed with Benthall paying court charges. (p. 125b)

Major Tilney left court for the following action:
Danll. Clansie was ordered to receive corporal punishment for his abusive behavior to Major Jno. Tilney. Since Clansie was sick, his punishment was delayed till the next court. Ordered the he remain in custody till posting bond for his appearance at next court and paying court costs. (p. 125b)

Capt. Bowman left court for the following action:
Certificate was granted to Capt. Edmond Bowman for 700 acres for transporting:

| Jno. Arundell | Mary Bagley | Mary Chayr |

Samuell Cosworth
Wm. Gosling
William Harris
Jane Hill

William Hine
Henry Jones
John Roberts
William Tredin

John Trelany
John Wheeler
Tho. Wilson
(p. 124b)

Certificate was granted to Mr. Southy Littleton for 1500 acres for transporting:

Jno. Arundell
Rich. Atkinson
James Billet
Hugh Biscaco
Thomas Blaet
William Bosca
John Bouthen
Haniball Buggins
Nich. Burlace
John Carnsew

Hugh Courtney
John Edgecomb
Gumsted (Negro)
Michaell Hill
Mary Holt
John (servant)
Thomas Kester
Southy Littleton
Richard Pendarnis
Wm. Pendarnis

John Penrose
James Prade
John Rash
Henry Roberts
John Roscar
Rich. Rouse
Rowland Savage
Henry Spurr
Thomas Trefy
William Trenisa
(p. 125b)

Certificate was granted to Henry White for 1300 acres for transporting:

Richard Arundell
John Billing
Francis Buller
John Burgess
John Carfeild
William Cotten
Peter Courtney
Wm. Courtney
John Elliot

Charles Grills
James Grinvill
Thomas Hoblin
Walter Kendall
Jonathan Laws
Ridgeby North
Humphry Noy
Hugh Piper
Rich. Prideaux

Jonas Rashly
Thomas Robinson
Wm. Scawen
Mark Silby
John Spekort
Arthur Spry
John Verman
James Wrey
(p. 125b)

Certificate was granted to John Jenkins for 800 acres for transporting:

Jno. Bligh
Anthony Chinow
James Harris
George Hele
Francis Jones
Tho. Langly

James Lear
Robert Long
Nath. Mohum
Jno. Moulsworth
Hugh Pomeroy
John Prideaux

Thomas Standford
Hugh Travanion
Thomas Willis
Jno. Willoughby
(p. 126a)

On 17 April 1666, Col. Scarburgh, at the suit of Jno. Anderson, issued attachment against the estate of James Andrews for 3000 lbs tobacco, and since no plea had been made against it, ordered that judgment proceed. John Anderson posted bond; if his plea was illegal he would repay everything including court charges. (p. 126a)

Several persons were delinquent in bringing in their lists of tithables. As it was necessary to have complete lists to turn in to James City, it was ordered that the sheriff send the negligent persons to the court clerk so the list could be finished. Ordered that the sheriff obtain the list taken by Capt. West and Mr. Wise. Ordered that persons neglecting to submit their lists be fined 35 lbs tobacco. (p. 126a)

Document written by "Edm. Scarburgh of the County of Accomack in Virginia, Esquire" regarding the estate of John Die, of the same county, who died intestate and left behind an estate in the care of Laurance Robinson, who married Die's widow. Robinson requested to be administrator of the estate, which was granted. Ordered that at the next court Robinson present an inventory of the estate which had been appraised by four men appointed by the court. Robinson was to pay all just debts and then bring in an account of the surplus. Signed 2 October 1666, Edm. Scarburgh.

On 2 October 1666, Richard Hill, George Truet, Fran. Benstone, and Robt. Hutchinson appraised the estate of John Die, deceased. Among other things the estate included: 15 cows (two of which were at Muddy Creek), 43 pigs, a musket, 10 pots and pans sized small to 10 gallons, hoes and axes. 7 small pewter dishes and 6 pewter porringers (bowls), a candlestick, a featherbed and accessories, a Dutch chest, various tubs, and a milk bucket. The following persons owed debts to the estate: Roger Turnon, William Abram, Richard Kellum and Edward Sacker. The entire estate was valued at 9434 lbs of tobacco. Recorded 9 January 1666/67, by Robt. Hutchinson. (p. 126a, b)

INDEX

BOUCHER, Alice iii 27; William 9 10 59
BOURES, Christian 123
BOURN, Geo. 151
BOUTCHER, Alice 45; William 45; Wm. 62
BOUTHEN, John 168
BOWIN, Hugh vii 146; John 83; (servant) 139
BOWLE, Rich. 102
BOWLES, Jno. 102; Thomas 163
BOWMAN, Capt. 5 119 134 139 148 167; Edm. iii 17 40 41 52 65 69 73 74 83 85 90 92 96 98 112-115 117 119 123 124 128 130 133 147 148 153 162 164 166; Edmond 18 41 43 51 65 69 74 152 166; Eliza. 37 114; Mr. 3 26 27 89
BOYCE, Wm. 101
BOYD, James 112
BOYES, John 101 150
BOYLE, Jno. 102
BOYS, Jno. 73 151; John 72 73; Mr. 71
BRACE, Mr. 113; Phillip 93; Robert iii 7 18 21 27 28 46 91 96 97 106 107 117; Robt. 39 121 129
BRACY, Walter 102
BRAD, Jno. 93
BRADFORD, Alice 39 95; Nath. 15 16 20 25 29 31 34 40 52 89 129 164; Nathaniel 5 92 122 123; Nathaniell 39 64 109 122
BRANDFORD, Nathaniell 95; Nathaniell Jr. 96
BRANDORD, Nathaniell 95
BRADSHAW, Roger 150
BRAENS, Arnold 151
BRAG, Edward 100
BRAMS, Arnold 101
BRAMSTONE, Jno. 152
BRANANE, Wm. 74
BRANDLOW, Arthur 23
BRANFIELD, Ralph 87

BRANGWELL, Mary 75 106 111
BRANSON, Frances 46; Francis 23
BRASE, Robt. 89
BREALER, Tho. 150
BREET, Charles 88
BRENT, Stephen 150; Wm. 101
BRETT, Claus 80; Stephen 102; Tho. 150
BREVETON, Tho. 65
BREWER, Tho. 101
BRICKHOUSE, Geo. 41 106 107 130; George iv 15-17 26 90 108
BRIDGES, 145; Robt. 43; William 152
BRIDGNORTH, Mary 2
BRIDWELL 112
BRIGG, Geo. 123
BRIGHT, Eliza. 160
BRISCOE, Edw. 149
BRISTOLL, Jno. 150
BRITAIN, Thomas 3
BRITAINE, Wm. 107
BRITINGHAM, Wm. 75
BROADNAX, Tho. 152
BROADNECK, Tho. 102
BROCKLEY, Arthur 155
BRODERICK, Nich. 87
BROOK, Thomas 4
BROOKE, James 101 150; John 152
BROOKES, Edward 161; Humphery 102; Jno. 40 129; Joane 45; John 52 89 94 153; Jone 45; Mr. 4 149; Sisley 84; William 115
BROUGHTON, Jno. 94
BROWN, Devoroux 12; Ellen 1; Henry 1; Mr. 1; William 26
BROWNE, Anto. 152; Charles 88; Deveorax 106; Deverax 72 106; Deverx. 5 96; Devorax 3 5 12 13 22 23 41 42 54 61 62 64 69 74 98 103-106 108 110 136 147 162; Devorx. 1 12 28

NEEDHAM, Jno. 103
NEGRO viii 9 36 52 61 65 115
    117 121 127 139 164
NEPAIR, Roger 135
NEREGON, Nora 60
NEVELL, John 103
NEWBY, William 103 104
NEWMAN, Geo. 103 151; James
    150
NEWTON, James 93; John 101;
    Joseph 76; Sara 93; Tho. 40
    89; Thomas 9
NEWWORTH, Wm. 23
NICHOLAS, Edw. 103; John 22
NICHOLS, Anne 13; Edward 13;
    John 3 4 10 13 19 95; Randall
    13
NICOLAIJ, Hans 47
NOELL, Edw. 152
NORAH v 21 24 25
NORDELL, Jno. 103; John 135
NORDES, Toby 151
NORINE 78
NORRIS, John 99
NORTH, Richard 161; Ridgeby
    168
NORTHGATE, Lewis 160
NORTON, Jeffry 80; Jno. 151;
    Tho. 151; William 131
NOSEENE, Joane 79
NOSWORTHY, Joan 94
NOTLEY, Edw. 103
NOTRES, Tho. 151
NOWCHETRAWEN, 22
NOWELL, Jno. 150; Roger 36
NOY, Humphry 168
NULL, Thomas 88
NURSE, Rowland 116; Tho. 152
NUSWATTOCKS 77 164
NUSWATTOCKS CREEK 39 47
    92 95
NUTTER, Xper. 164
NUTWELL, John 85
OAKE, Thomas 160
OAKELAND, Alice 155; Tho.
    160

OAKLY, William 99
OBIN, Folcot 5 40; Fulcand 90;
    Fulcot 107 129
OCCAHANNOCK 80 86 113 125
    145 164 166
OCCAHANNOCK CHURCH 19
    66
OCCAHANNOCK CREEK 95
    125
OCCAHANNOCK NECK 22
OCCAHANOCK 145 160
OCCAHANOCK CREEK 95 96
OCCAHONNOCK 99 122 140
    146
OCKAHANNOCK CREEK 39
OCOLMAN, Owin 89
OGLE, Cutbert 151
OGLESBY, Abram. 160
OGRAHAM, Daniell 40; Danll.
    89 128 139
OKELY, Sisly 138
OLDIS, Jno. 161
OLESTER 77
OLIVER, Robert 103; Robt. 150
OMISCALL, Teage 22
ONANCOCK 46
ONOUGHTON, William i vii 22
    26 30 42 74 126 131 132 133
    136 137 149; Wm. iv 21 101
    104 132
ONSLOW, John 87
OPHISH, Stephen 88
ORDELL, Thomas 165
ORIOTT, Tho. 93
ORLY, William 138
ORTON, James 101 William 116
OSBALD, Jno. 100
OSBORN, Oliver 127
OSBOURNE, Thomas 29 30
OSSETT, Jone 36
OSTIPE, Anne 115
OTAWAY, John 135
OTHER, Thomas 149
OTLEY, Richard 100
OTTERDAM 3
OTTERDAM BRIDGE 149

18
5,3

Made in the USA
Charleston, SC
24 July 2012